Vygotsky Philosophy a

The Journal of Philosophy of Education Book Series

The Journal of Philosophy of Education Book Series publishes titles that represent a wide variety of philosophical traditions. They vary from examination of fundamental philosophical issues in their connection with education, to detailed critical engagement with current educational practice or policy from a philosophical point of view. Books in this series promote rigorous thinking on educational matters and identify and criticise the ideological forces shaping education.

Titles in the series include:

Vygotsky Philosophy and Education
Jan Derry

Education Policy: Philosophical Critique
Edited by Richard Smith

Levinas, Subjectivity, Education: Towards an Ethics of Radical Responsibility
Anna Strhan

Philosophy for Children in Transition: Problems and Prospects
Edited by Nancy Vansieleghem and David Kennedy

The Good Life of Teaching: An Ethics of Professional Practice
Chris Higgins

Reading R. S. Peters Today: Analysis, Ethics, and the Aims of Education
Edited by Stefaan E. Cuypers and Christopher Martin

The Formation of Reason
David Bakhurst

What do Philosophers of Education do? (And how do they do it?)
Edited by Claudia Ruitenberg

Evidence-Based Education Policy: What Evidence? What Basis? Whose Policy?
Edited by David Bridges, Paul Smeyers and Richard Smith

New Philosophies of Learning
Edited by Ruth Cigman and Andrew Davis

The Common School and the Comprehensive Ideal: A Defence by Richard Pring with Complementary Essays
Edited by Mark Halstead and Graham Haydon

Philosophy, Methodology and Educational Research
Edited by David Bridges and Richard D Smith

Philosophy of the Teacher
By Nigel Tubbs

Conformism and Critique in Liberal Society
Edited by Frieda Heyting and Christopher Winch

Retrieving Nature: Education for a Post-Humanist Age
By Michael Bonnett

Education and Practice: Upholding the Integrity of Teaching and Learning
Edited by Joseph Dunne and Pádraig Hogan

Educating Humanity: Bildung in Postmodernity
Edited by Lars Lovlie, Klaus Peter Mortensen and Sven Erik Nordenbo

The Ethics of Educational Research
Edited by Michael McNamee and David Bridges

In Defence of High Culture
Edited by John Gingell and Ed Brandon

Enquiries at the Interface: Philosophical Problems of On-Line Education
Edited by Paul Standish and Nigel Blake

The Limits of Educational Assessment
Edited by Andrew Davis

Illusory Freedoms: Liberalism, Education and the Market
Edited by Ruth Jonathan

Quality and Education
Edited by Christopher Winch

Vygotsky Philosophy and Education

Jan Derry

WILEY Blackwell

Contents

Series Editor Preface

Anyone who trained to be a teacher in the latter half of the twentieth century is likely to have studied developmental psychology, and within this one name stood out: that of Jean Piaget. But alongside Piaget, and not entirely overshadowed, another figure was apparent, someone whose work was less readily assimilated, less easily reduced to simple stages, and whose profound innovations in psychology came only dimly into view: this, of course, was Lev Semyonovich Vygotsky. For psychologists, Vygotsky has remained a key, though controversial, thinker, and estimations of the value of his work have fluctuated. For philosophers, he has continued to be perceived as a marginal figure: in the *Stanford Encyclopedia of Philosophy* the only reference to him is in Denis Phillips's entry for the philosophy of education, and there he is just one in a list of theorists and researchers who are not philosophers. In fact Vygotsky's theoretical innovations had implications for the philosophy of mind, but this philosophical importance of his work has for the most part simply been missed. Institutional boundaries within the academy have not eased the reception of his work, and they have hidden its interdisciplinary richness, while political prejudice has in contrary ways blocked the path of its wider recognition. In consequence, the lines along which Vygotsky's thought has been inherited have been various, and the perspectives that have held sway have been decidedly partial.

Against this background, and in the light of an ever-burgeoning secondary literature, it is the unique achievement of Jan Derry's *Vygotsky, Philosophy and Education* to have brought together these disparate lines of thought. In particular, it is through her reassessment of the significance of Vygotsky's philosophical background that a more coherent reading becomes possible. The robustness of the critique this generates is such as to rebut some leading accounts of the work, and in consequence it paves the way for a renewal of Vygotsky studies. What should be apparent also, from the plethora of classroom examples that Derry works through, is that she approaches these discussions with the benefit of varied experience as a practising teacher. This helps to make the practical implications of the study all the more apparent.

It was an important step forward for Vygotsky when he came to see the implications of Marx's 'reverse method', according to which things need to be understood not as progressive increments to an initial state but rather in terms of their higher form: human anatomy is the key to the anatomy of the ape. Vygotsky's 'zone of proximal development' provides a small-scale, familiar example of this, but the conceptual and methodological implications are far wider. It is a related strength of Derry's text that it avoids a developmental historical account of Vygotsky's thought in favour of an approach that exploits the vantage point of the present: it is from here that the diverse and disparate paths of enquiry that have been associated with Vygotsky's name can coherently be brought into view. Contemporary debates in learning theory can then be read in the light of leading-edge philosophy of mind, while philosophical psychology can be seen to dovetail with aspects of Spinoza, Hegel and Marx. Indeed, Derry's appreciative account of the philosophy of John McDowell, Robert Brandom and, behind them, Wilfrid Sellars, reveals the background significance of Hegel, a philosopher whose determining importance for Vygotsky has been wildly underestimated. In its affirmation of this and in its understanding of the diverse traditions of thought that are crossed here, Derry's book complements and extends the lines of research elaborated in David Bakhurst's *The Formation of Reason*, published in this series in 2011.

In sum, Derry has undertaken a fascinating study. She has written a book that challenges received ideas in learning theory, that overturns the positions held by leading Vygotsky scholars, and that reveals more fully the congruence of current philosophy of mind with the insights of this remarkable Russian psychologist who was working nearly a century ago and whose potential importance has still not fully been realised.

Paul Standish, Series Editor

Preface

It was at the Institute of Education, London, that I was introduced to Vygotsky's work by Jane Miller. Later my interests in his work deepened, especially through lively discussions and disagreements with colleagues – David Guile, John Hardcastle, Tony Burgess, Anton Franks, Arthur Bakker, Richard Noss, Bob Cowen, Celia Hoyles, Gunther Kress, Shirley Franklin and Carey Jewitt. It is particularly important for me to have worked with Michael Young and Harry Daniels. In 1999 I benefited greatly from being a member of the Sociocultural Theory Seminar Series, funded by the Economic and Social Research Council.

Aware of my interests, the late Michael Cowen mentioned a book to me by John McDowell called *Mind and World*. This led me to see links with the work of David Bakhurst, whom I had come to know of through his work on Vygotsky and Ilyenkov. Later, when I met David, I learnt that the connection was not merely coincidental as David had been supervised by John McDowell at Oxford. David is one of the few philosophers who appreciate that systematic speculative reflection on the nature of education has an invaluable contribution to make to philosophy and philosophical anthropology. His work has proved highly influential amongst educationalists interested in Vygotsky. Unfortunately the time needed for the philosophical reflection that David's work suggests is necessary is tantalisingly difficult to secure.

This book draws on Hegel, and I have benefited from being a member of the Hegel Society of Great Britain, which provides a forum that does full justice to the richness of his thought. My appreciation of Hegel has been deepened by listening to members of the Society, in particular Ken Westphal. I have also benefited from the lively discussion list on Cultural Historical Activity Theory, organised by Michael Cole. In addition, personal discussions with Anne Edwards, Mariane Hedegaard, Peter Medway, Yrjö Engeström, Johan Muller, Joseph Dunne, Uffe Juul Jensen, Peter Jones and Charles Crook have always helped me greatly.

I am particularly indebted to Paul Standish, who read the manuscript, and to Andrew Davis and Seth Chaiklin, who read substantial sections of it. They made extremely helpful suggestions. The errors that remain are, of course, my own.

My heartfelt thanks to my family, especially my brother Colin Dubery, for their forbearance when my work consumed me and I had little time for family life.

Finally, my thanks to Geoff Kay, who was my teacher 40 years ago and whose friendship and conversations over the years have enriched my life.

Jan Derry
London, May 2013

1
Introduction

This book is a response to the claim that Vygotsky holds abstract rationality as the pinnacle of thought. The claim is based on the belief that Vygotsky subscribed to what is referred to as the 'Enlightenment project'. The book aims to show that Vygotsky had a far more sophisticated appreciation both of reason and of its remit than this fashionable characterisation implies. Its argument is developed through an exploration of some aspects of the philosophy of Hegel and Spinoza, to both of whom Vygotsky acknowledges a debt. In the dominant, predominantly psychological research literature, the nature of the philosophical underpinnings of Vygotsky's work tends to receive little attention. Not only is that neglect contested here, but the argument is carried a stage further, claiming that the limitations that critics see in Vygotsky's work are based on misapprehensions of his understanding of reason. In support of this it is argued that Hegel's investigation of the presuppositions of claims to knowledge already contains a critique of the frame of reference used by these commentators – commentators who view Vygotsky, in this aspect of his work, as having an 'old-fashioned' conception of reason that cannot do justice to diversity.

A recurring theme of this book is Vygotsky's conception of the nature of abstract reason, but such are the ramifications of this that it is necessary to go well beyond an examination of any particular aspect of Vygotsky's work. Vygotsky was concerned above all with questions of education. While education may appear to be non-philosophical and certainly to lie outside the range of what most philosophers write about, it has, by virtue of its direct involvement with thought and intellect, a philosophical dimension. As education leads towards philosophy, so philosophy can gain from an engagement with education, precisely because the latter is not only engaged with questions of mind and world but engaged with them in a real and practical sense.

Vygotsky Philosophy and Education, First Edition. Jan Derry.
© 2013 Jan Derry. Editorial organisation © Philosophy of Education Society of Great Britain.
Published 2013 by John Wiley & Sons, Ltd.

It was Piaget, with his genetic epistemology, who brought the study of the development of faculties into direct contact with philosophy. Vygotsky, Piaget's contemporary, appreciated that any inquiry on the part of philosophy into the nature of mind and world could not be separated from the study of the mind in its development. Those familiar with Vygotsky's work will appreciate the extent of his influence within education and also be aware of the debates about pedagogy and knowledge that his work has generated. Accordingly, although this book focuses on the question of abstract reason in Vygotsky, it concludes by illustrating how the philosophical tradition that inspired Vygotsky has significant implications for these debates.

While Vygotsky was explicit about the importance of philosophy for theory, he did not actually spell out the philosophy that informed his argument, yet this omission, if this is how it is to be judged, does not detract from the subtlety and sophistication of his approach. The dualism of the ideal and real, of mind and world, that has underpinned criticism of Vygotsky both in his own time and in the current period has been taken up not only by his follower Evald Ilyenkov, but also by contemporary analytical philosophers. David Bakhurst has written on this directly: in claiming normativity to be a necessary element of the sociogenesis of mind, he has brought to our attention links between the philosophy of John McDowell and Ilyenkov. For modern philosophy the questions requiring careful analysis concern empiricism and knowing. The two contemporary philosophers whose work is most important in this book have both taken a Hegelian approach to make explicit points, which, though unexpressed, are necessarily assumed in the forms of argument that they analyse. In *Mind and World* McDowell addresses the problem of how a separate mind can connect with a world by working through a number of highly developed arguments about how we come to know. His enquiries lead to the unusual conclusion that, rather than possessing the means of thought solely in one's head, 'the dictates of reason are there [in the world] anyway, whether or not one's eyes are open to them' (McDowell, 1996, p. 91). Following Wilfrid Sellars, he refers to this sphere as 'The Space of Reasons'.

For McDowell and also for Robert Brandom, the other contemporary philosopher whose work I shall highlight, this concept plays a crucial role. Simply summarised, the gist of the argument is that in order to make a claim of knowing we are not, as commonly thought, giving a description of an event but placing our claims about it in a space of reasons – that is to say, making claims on the basis of knowing what follows from them and what it is necessary to assume in order to make them in the first place. Where a word is used without the user being aware of its conceptual connections to other concepts, these connections are still present. The implication of Brandom's argument is that context, not simply conscious intention, imparts reason. This approach, which results from bringing a Kantian argument to bear upon a Humean residue in empiricist conceptions of knowledge, identifies human knowing as fundamentally different from the 'knowing' of machines. For example, a human shout of 'Fire!' is fundamentally different as far as general awareness is concerned from the *differential response* of a fire alarm, though both are an alert to the same danger. For Brandom, what is distinctive about human beings is the ability to operate in the light of reasons rather than to respond simply to causes. McDowell refers to this as our second nature, emphasising our being human as something other than pure matter yet still part of nature.

When the distinction between the human and the natural is dualistically drawn as a distinction of mind and world, a clear boundary exists between the conceptual (mind) and the nonconceptual (nature). Such a distinction exists for Kant, but for McDowell, who adopts a Hegelian standpoint *in Mind and World* and speaks of the 'unboundedness of the conceptual', it is fundamentally misconceived. McDowell rejects the separation of mind and world underlying so much philosophy in favour of a frame of thought in which reasons exist in the world that humans have developed. In adopting this frame of thought McDowell takes up a position similar to Vygotsky's. For both, mind is social and to give an account of mindedness and intellect it is necessary to look beyond the individual and to attend to external mediation in the formation of higher mental functions.

The arguments of McDowell, Brandom, Sellars, Bakhurst and, with them, Vygotsky cast a distinctive light on rationality and reason.[1] In their hands these concepts take on quite a different shape from the mainstream of philosophical thought that comes through Descartes, Locke, Hume and Kant down to modern analytical philosophy. To give a bare outline, a once prevailing view in analytical philosophy presents rationality as abstract and decontextualised: it relies on the idea that reason is separated from the world and can be applied to it with greater or lesser degrees of adequacy. When applied to education such a position can lead to the most extreme forms of formalised teaching.

It is beyond the remit of this book to begin to spell out the many practical implications of the philosophical issues it considers. However, one topic must be mentioned that confirms that there are such implications and that these are of crucial importance. This is the way 'abstract' reason has been made the culprit for the poverty of educational practice in mass schooling. McDowell's claim that receptivity – our experience of the world through our senses – is already 'conceptual' involves a conception of reason quite different from that with which critics such as James Wertsch quite correctly take issue – the extreme of a decontextualised schooled knowledge, presented without regard to its genetic development or any sense that learning involves actualising concepts. This matter of decontextualisation is taken up in Chapter 2, which presents the critique of Vygotsky's alleged abstract rationalism and considers the theory of situated cognition which has been proposed in its place.

Chapter 3 turns to 'constructivism', which plays a central role in much post-Vygotskian thought. Criticism here is directed against what is argued to be the 'representationalist paradigm' implicit in conceptions of the active construction of meaning into a bare 'given'. It is argued that constructivism leads to particular pedagogic strategies that, though not part of a more sophisticated analysis, are influential in the rhetoric of classroom practice, specifically the undermining of the authority of the teacher, of knowledge (in texts) and of the belief that knowledge is a matter of plurality in the sense that no one approach is superior to any other.

Chapter 4 uses the debate between Vygotsky and Piaget on conscious awareness, egocentrism and development to illustrate the differences between their philosophical backgrounds. The purpose of this chapter is to show how the different philosophical presuppositions of each author lead to different theoretical positions.

Chapter 5 turns to elements of Spinoza's philosophy that influenced Vygotsky. In particular it is concerned with Spinoza's formulation of knowing in terms of a holism of one substance of which everything is a part, as opposed to a dualism that assumes fundamental separations. Spinoza's approach leads to a conception of truth not as an attribute but as an actualisation of a process understood as many-sided. From this standpoint, freedom appears quite differently from the Cartesian conception of wilful agency. It is understood as self-determination: to be free is to be the cause of oneself rather than subject to external causes, and this depends upon 'adequate ideas'.

Chapter 6 turns to Hegel, who follows a similar approach to Spinoza, progressively 'exorcising' claims to know to reach a distinctive conception of knowing. This conception, rather than being based on secure foundations, sees new knowledge arising out of a working through of existing claims to knowledge to show that more is implicated than appears initially to be the case.

Chapter 7 considers this anti-foundationalist character of the philosophy of Spinoza, Hegel and Vygotsky in order to argue that the conception of reason central to Vygotsky's work bears no relation to the caricature of abstract rationality criticised by contemporary post-Vygotskian researchers.

This order is not a linear sequence as the criticisms levelled against situated cognition and constructivism in Chapters 2 and 3 presuppose philosophical ideas that are not discussed until Chapters 5 and 6. On the other hand, those philosophical ideas would not make sense in the context of this book without an examination of post-Vygotskian research. Furthermore, it must be stressed that the later chapters are intended only to address those parts of Spinoza and Hegel that are relevant for understanding Vygotsky's work. The aims of this book are: first, to show that Vygotsky was influenced by a different tradition of philosophy from that which has influenced post-Vygotskian research; and second, to demonstrate that this difference is significant and has implications for educational practice.

Apart from the complexities of the differences between the philosophical traditions, there is the additional difficulty that neither Vygotsky nor post-Vygotskian researchers spell out their philosophical presuppositions in detail. Vygotsky, it is true, acknowledged the philosophic influence on his thinking, and it is often only a matter of following the leads he gave to find his sources. With his commentators, however, things are much less clear and the scope for attributing to them positions they do not hold is necessarily that much greater. But it must be stressed that the criticisms made of various works of commentary on Vygotsky for failure to appreciate the significance of the philosophical traditions in which he was working stop far short of denying the value of the contribution of those traditions to the understanding of the nature of reason.

NOTES

1 Bakhurst's *The Formation of Reason* (2011) offers an original defence of a sociohistorical account of mind that utilises the work of all the thinkers here mentioned, especially McDowell.

REFERENCES

Bakhurst, D. (2011) *The Formation of Reason* (Oxford: Wiley-Blackwell).
McDowell, J. (1996) *Mind and World* (Cambridge, MA: Harvard University Press).

2
Situated Cognition and Contextualism

The interpretation of Vygotsky raises issues at the heart of contemporary debates in educational theory and practice, and nowhere is this more true than in connection with situated cognition and constructivism. The critical question here is how knowledge and understanding are related to immediate context, whether causally or constitutively or in some combination of these (Robbins and Aydede, 2009). This chapter and the next consider the division of opinion concerning situated cognition, contextualism and constructivism. But first, and in order to better place these matters within the main theme of this book, consideration is given to what has been termed 'decontextualised rationality'. This will demonstrate the importance of placing Vygotsky's work in its proper *philosophical* context and, hence, preventing the foreclosure of areas of investigation by commentators who do not pay it due regard.

'Decontextualised rationality' is a term used by Wertsch to characterise a 'voice' (in Bakhtin's sense) or 'social speech type' that emerged with the Enlightenment:

> The defining characteristic of the voice of decontextualised rationality is that it represents objects and events (i.e. referentially semantic content) in terms of formal, logical, and, if possible, quantifiable categories. The categories used in this form of representation are decontextualised in the sense that their meaning can be derived from their position in abstract theories or systems independent of particular speech contexts.[1] (Wertsch, 1992, p. 120)

Wertsch goes on to write that 'the voice of decontextualised rationality contrasts with "contextualised forms of representation" in that the latter represent events and objects in terms of their concrete particularity' (p. 120). He sees the distinction between decontextualised rationality and contextualised forms of representation as particularly significant in the case of schooling: there, it seems, even when 'other forms of representing the objects and operations at issue would do equally well

Vygotsky Philosophy and Education, First Edition. Jan Derry.
© 2013 Jan Derry. Editorial organisation © Philosophy of Education Society of Great Britain.
Published 2013 by John Wiley & Sons, Ltd.

or better' (p. 120), decontextualised modes of discourse are privileged. The focal point of Wertsch's argument is forms of 'representation', and, as we shall see below, the emphasis that he lays upon them has a decisive influence on his account of decontextualised rationality. The question of what precisely decontextualised rationality is and how it is best understood is not clearly worked out, but for Wertsch it has significant ramifications as his references to teaching and learning make clear.[2] In the context of schooling the natural sciences and mathematics would typically fit Wertsch's description of decontextualised rationality. For example, the concept *electron* takes its meaning from its position within a tightly bounded atomic theory. The application of the concept *electron* does not rely on any specific personal context for its sense. This can be distinguished from what Wertsch describes as 'contextualised forms of representation ... that ... represent objects in terms of their concrete particularity' (p. 120). In schools this might be associated with expressive subjects such as literature or art where the legitimacy of what Wertsch would call a different *voice* is not only acceptable but required. Wertsch's concern is with the dominance of 'the voice of decontextualised rationality' in schooling. It is important to note that Wertsch's work is set within a broader context of thought dealing with the nature of *rationality*. For instance, referring to Habermas's analysis of instrumental rationality and to Lukács's examination of reification, Wertsch points beyond formal instructional settings to a wider tendency in modern society to privilege the 'decontextualised, rational voice' (p. 121). In an educational context this theme appears in various works concerned with theoretical knowledge – for example, in Donald Schon's critique of technical rationality (1983) and in Paul Hirst's rethinking of the character of reason (Hirst, 2008) and its place in education.[3] Here we are particularly concerned with Wertsch and his reading of Vygotsky and related literature. To grasp the nature of the issues involved it is necessary to consider the following: decontextualisation, theorising the institutional, historical background, situated cognition, the transfer problem and the question of determination.

The issue of decontextualisation appears in various ways in the literature relating to general questions about curricula and pedagogy, but here our specific concern is to consider the charge of decontextualised rationality levelled against Vygotsky.

DECONTEXTUALISATION

Decontextualised rationality is a recurring theme in those critical interpretations of Vygotsky that pay little attention to the philosophical tradition in which he formulated his ideas.[4] Contemporary discussion of Vygotsky's work is influenced by developments in postmodernist thought, which, in attempting to supersede the problems of abstract rationality, has often failed to give thought and reason proper consideration. Postmodernism has caricatured the tradition of the Enlightenment, which has more to say than some texts on Vygotsky have recognised. But the examination of what exactly is meant by decontextualised rationality is underdeveloped.

The question of Vygotsky's commitment to an ideal of development characterised by abstract universal reason is typically addressed against a background of sociogenetic accounts of the development of mind. Although it is accepted that Vygotsky revealed the sociogenesis of thought, recent commentaries raise the question of how far his commitment to absolute reason limited his conception of the variety and multiplicity of modes of thought. Is Vygotsky's commitment to universal reason simply an expression of the context in which he worked, a time when the unenlightened understanding characteristic of colonialist perceptions of the primitive was pitted against the modern? Or does it derive from the instrumental Marxism of Soviet practice, concerned with the possibility of the creation of 'socialist man'? Or, again, is its fundamental role in his thought rooted in the philosophical tradition from which he came? And if this last is so, does it stand in direct contradiction to his concept of sociogenesis?

Jay Lemke, a prominent researcher in the field and a semiotician, who interprets Vygotsky from an explicitly postmodern standpoint,[5] appears to adopt the first of these alternatives: 'Despite the optimism that Lev Vygotsky undoubtedly shared with his times, I hope that he did not believe that abstract symbolic formulations were the highest goal of meaning-making' (Lemke, 1999, p. 91). Like Lemke, Wertsch is concerned with what he sees as ambivalence in Vygotsky's writings. He presents Vygotsky as an Enlightenment rationalist who 'embraced human rationality as the *telos* of human development', adding that 'as a Marxist he also viewed rationality as an essential *tool* for constructing a centrally planned economy and state' (Wertsch, 1996, p. 25, italics added).[6] But he believes that Vygotsky's theory of sociogenesis can be detached from what he construes as the instrumental aspect of Vygotsky's ideas. My own account takes issue with this reading of Vygotsky's work and develops this criticism by exploring the meaning of rationality for Vygotsky. It argues that his work forms a coherent unity. It exposes the influences on Vygotsky's work of German idealist philosophy in order to show that Vygotsky's understanding of rationality was far more sophisticated than the instrumental and decontextualised concept of reason attributed to him.

The claim that Vygotsky's work is coloured by its period can, of course, be turned against those who make it: the argument that his embrace of universal reason is simply an expression of modernism can be met with the rejoinder that its rejection is an equally simple expression of postmodernism. Certainly the impetus to disengage from universalising reason within educational research and the social sciences emerged in the context of research conducted in the milieu of multiculturalism, partly out of a concern to do justice to the variety and legitimacy of human response and creativity, particularly in the case of American schooling. It also drew inspiration from anthropological critiques of colonialism. But what is more important than historical name-calling is recognition of the fact that the validation of the multiple ways in which individuals make meaning through their activities can lead to exactly the same sort of determinism believed to be inherent in the idea of universal reason.[7] The idea that an individual's thought processes are directly and causally the result of the context that provides their genesis is a mirror image of the determinism in Stalinist practice that Wertsch, for example, opposes so strongly.

In contrast to Wertsch's conflation of Marxism and Soviet practice, David Joravsky argues that Vygotsky looked to Marx rather than Stalinist reductionism for inspiration. Highlighting the difference between, for example, Marx's aesthetic theory – which saw the 'young Marx ... ask[ing] the same question about the persistent appeal of Greek classics that he [Vygotsky] was asking about *Hamlet*. How could it be that the beautiful works of a slave owning society are still beautiful in a capitalist society and will be under socialism?' – and the crude base–superstructure metaphors that were adopted as orthodox Marxism by the Third International, Joravsky challenges the ground on which Wertsch levels his charges of instrumentalism (Joravsky, 1989, pp. 256–257). Universalising rationality comes under attack from those for whom the most critical dimension of the constitution of thought is context.

In addition to the antinomy between causal accounts and the understanding of art and imaginative literature that troubled Vygotsky, a further issue stands behind readings of rationality, that of the poverty of mass schooling. Although the present chapter examines the way that the notion of context is counterposed against decontextualised rationality, it is also important to note that much of the literature on Vygotsky has developed in relation to issues raised directly by schooling. Inevitably, when Vygotsky's work is being quarried for ideas about change and intentional development in schooling, the way in which it is construed must be affected. Once it is accepted that education is the decisive factor in the development of intellect, then the responsibility for failure cannot be blamed on the innate capacities of students; responsibility falls on educational practices and the conditions in which those practices take place.[8] Because so much of the work making use of Vygotsky addresses the failures of schooling, the arguments developed are inevitably influenced by the current poverty of practice of mass schooling. The failure of schooling for large numbers of children tends to be explained by the inadequacy of curriculum content, particularly in terms of its relevance for the lives of learners. As a result abstract rationality is blamed and more concrete conditions, such as the condition in which teachers work and the constraints on their practices, are absolved.

The counter-position to abstract rationality calls for an approach that takes account of the context in which human activity takes place – that is, within institutions – and it is to the demand for such an approach that we now turn.

THEORISING THE INSTITUTIONAL

Particular questions about Vygotsky's work are raised within such different agendas that a variety of readings of Vygotsky has emerged (Burgess, 1993). In their effort to understand the work of Vygotsky in its complexity and cultural-historical context, Jaan Valsiner and René Van der Veer note the 'various myths circulating among the fascinated followers of [this] interesting scholar' (Valsiner and Van der Veer, 2000, p. ix). My concern here, as has been indicated, is with that tendency in the reading of Vygotsky that sees his conception of rationality as decontextualised. In order to examine this, we need initially to understand the background against which decontextualisation is construed by various commentators – first, in the work on situated cognition and, second, in the theorisation of context.

Vygotskian research raises crucial questions about aspects of cognition that are not covered in cognitivist approaches to the nature of thinking. The idea that processes of thought are generated and sustained externally raises the question of how this comes about. Interest in externalist accounts of mind has led researchers to examine the way that cognitive achievements are made collaboratively and through the medium of external artefacts (Clark, 1997, 1998; Wilson and Clark, 2009).[9] The quest to specify causes and effects within this field is compelling since one of its driving forces is the pressure to operationalise theory for development and change.[10]

The commitment to providing a clear account results in the fact that a key demand of contemporary Vygotskian research has been to fill what may be considered a gap in Vygotsky's original project – namely, to identify the specific mechanisms and relations to context through which the sociogenesis of mind takes place. Thus James Wertsch, Norris Minick and Flávio José Arns write:

> A complete account of the organization of human cognitive activity, manifested in a task carried out on either the individual or the social level, must go beyond narrowly defined psychological phenomena and consider the forces that create the context in which human cognition is defined and required to operate at the level of societal and cultural organisation. (Wertsch, Minick and Arns, 1984, p. 171)

The fact that Vygotsky saw language as a 'generalised semiotic system' rather than as 'a multitude of speech genres and semiotic devices that are tightly linked with particular institutions and … social practices' (Forman, Minick and Stone, 1993, p. 6) is viewed as a limitation of his work. According to Michael Cole, 'One cannot develop a viable sociocultural conception of human development without looking carefully at the way … institutions develop, the way they are linked with one another, and the way human social life is organized within them' (Cole, 1996, p. 6).

Wertsch, Tulviste and Hagstrom criticise Vygotsky for limiting his analysis of the relationship between intermental and intramental functioning to small groups, arguing that 'he did relatively little to specify how intermental functioning and mediational means fit into a broader framework of sociocultural processes' (Wertsch, Tulviste and Hagstrom, 1993, p. 343). For them Vygotsky's failure to provide an account of the causal role of each of the contextual elements in the development of specific modes of mind is evidence of universalism, which they view in a negative light:

> we think it is essential to recognise that, in isolation, a concern with this level of social process suggests a kind of universalism that is antithetical to the argument for social situatedness that Vygotsky himself was pursuing. This is because it fails to specify any reason to expect semiotically mediated intermental functioning to vary as a function of cultural, historical, and institutional setting. (Wertsch *et al.*, 1993, p. 343)

Wertsch *et al.* go beyond theorising the institutional to demanding the theorisation of some concrete mechanism: 'In order to avoid this shortcoming [i.e. the lack of such mechanism] a sociocultural approach must posit some concrete mechanism for connecting cultural, historical, and institutional processes with mediated intermental and intramental processes' (p. 343).

But in a later article Hatano and Wertsch note the need for an alternative to 'some form of simple, mechanistic transmission' (Hatano and Wertsch, 2001, p. 79). Nevertheless they run into difficulty in offering an alternative when it comes to explaining the means laid down by human activity in facilitating and sustaining mental processes. Any alternative cannot rely on a reductive image of mind that understands things in terms simply of mechanical response. There are grounds for believing that the concept of representation implicit in their analysis of cultural tools leads to precisely the type of 'mechanist transmission' from which they seek to distance themselves. Take the following sentence: 'This knowledge or system of representation can be regarded as a form of culture in mind, something constituted through participation in practice' (Hatano and Wertsch, 2001, p. 79). It is revealing in two closely connected ways. The first involves the equation of knowledge with a system of representation; the second, the idea that this knowledge or system of representation or form of culture in the mind is constituted through participation in practice. Both these themes are discussed further in Chapter 3. For the moment our immediate concern is with anticipations of these lines of argument in the history of Vygotskian debate and research, with reference in particular to two themes in the literature: the debate between John Anderson and James Greeno regarding the contrast between abstract knowledge and contextualised knowing, and Wertsch's account of the shaping of cognition by mediational means.

Before considering the idea that knowledge (understood as a system of representation) is constituted through participation in practice, we need to be clear about different interpretations of Vygotsky's work and the different evaluations of how it can most profitably be built upon. Furthermore, it is important to remember that the same terms have different meanings in different branches of Vygotskian research. For instance, for contemporary American scholars the phrase 'the institutional framework' does not have the same ring as it did amongst scholars in the 1930s, connoting, as it did then, historical and class background (Van der Veer, 2000). At the same time, some scholars in the 1920s would, under the rubric of Marxism, have accepted the arguments put forward by their contemporaries as non-Marxist or even anti-Marxist claims. The pattern is confused and confusing. Hence it is often necessary, when using a term, to qualify its meaning even when it appears self-evident.

As noted already, Vygotsky has been accused of neglecting the institutional framework in favour of the semiotic system. His focus on a semiotic system as opposed to a more specific account of the relationships between institutions, social practices and mind has a deep history. It is not by chance that two expressions, 'cultural-historical' and 'sociocultural', characterise Vygotskian research.[11] The differences between these expressions reflect different traditions, the former stressing the importance of the historical, and the latter the contextual. In order to gain an understanding of the reasons for the difference between these traditions of research it is necessary to appreciate the historical background to post-Vygotskian research.

THE HISTORICAL BACKGROUND

Wertsch *et al.* (1993) sketch the rationale for using the distinct expressions 'cultural-historical' and 'sociocultural' to characterise post-Vygotskian research. It is important to appreciate the different traditions in which these distinct expressions arose and the extent to which the interpretation of the cultural-historical tradition has been influenced by the experience of Stalinism. It is telling that Wertsch associates sociocultural research with 'the notion of culture derive[d] from the tradition of Boas' (Wertsch, del Rio and Alvarez, 1995, p. 10).[12] It is this tradition in anthropology that proved so influential for the criticism of 'evolutionism' and the assumptions of the 'psychic unity' of humankind made in anthropology. It is this aspect of evolutionism – that is, the view of history as universal human progress – that Wertsch claims to find in Vygotsky's work and that he associates with his philosophical commitment to the Enlightenment. Of the tradition stemming from Vygotsky's Russian followers, if not from Vygotsky himself, Wertsch writes:

> it assumed a notion of culture that is clearly in line with universalistic assumptions about the psychic unity of humankind and evolutionist claims associated with these assumptions ... The evolutionist assumptions indexed by the term 'sociohistorical' and 'cultural-historical' are one place where most authors in this volume part ways with Vygotsky's followers, if not Vygotsky himself. It is for this reason that we prefer the term 'sociocultural'. (Wertsch *et al.*, 1995, p. 10)

This passage illustrates two reasons why Wertsch wishes to keep the terms 'sociocultural' and 'cultural-historical' distinct: first, there is the rejection of what he and other contemporary commentators perceive as evolutionism; and second, and associated with this, there is his rejection of the psychic unity of humankind. Reaction against any suggestion of psychic unity goes hand in hand with a distancing from the notion of mind as universal. There are, however, problems with understanding exactly what is meant by 'universal' here. What 'psychic unity' might mean in Vygotskian terms is considered in Chapters 5 and 6, where it will be argued that the distinctive feature of human beings' 'experiencing' of the world is that it is via second nature. It is to this – experiencing the world via second nature – that the claim of universalism is attached.

Within the field of research under consideration, much of the terminology is underspecified and carries the historical baggage of political events, particularly of the history of Marxism and of the various practices justified in its name. Apart from 'universal', there are other terms, such as the aforementioned 'evolutionism', that inform consideration of Vygotsky's work, and the negative connotations associated with them are evident in the ambivalence of Wertsch's efforts to situate Vygotsky. When it comes to questions of development and history, politically positioned conceptions and terminology are apt to inform analysis. While noting Scribner's argument against any crude caricature of Vygotsky's understanding of history as recapitulationist,[13] Wertsch *et al.* still claim that Vygotsky's work with Luria on 'primitive thinking ... [made] strong assumptions about universal rationality and progress' (Wertsch *et al.*, 1995, p. 8). On the other hand, Wertsch *et al.* acknowledge that 'Vygotsky seemed to recognise historical processes other than those that fall under the heading of universal human progress' (p. 8). Scribner emphasises that Vygotsky's conception of history was sophisticated and that Vygotsky argued that 'only "sloth" ... would assimilate his theory to recapitulationist or parallelist positions'[14] (Scribner, 1985, p. 138). Wertsch *et al.* also recognise that Vygotsky did not accept the view that primitive languages were 'simpler or less adequate in all ways'; on the contrary, he adopted the opposite position (Wertsch *et al.*, 1995, p. 9).

Vygotsky's comment that only a form of intellectual sloth could lead a commentator to reduce his approach to a simplistic notion of development indicates that he was working towards a more complex view – one that was far from the caricature that aligns his work with what became Soviet practice. This more complex view put him at odds with his colleagues and those followers who formed the Kharkov school. In relation to Vygotsky's followers, Kozulin notes that:

> The Kharkovites solved the problem of the relation between consciousness and activity in the following way: 'The development of the consciousness of a child occurs as a result of the development of the system of psychological operations, which, in their turn, are determined by the actual relations between a child and reality.' This insistence on 'the actual relations of reality' became a major point of disagreement between the Kharkovites and Vygotsky. (Kozulin, 1986, pp. xliv–xlv).[15]

Kozulin argues that when the disagreement between the Kharkov school and Vygotsky is considered in the context of the Soviet Union, it can be seen necessarily to have specific consequences. As he puts it: 'the thesis of "actual relations with reality" fitted the Soviet dialectical materialist credo of the 1930s much better than Vygotsky's more complex cultural-historical model'[16] (Kozulin, 1986, p. xlv). The members of the Kharkov school of Soviet colleagues and followers of Vygotsky (Leontiev, Luria, and Zaporozhets) argued that 'activity' should be used as the basic analytic unit in psychology. There was debate in the Soviet Union over whether this extended or distorted Vygotsky's basic ideas (Wertsch, Minick and Arns, 1984, p. 154; Bakhurst, 1990).

Kozulin alerts us to the possibility that there might be rather more in what Vygotsky was working towards than what in fact developed in the work of his followers, who were inevitably compromised by the difficult political conditions of Stalinism. The attempt to work out the *mechanics* of the relationship between the historical, social and cultural determinations of mind took place against the background of differences emerging in Vygotskian research conditioned by political events in the Soviet Union. In the early 1930s Leontiev and many others loosened their connection with Vygotsky and moved from Moscow to Karkhov to create a scientific school and to develop the 'activity approach'. This change of focus from the consciousness of the cultural-historical school of Vygotsky towards a more 'materialist' approach occurred in a climate of terror that had become life-threatening (Zinchenko, 1995, p. 39). The issue that more than any other divided these schools was to do with whether research should focus on the problem of con-sciousness and on the problem of 'object-orientedness, in both internal and external mental activity' (Zinchenko, 1995, p. 41). The Kharkov school moved from the former to the latter. The differences occurred during a period of intense political pressure, at a time when some of Vygotsky's work had already been banned.

A sharp distinction was drawn between *materialism* and *idealism*, as these were then conceived. According to Zinchenko:

> The psychological theory of activity was concerned with the problem of real (i.e. concrete) tools and objects that humans, also in accordance with Marxism, place between themselves and nature. In other words what makes a human human? Symbol or thing? The crucifix or the hammer and sickle? If it is the symbol, then this is idealism. If it is the thing, then this is materialism or perhaps dialectical materialism. (Zinchenko, 1995 p. 44)

This stark separation of the material and the ideal played a central role in the failure to appreciate aspects of Vygotsky's work in the Soviet Union. But of particular relevance here is Zinchenko's awareness of the reductive and dehuman-ising implication of accounting for mind solely in terms of object-oriented activ-ity. He illustrates the implication of viewing what it is to be human as the outcome of a solely mechanical and material process by referring to the way in which research 'analogous to the theory of activity' was carried out under German and Italian totalitarian regimes. Intrinsic to the research was the aim of developing the kind of conformist personality that would acquiesce in the push to collectivisation. Activity was reduced to the notion that the 'human being was nothing more than a … functional organ that served as a means for carrying out activity that had been ordered' (Zinchenko, 1995, p. 51). Zinchenko emphasises the extent to which communist ideology pushed towards the removal of the subject from the under-standing of activity. Such an ideology was plainly alien to the views of Marx, who writes: 'We have fallen into a difficult position owing to the fact that we examined persons only as personified categories and not as individuums' (Marx, cited in Zinchenko, 1995, p. 51). It would be easy enough to relate Zinchenko's apprecia-tion of the potential determinism presented by a mechanical 'materialist' account of mind to practice today. There is, for instance, pressure to provide behaviourist accounts of human action in order to develop 'teacher-proof' practice: such accounts advocate standardised techniques and methods that do not depend on the capability of the teacher. Of immediate concern here, however, is the area of research concerned with bringing the situated nature of cognition to our attention and with contesting the idea of abstract rationality.

SITUATED COGNITION

Abstraction and decontextualised knowledge have been brought to the fore by work on the situated character of cognition. Jean Lave, with her focus on cognition as situated, argues that it is possible for the issue of abstraction to be dissolved and for all knowledge to be understood solely as situated. Lave notes that:

> Usually contextualised learning is not discussed alone, but as part of a duality of which decontextualised learning forms the other half. But the theories discussed in the previous section [and among these Lave includes activity theory] are intended to apply broadly to all social practices. They claim that there is no decontextualised social practice. Such a claim commits us to explaining what has often been taken to be 'decontextualised knowledge' or 'decontextualised learning' as contextualised social practices. (Lave, 1996, p. 22)

Situated cognitivists address a significant claim made by Vygotsky, namely that mind cannot be conceived as an attribute of an isolated individual. In line with this, situated cognitivists argue that thinking is conceived differently once the sociality of thought is taken properly into account. Their aim is to decentre cognition. This would resolve the learning paradox of explaining how we can come to know anything that we do not already know, by removing the dualism of *thought acting on world* and replacing it with *activity in context*. The work of Lave and Wenger counts as an important initiative in the understanding of learning, in shifting the focus from cognitive functions to *communities of practice*. The latter emphasises the situated character of knowledge production and reproduction. Lave and Wenger see this decentring of the analysis of learning as opening 'an alternative approach to the dichotomy … between learning by doing and learning by abstraction' (Lave and Wenger, 1991, p. 105). For Lave and Wenger, this is a part of 'a folk epistemology of dichotomies, for instance between "abstract" and "concrete" knowledge' (p. 104). They aim to dissociate learning from formal pedagogical intention and to understand situated learning activity as 'legitimate peripheral participation' in communities of practice. From this standpoint learning should be viewed less as a conscious or artificial process constructed via a specific pedagogical form and more as an event arising naturally from changes in activity within a specific domain of practice. Lave argues that it is difficult

> to avoid the conclusion that learning is ubiquitous in ongoing activity though often unrecognised as such. Situated activity always involves changes in knowledge and action … and 'changes in knowledge and action' are central to what we mean by 'learning'… We have come to the conclusion … that there is no such thing as 'learning' sui generis, but only changing participation in the culturally designed settings of everyday life. (Lave, 1996, p. 6)

Two points follow from Lave's view: first, what was previously seen as decontextualised is subsequently considered as just another form of contextualised knowledge; and second, learning is viewed as a more naturalised, less artificial, process. Hence, 'Conventional theories of learning and schooling appeal to the decontextualised character of some knowledge ... whereas in a theory of situated activity, "decontextualised learning activity" is a contradiction in terms' (p. 6). This view of all learning as contextualised attempts to replace the dualism of a mind acting on a world by way of a reconceptualisation of knowledge. The resulting view of knowledge as the outcome of situated practice lends itself to an anti-realist stance, even in its conception of science:

> The idea of learning as cognitive acquisition – whether of facts, knowledge, problem-solving strategies, or metacognitive skills – seems to dissolve when learning is conceived of as the construction of present versions of past experience for several persons acting together ... And when scientific practice is viewed as just another everyday practice ... it is clear that theories of 'situated activity' provide different perspectives on 'learning' and its 'contexts'. (Lave, 1996, p. 6)

Although the idea of scientific practice as 'just another everyday practice' implicates scientific knowledge in the constructive activity of individuals in contexts, the relativisation of scientific knowledge does not automatically follow. Attention to the way in which cognition is situated and formed by context allows different attitudes towards realism. In clarifying different viewpoints on context as situated activity, Lave indicates two different positions found in contextual approaches. She paints one approach as holding to a world out there, independent of human activity, and the other, 'social constructionist' approach, as a far more limited conception of the context in which humans engage in activity. In the first case, world history is the context in which human activity takes place, but, in the second, activity creates its own context since intersubjectivity serves as the basis of what the world means to humans. To reiterate the relation between these contrasting views:

> One argues that the central theoretical relation is historically constituted between persons engaged in socioculturally constructed activity and the world in which they are engaged. Activity theory is a representative of such a theoretical position. The other focuses on the construction of the world in social interaction; this leads to the view that activity is its own context. Here the central theoretical relation is the intersubjective relation among co-participants in social interaction. This derives from a tradition of phenomenological social theory.[17] (Lave, 1996, p. 17)

Lave is well aware that the view of context developed within the phenomenological tradition can lead to the 'eras[ing] of historical processes, both large and small' (p. 20). She explains:

> The major difficulty of phenomenological and activity theory in the eyes of others will be plain: Those who start with the views that social activity is its own context dispute claims that objective social structures exist other than in social-interactional construction in situ. Activity theorists argue, on the other hand, that

the concrete connectedness and meaning of activity cannot be accounted for by analysis of the immediate situation. (Lave, 1996, p. 20)

What is clear is that the trend away from abstract knowledge towards a 'distributed form of knowledge production' raises issues that are so far unresolved. The latter examines knowledge as distributed and sustained across a variety of artefacts, discourses and social practices in 'context'. Of particular importance in this respect is the attempt to account for the mechanics of such a relation of different elements involved in the production of knowledge. This attempt involves questions concerning representation, affordance, and cause and effect, all of which are undertheorised at present (Derry, 2008). But more importantly it involves human freedom and agency to the extent that these play a critical role in any proper consideration of these questions.

As the historical background to the field of Vygotskian studies illustrates, the question of freedom has been at issue in both the cultural-historical and activity-theory traditions. The question of agency has remained particularly pertinent in the light of the claims made for artificial intelligence. Artificial intelligence researchers have also adopted a conception of cognition as emergent in an environment rather than programmable in advance. Wertsch, Tulviste and Hagstrom (1993) remark on how the use of computers to take over tasks formerly carried out by humans raises questions concerning whether computers can be agents with consciousness. At the same time that commentators entertain the idea of an artificial intelligence on a par with human intelligence, the role of theory in facilitating thought and action is subordinated to emphasis on *participation* in a *community of practice* as the key to learning.

Once the contextual and embedded character of mind is emphasised, the question arises of how knowing as a process (as opposed to an abstract set of principles contained in a system of knowledge) can be transferred between different domains.

THE TRANSFER PROBLEM AND THE IMPLICATIONS FOR POLICY

The issue of decontextualisation is posed most sharply by what is known as the transfer problem (Guile and Young, 2003; Tuomi-Gröhn and Engeström, 2003). In effect, once knowledge is understood as contextualised then the issue of its application in different domains becomes critical. Once the conception of mind and world has been radically rethought – first, in relation to the intellect's development and sociogenetic origin, and second, in relation to knowledge conceived as existing only in processes of human construction/intervention – a number of policy implications follow. Writers concerned with the transfer problem contest the idea of knowledge being delivered by an expert, acquired by the learner in a general form, and then applied in a variety of specific circumstances. They reject the idea of a universally applicable knowledge capable of *transfer* across domains.

Kirshner and Whitson understand what is termed *decontextualised* knowledge in terms of transfer across contexts – that is, with the idea that knowledge is not locally bound, but rather is tied to a specific form of pedagogic practice (for example, a passive transmission mode of learning):

> If abstract decontextualised knowledge is theorised to be the means by which people transfer learning from context to context, then schools will set their goal to provide as much of it as possible with the greatest possible efficiency. Thus teaching becomes telling and learning becomes listening and memorizing. (Kirshner and Whitson, 1997, p. viii)

The argument here relies on equating decontextualised knowledge with an impoverished instructional mode of teaching restricted to rote learning. The complications that surround the issue of decontextualisation can be seen in the debates about how knowledge can be transferred from one domain and applied in another. Attempts have been made to overcome the polarised character of the discussion that has emerged around the transfer problem. An influential discussion in the literature was conducted between John Anderson and colleagues and James Greeno. It relates to concerns over the value of what is described as propositional and abstract knowledge, and to the claim that this mode of representation (dressed up as universal knowledge) is the result of elite interests and fails to respond to the diversity of learners (Anderson, Reder and Simon, 1996).

Greeno has argued that the polarisation of arguments about 'situativity' results from the different usage of the same terms and from confusion over levels of analysis. Anderson, although not expressly rejecting the argument for situativity out of hand, offers examples of boundary crossing and successful applications of generic learning. Greeno responds that Anderson sets up a straw man on the grounds that his argument employs a cognitivist model. But Greeno's response neglects important issues. By shifting attention to the communicative dimension of knowledge, the situative approach finds it difficult, if not impossible, to avoid a model that restricts understanding to cognitive states as the outcome of situated contexts.

Anderson remarks on the frequently cited example of Carraher, Carraher and Schliemann's (1985) account of Brazilian street children, who can perform mathematics when making sales in the street but are unable to solve similar problems presented in a school context. The example is famously used by Lave for the more familiar purpose of criticising the failures of schools to offer learning that is of use to the learner (Lave, 1988, p. 149). The extent to which discussions of decontextualised knowledge are implicated in key education policy decisions is indicated by Anderson's critique of what he sees as Lave's value-laden interpretation:

> The literature on situation-specificity of learning often comes with a value judgment about the merits of knowledge tied to a non-school context relative to school-taught knowledge and an implied or expressed claim that school knowledge is not legitimate. Lave ... goes so far as to suggest that school-taught mathematics serves only to justify an arbitrary and unfair class structure. (Anderson *et al.*, 1996, p. 6)

Greeno takes issue with the way in which a cognitivist framework is used to support an argument that, he suggests, could equally well be read within a framework of situativity. So where Anderson cites evidence that 'it is not the case that learning is wholly tied to a specific context' (Greeno, 1997, p. 7), Greeno turns the point around to argue that, on the contrary, the findings can be read as 'supporting the view that activities in some situations include aspects of practices that have been learned in different types of situations' (p. 7), thus maintaining that what might appear to be abstract knowledge can be understood in terms of a discourse. The most important question here is whether the phenomenon that Greeno views as a case of discourse and Anderson a case of abstraction is really one and the same.[18]

Greeno attempts to reconcile what appear to be contradictory positions by arguing that generality is conceptualised differently in the two perspectives. However, the situative understanding that he claims is capable of moving beyond context presupposes some commonality between contexts: it is this common ground that makes possible a transfer from one context to another. As a result, Greeno ends up in a position close to Lave's, and he actually quotes her results to the effect that reasoning activities can reach mathematically correct conclusions without making significant use of the algorithms typically taught in school. And, to underline the point, he goes on to argue that 'if a goal of education is for students to reason successfully in their everyday activities outside of school, school mathematics programs that are limited to teaching algorithmic skills do not reach important aspects of those reasoning activities' (Greeno, 1997, p. 7).

Greeno sees a problem with the terminology used in this area when he takes up what he terms a 'cognitivist position' regarding 'knowledge'. The quotation marks here are apt because he argues that, from within a situative framework, the term 'knowing' is a better way of evoking a process than 'knowledge', and 'generality of knowing' is a better term than 'transfer of knowledge': '"knowing" refers more appropriately to regular patterns in someone's participation in interactions with other people and with material and representational systems, and "generality of knowing" is a more accurate phrase than "transfer of knowledge"' (p. 11). What is missing here is a sense of a transformative or creative capacity of the knower making the move from one context to another possible and in the absence of this the gap left is filled sociologically by the idea of transferring 'patterns of participation with people and objects'. This suggests that the knower is able to appear knowledgeable in the new context by replicating patterns of activity as though, in Brandom's example used earlier, the repeating of the shout 'Fire' is sufficient to be read as *knowledge* of combustion on the part of the shouter.

It may be the case that, when the inadequacy of schooling is judged in terms of failing to prepare learners for jobs, the replication of 'patterns of participation' would be appropriate. However, on such a conception of schooling, learning is seen in reductive terms: it attempts to meet certain ends but not to go beyond them. Such an instrumental view of schooling is evident in Greeno's argument: 'we need to take into account the kinds of activities in which we want students to learn to be successful, and develop learning environments in which they can develop their abilities to participate in certain kinds of practices that are important to them' (p. 13).

Greeno takes issue with the significance to be attributed to the terms 'specific' and 'abstract'. For instance, when he refers to the transfer of knowledge between domains, the emphasis is not upon a concept of abstract knowledge that can be applied in different specific conditions but upon the generalisability of patterns of experience. As he puts it, 'It seems more likely that knowing how to use abstract representations can be a significant part of general knowing, but that knowing abstraction is neither sufficient nor necessary for generality' (p. 13). The problem here centres on what is meant by 'knowing abstractions' or 'knowing how to use abstract representations'. Greeno advances his argument by making a parallel connection between abstract knowledge and abstract representations. In response to this, Chapter 3 takes up the work of Robert Brandom, who, building on Wilfrid Sellars, argues that knowing is never merely a matter of knowing a representation but always involves the reasons that follow and the reasons that support it. A significant point to note here is what is in effect Greeno's identification of abstract knowledge and abstract *representation* – as though the ability to understand and apply quadratic equations is the same as the capacity to reproduce them mechanically as a purely formal exercise, or, to use a recurrent example, as though the significance of the shout of 'fire' by an adult is the same as the same cry made by an infant.[19]

Greeno uses John Searle's parable (1980) of the Chinese room to illustrate the poverty of mass education. The Chinese room is a thought experiment developed by Searle in order to counter the view, in philosophy of mind and artificial intelligence, that the mind is an information-processing system. Searle's thought experiment is designed to show that a computer cannot possess mind or understanding. Searle criticises the view, advanced by advocates of artificial intelligence, that by following rules machines can transform strings of characters to produce responses that could have the same form as those that a human being would make in similar circumstances. Searle intended his example to be used to illustrate that a machine cannot have understanding or consciousness and that, as a result, what it does cannot be described as thinking.

However, while Greeno uses the parable to attack abstract knowledge, Searle's purpose is the different one of distinguishing between human and machine activity. The parable shows that a process of transmitting instructions does not require human understanding and that human activity is not reducible to that of a machine. For Greeno this parable is an illustration of the shortcomings of abstract knowledge, that is – in the case of mathematics – of the apprehension of formal rules and procedures without the pupil having understood their meaning (Greeno, 1997, p. 14). But what Greeno calls abstract knowledge is really only abstract representation, and his failure to distinguish the one from the other calls into question his general criticism of abstract knowledge. Machines process 'representations' without any knowledge of what they mean. His case against abstract representation may be valid, but this is not sufficient to justify its use as a critique of abstraction as a general practice.

Within the field of Vygotskian studies there are other influential conceptions of knowledge: some take the view, for instance, that decontextualisation does not render knowledge inert. For instance, the cultural-historical tradition emerging from the Soviet Union, particularly the work of Davydov (1988) and Hedegaard (1998), stresses conscious instruction rather than tacit apprenticing. Teaching, according to this tradition, is not simply a matter of telling, but requires expertise and deep knowledge of the subject.[20] This 'deep knowledge' is necessary for the teacher to be in a position to unpack and open up the genetic development of ideas and to provoke students into acquiring scientific concepts through a process that recapitulates that of their development. An appreciation of the depth of knowledge of the subject on the part of the teacher is necessary for pupils to acquire scientific concepts.

When Vygotsky talked of scientific concepts (as part of the content of school curricula), he did not believe that abstraction entailed decontextualised rationality in the sense of being totally separate from context. At stake here is the meaning to be attached to the term 'context'. Even Lave and Wenger, who reject any form of decontextualisation, concede that what constitutes a community of practice need not be specifically geographical or temporal. For Vygotsky, however, concepts are only meaningful, and hence only concepts, when they comprise elements of a system of connections that is historically constituted. This is totally different from the shallow notion of 'concepts as representations' criticised as part of the transmission mode of pedagogy found in formal schooling. Vygotsky was clear about the need to challenge conceptions of knowledge based on our senses, where knowledge is taken to be inert and to be appropriate to passive absorption. This point is taken up in Chapter 3 in relation to Brandom's discussion of the dominance of the concept of representation. For Vygotsky concepts are mediators:

> with the help of the concept, we are able to penetrate through the external appearance of phenomena to penetrate into their essence, just as with the aid of a microscope, we disclose in a drop of water a complex and rich life, or the complex structure of the cell hidden from our eyes. (Vygotsky, 1998, p. 54)

Vygotsky often cites Marx's claim that science would be unnecessary 'if the form of a manifestation and the essence of things coincided directly' (1998, p. 54). He makes the anti-positivist claims that things cannot be understood independently of one another and that concepts do similar work to technologies such as microscopes:

> For this reason thinking in concepts is the most adequate method of knowing reality because it penetrates into the internal essence of things, for the nature of things is disclosed not in direct contemplation of one single object or another, but in connections and relations that are manifested in movement and development of the object, and these connect it to the rest of reality. The internal connection of things is disclosed with the help of thinking in concepts, for to develop a concept of some object means to disclose a series of connections and relations of the object with the rest of reality, to include it in a complex system of phenomena. (Vygotsky, 1998, p. 54)

Given his point of view, it would be difficult to believe that scientific concepts could be taught without disclosing their relationships to one another – what

Brandom calls their inferential form (see Chapter 3). Kirshner and Whitson may be correct in characterising the dominant form of pedagogy as 'transmission', but it does not follow that this mode of pedagogical practice is the result of the particular type of (decontextualised) knowledge.

There is no doubt that researchers in the area are correct to point to the needs, first, for the active and positive involvement of learners in their learning and, second, for any learning to be infused with purpose. Clearly an impoverished conception of knowledge entailing poor teaching practices demands critique. However, this critique is inevitably affected by the demands of policy, which in contemporary conditions invariably requires a deterministic scientific approach.

DETERMINATION, CONDITIONING OR SHAPING?

The advocates of situated cognition are not free from the dualism they oppose so strongly. As Kirshner and Whitson point out, many issues remain unresolved. One of these is the overly determinist conception of what it is to be human that arises from the attempt of post-Vygotskian researchers to work out the mechanics of cognition arising in activity. Kirshner and Whitson use Collins's critique of Pierre Bourdieu's work as an example of what they criticise, namely the understanding of the discursive as ultimately reducible to something else such as class conditions, capital composition or habitus (Collins, 1993, p. 123). They suggest that the 'Vygotskian tradition is similarly weighted toward a deterministic social plane' (Kirshner and Whitson, 1997, p. 8), citing the often quoted passage in which he argues that functions in the child's development appear twice, first between people and then within the child: 'Social relations or relations among people genetically underlie all higher [mental] functions and their relationships' (Vygotsky, cited by Kirshner and Whitson, 1997, p. 8). However, they also note both that proponents of situated cognition are fully aware of the challenges they face in attempting to move away from the mind–body dualism underlying traditional cognitive psychology and that situated cognition theory is generally viewed by its proponents as a work in progress.

The problems of determinism, which were already present in classical socio-logical theory, have become far more serious with explanations of human activity in terms of enculturation through a community of practice. In sociol-ogy, where enculturation is explained in terms of socialisation rather than activity, criticisms were levelled against what were taken to be overly deter-minist characterisations of how humans become fully human. Dennis Wrong's classic commentary, 'The Oversocialized Conception of Man in Modern Sociology' (Wrong, 1969) offers a particularly clear example of how sociol-ogy, by virtue of its attempt to explain socialisation as a causal and constitutive process, was forced into a highly deterministic conception of what it is to be human. Wrong especially challenged the view developed by Talcott Parsons. Drawing on Durkheim, Parsons had argued in *The Structure of Social Action* that social rules are constituted by the actors' ends and do not arise externally. Wrong discussed the variety of ways in which internalisation has been equated by sociologists with 'learning' or 'habit formation'. He argued that, although Freud became influential for sociology (and for Parsons) with regard to explanation of the internalisation of social norms, none of these ensuing sociological accounts has any real sense of inner conflict and tension between powerful impulses in the way that Freud construed them (Wrong, 1969, p. 125). For Freud, Wrong notes, internalisation means that a norm has been introjected to become part of the superego, so that individuals suffer guilt feelings if they fail to live up to it. Internalisation does not, of course, mean that a person will actually live up to the norm. Wrong's methodological claim is that the psychoanalytic approach, which admits tensions and repression and sees 'inner life as a battle-field of conflicting motives' (p. 125), is less determinist than the sociological approach.

The determinism that Wrong criticises in sociology is carried further by writers such as Lave who take as their brief not simply the explanation of behaviour but also the apprehension, at least by implication, of the nature of mind. Enculturation for Lave entails the development of mind in context. For Lave, 'Understanding-in-practice looks like a more powerful source of enculturation than [socialisation through] the pedagogical efforts of caregivers and teachers' (Lave, 1997, p. 32). Citing Ortner's (1984) argument, Lave believes that the concept of socialisation has been replaced by the claim that everyday practices 'embody within themselves, the fundamental notions of temporal, spatial and social ordering that underlie and organise the social system as a whole' (Ortner, cited by Lave, 1997, p. 32). The incorporation of psychology in the work of Lave and Wenger, however, leads to potentially an even deeper level of 'oversocialisation' since *learning-in-practice* is taken to build higher mental functions and modes of identity and is not limited to one aspect of a person's activity. Activity in a social context is a form of apprenticeship, albeit one involving conflict, though this is seldom theorised. Insofar as Wrong's criticism deals with methodology, however, it covers Lave's position as well.[21]

Nardi shows similar concern about the potentially determinate nature of explanation that is implicit in activity theory when she raises questions about the limitations of that theory.[22] She criticises its emphasis on object-oriented action and the reduction of activity to three levels. According to Nardi, 'activity theory excels at describing object-related activity but says little about how we are diverted, distracted, interrupted, seduced away from our objects, subject to serendipity and surprise' (Nardi, 1997, p. 377). It is not by chance that she draws on a passage from George Eliot's *Middlemarch* to illustrate the complexity of consciousness. Eliot was greatly influenced by Spinoza and was the first to translate his *Ethics* into English. In the passage Nardi selects, the protagonist is thinking of three totally different things at the same time as well as experiencing 'a powerful emotional response that reverberates through his body to his very fingertips. Indeed, Eliot avers that "every molecule in his body" is affected, thereby asserting the primacy of the body in our activity, our responses to events' (Nardi, 1997, p. 377). Nardi seeks to emphasise the ambivalence and contradictory variables that the protagonist is facing at a decisive moment.

For Wertsch *et al.* the issue of determinism comes up in the role played by artefacts within sociocultural explanations. They write, for example:

> While the cultural tools or artifacts involved in mediation certainly play a central role in shaping action, they do not determine or cause action in some kind of static, mechanistic way... such cultural tools are powerless to do anything. They can have their impact only when individuals use them. (Wertsch, del Rio and Alvarez, 1995, p. 22)

But at the same time that they resist determinist explanation, Wertsch *et al.* seek to credit cultural tools with the capacity to constrain our actions: 'We can never "speak from nowhere", given that we speak (or more broadly act) only by invoking mediational means that are available in the "cultural tool kit" provided by the sociocultural setting in which we operate' (Wertsch, del Rio and Alvarez, 1995, p. 25). For Wertsch the social character of mind requires a conception of agency extending beyond the individual. This agency can be understood only if the mediational means that are party to it are seen as both products and sources of social-cultural contexts.

Wertsch, Tulviste and Hagstrom argue in favour of the sociocultural situatedness of agency: 'The line of argument we pursue is that the mediational means that shape human mental functioning reflect and are fundamentally involved in creating and maintaining cultural, historical and institutional contexts' (Wertsch, Tulviste and Hagstrom, 1993, p. 344).[23] They present this claim as the alternative to the poverty of the 'typically modern notion of freedom, as the ability to act on one's own, without outside interference or subordination to outside authority (Taylor, 1985, p. 5) which underlies psychology and limits the possibility of dealing adequately with how sociocultural forces shape or constitute individuals' (p. 338).

As we shall see in Chapter 5, the crucial issue for Wertsch *et al.* is the conception of human freedom as acting without 'subordination to outside authority'. In rejecting such a view of free will, it is not unexpected that, in an effort to recognise that human will does not work in conditions free of constraint, they turn to crediting cultural tools with a form of agency. However, Spinoza, who was particularly important for Vygotsky, was able to acknowledge constraint on human activity yet see freedom as an altered position within this restraint. Thus the attempt theoretically to credit mediational means with the capacity to shape human activity may press its case too far if it overlooks the distinguishing feature of human beings: that they are free. Wertsch *et al.* are fully aware that the implicit assumptions of psychology harbour problems, and they cite Joravsky approvingly for lamenting the neglect of fundamental questions: 'Sophisticated people have learned to evade questions that seemed urgent a century ago' (Wertsch, Tulviste and Hagstrom, 1993, p. 336). Nevertheless, instead of exploring the concept of freedom, they restrict themselves to examining instances where freedom appears to be curtailed by mediational means. In a sense it can be said that, to use the language of Gregory Bateson (1972), they embrace a conception of will that 'extends it beyond the skin' to include mediational means (Wertsch *et al.*, 1993, p. 352). The argument of Wertsch *et al.* is that the boundary of agency must be extended to include an 'irreducible aggregate of individuals (or individuals in intermental functioning) together with mediational means' (Wertsch *et al.*, 1993, p. 341).[24] For this argument they find further support in Bakhtin's notion of speech genres.

Wertsch *et al.* recruit this notion of Bakhtin's, which they liken to Basil Bernstein's account of language codes, to support their claim of a determinate relation between particular social forms and specific genres. Citing Holquist and Emerson (1981, p. 430), they claim that social languages are 'peculiar to a specific stratum of society ... within a given social system at a given time' (Wertsch et al., 1993, p. 346).[25] Drawing first on Bakhtin's distinction between a social language and a national language, and second on Bakhtin's view that when a word is used it is neither neutral nor impersonal but 'rather exists in other people's mouths, in other people's concrete contexts, serving other people's intentions' (Wertsch *et al.*, 1993, p. 345), they claim for words a determining effect on the intramental. Bakhtin called this 'ventriloquism', and Wertsch *et al.* see it as a special kind of dialogicality, which they term 'double voicedness'.

The importance of mediational means in forming and shaping the means of thought is carried further in Tulviste's work. Wertsch and his co-authors cite Tulviste in support of their argument about the cultural domain as the context of activity and as a factor of crucial importance for specific modes of thinking:

> Tulviste ... has argued that various modes of thinking correspond functionally to an array of 'cultural activities' and are created by them. Each cultural activity (e.g. science, arts, everyday life, religion) poses specific tasks that can be solved only by using the corresponding modes of thinking. For instance, practical thinking or common sense is not sufficient to solve scientific tasks, whereas scientific thinking is of little use when writing a poem or a sermon or when solving most everyday problems. (Wertsch *et al.*, 1993, p. 351)

This degree of specialisation in the modes of thought is viewed by the authors as antithetical to universal rationality since 'mental functioning and the mediational means it employs are viewed as being domain-specific' (Wertsch *et al.*, 1993, p. 351). The point is put most strongly when they write: 'In an important sense, individuals can be no more intelligent than the psychological tools they employ' (Wertsch *et al.*, 1993, p. 352). This statement is particularly significant for the degree of determination and power it attributes to mediational means – sufficient to affect potential intelligence. Great weight is placed on the meditational means, while consideration of the implicit assumption about the nature of agency and freedom is neglected. The impetus to explore the extent of the contribution of mediational means is a powerful one. As Wertsch points out, the approach used in post-Vygotskian research is quite distinct from mainstream cognitive psychology and it opens up a completely new way of thinking about mind. But it is the implicit assumptions that Joravsky comments upon that are the key to development in this field.

This chapter has considered the question of abstract rationality. Once the idea of a free-floating abstract reason – that is, of one decontextualised from the practices that generate it – has been rejected, the question arises as to by what means does reasoning develop. What are the conditions of its constitution? Clearly a whole range of factors contribute to cognition and the pressure to provide a causal account of these is so overwhelming that implicit assumptions go unexamined. As Wrong reminds us: 'If our assumptions are left implicit, we will inevitably presuppose a view of man that is tailor made to our special needs' (Wrong, 1969, p. 131). A central theme of this book is that by not making underlying assumptions explicit, theoretical positions do not deal with their own internal contradictions.

The next chapter begins to examine these implicit assumptions by exploring the dualism implicit in the representational paradigm underlying post-Vygotskian and other areas of research. This is presented within the broader frame of constructivism and schooling since it is in relation to these that reason and universal rationality are brought into question.

NOTES

1 Wertsch provides the following examples; 'the meaning of *five* or *electron* or *interpsychological* can be and often is established by definitions that are abstract (i.e. independent of particular use) and hence identical across various contexts' (Wertsch, 1992, p. 120).

2 Wertsch introduces the idea of the 'privileging' of particular *voices* over others, arguing that it 'can be seen as implicitly lying at the foundation of many researchers' claims about difference between sexes (Gilligan, 1982), between schooled and nonschooled people ... and between cultures' (Wertsch, 1992, p. 122). He goes on to argue that there is a need for 'the development of a new theory of meaning'.

3 Hirst, renowned for his ground-breaking work on *forms of knowledge* and their significance for the development of mind, revised his position in recent years: 'it was the work of MacIntyre in *After Virtue* (1981) and *Whose Justice? Whose Rationality?* (1988), followed by Dunne's impressive *Back to the Rough Ground* (1993), that particularly led me to radically rethink the whole character of reason, its place in human life, and hence its proper place in education' (Hirst, 2008, p. 119).

4 Wertsch views Vygotsky's discussion of 'scientific concepts' as an indication of the belief that a universal human rationality was the *telos* of human development. For Wertsch the fact that Vygotsky recognises 'other' forms of mental functioning suggests inconsistency. Wertsch sees this inconsistency as due to 'a struggle between basic philosophical commitments [Enlightenment philosophy] on the one hand, and the results of analysing the complexities of human speech on the other' (Wertsch, 1996, p. 26).

5 'Post-modern theorists are mostly united by what we ... reject from modernism, and unanimously by our rejection of arguments for universally valid "master narratives", meta-theories or discourses of any sort that aspire to set the terms of the conversation for anyone else' (Lemke, 1999, p. 91).

6 It is revealing that Wertsch views Vygotsky's use of rationality as a tool. This immediately sets up the discussion about Vygotsky's emphasis on abstract rationality in a way that supports Wertsch's reading. To see rationality as a tool is to separate it from the world and then to suggest its artificial application. This is at odds with the reading of Vygotsky that this book develops.

7 This is due to the unproblematic use in explanation of the same relation critiqued in the case of abstract reason and the assumption of the causal character of local explanations.

8 The conditions in which practices take place range from pedagogical practice and curricula design, to funding and the restraints upon teachers and the wider society and are not exhausted by contexts provided by formal schooling.

9 John Haugeland expresses the demand of externalists, to free ourselves from prejudicial Cartesian commitments: 'if we are to understand the mind as the locus of intelligence, we cannot follow Descartes in regarding it as separable in principle from body and world ... Mind ... is not incidentally but *intimately* embodied and *intimately* embedded in the world' (Haugeland, 1998, pp. 236–237).

10 The relationship between policy and developmental change is not transparent as it is often assumed. The relationship between the intention to develop something and its own momentum of development is not isomorphic. See Cowen and Shenton (1996).

11 The distinction between the two phrases has been considered sufficiently important to warrant two separate international research organisations, which have now merged (http://www.iscar. org/en/Institutional_History_).

12 Anthropological literature has been important for debates about the nature of rationality because an influential strand in anthropology (following Boas, Sapir and Whorf) has argued for a relativist approach to culture. See Bloch (2005) for a critique of this approach. Wertsch recognises that Vygotsky would be at odds with such relativist positions.

13 'Recapitulation' refers to the theory that the development of the individual repeats the stages of the development of the species. This is expressed in the phrase 'ontogeny recapitulates phylogeny'.

14 'Parallelism' refers to the similarity between processes in the development of an individual organism and those in the development of the species. It can also refer to the parallel between a child passing through earlier stages of development in common with the development of adults in earlier epochs.

15 The quoted passage in the extract from Kozulin is from A. N. Leontiev, in a work published in 1935.

16 However, Kozulin notes that the ideological benefits of Leontiev's revisionism did have serious scientific underpinnings but that 'Ideological cautiousness, honest scientific agreement, and also a misunderstanding of Vygotsky's ideas – all were intricately interwoven in the phenomenon that later became known as Leontiev's theory of activity' (Kozulin, 1986, p. xlv).

17 These viewpoints replicate the classic polarisation in sociology between agency and structure.

18 Walkerdine, in her work on the learning of mathematics (1990), goes as far as to suggest that what are understood as highly abstract cognitive activities may be seen as a matter of discourse.

19 The identification of abstract knowledge with abstract representation or decontextualised knowledge in Greeno's account is in tune with the contemporary practice of mass schooling which he would of course criticise. Hence, his criticism of that practice is legitimate, while the way he construes abstract *knowledge* is not.

20 'Knowledge of the subject' is not the same as the conception of 'subject knowledge' currently laid down in British government prescriptions for teacher education. It is more akin to what is implied in the concept of *Bildung*, where a teacher pursues a subject or a topic with students in such a way as to allow a deep and developmental grasp of issues and concepts. Such knowledge is certainly not guaranteed by possession of a 'good degree', as the current criteria for teachers require. Indeed, research has indicated how passing examinations at degree level does not necessitate a proper grasp of a subject. For a discussion of the case of mathematical knowledge see Suggate, Davis and Goulding (2010, chapter 1).

21 'If our assumptions are left implicit, we will inevitably presuppose a view of man that is tailor made to our special needs' (Wrong, 1969, p. 131). The underlying argument informing this book is that by not making underlying assumptions explicit, theoretical positions do not deal with their own internal contradictions.

22 Nardi works within the activity theory field and utilises activity theory to address issues of design and pedagogy in the application of new technologies.

23 In a footnote Wertsch *et al.* attempt to clarify their conception of the power of agency as attributable to and inextricable from the mediation of tools: 'In our view, the psychological tools that mediate thinking, memory, and other mental functions are typically shaped strongly by forces

distinct from the dictates of mental functioning and for this reason import "foreign" structures and processes into this functioning' (Wertsch, Tulviste and Hagstrom, 1993, p. 353).

24 'The irreducible unit of analysis for agency is "individual(s) operating with mediational means"', and for convenience Wertsch *et al.* shorten this to 'mediated agency' (Wertsch, Tulviste and Hagstrom, 1993, p. 342).

25 Wertsch *et al.* view a language as a mediational means: 'The notion of social language is useful because it is a mediational means that is inherently tied to a sociocultural setting' (Wertsch, Tulviste, and Hagstrom, 1993, p. 346).

REFERENCES

Anderson, J., Reder, L. and Simon, H. (1996) Situated Learning and Education, *Educational Researcher*, 25:4, 5–11.

Bakhurst, D. (1990) Social Memory in Soviet Thought. In: D. Middleton and D. Edwards (eds) *Collective Remembering* (London: Sage), pp. 203–226.

Bateson G. (1972). *Steps to an Ecology of Mind: A Revolutionary Approach to Man's Understanding of Himself* (New York: Ballantine).

Bloch, M. (2005) Where Did Anthropology Go?: Or the Needs for 'Human Nature'. In: M. Bloch (ed.) *Essays on Cultural Transmission* (Oxford: Berg), pp. 1–20.

Burgess, T. (1993) Reading Vygotsky. In: H. Daniels (ed.) *Charting the Agenda, Educational Activity After Vygotsky* (London: Routledge), pp. 1–29.

Carraher, T.N., Carraher, D.W. and Schliemann, A.D. (1985) Mathematics in the Streets and in Schools, *British Journal of Developmental Psychology*, 3, 21–29.

Clark, A. (1997) *Being There: Putting Brain, Body, and World Together Again* (London: Routledge).

Clark, A. (1998) Magic Words: How Language Augments Human Computation. In: P. Carruthers and J. Boucher (eds) *Language and Thought: Interdisciplinary Themes* (Cambridge: Cambridge University Press), pp. 162–183.

Cole, M. (1996) *Cultural Psychology: A Once and Future Discipline* (Cambridge, MA: Harvard University Press).

Collins, J. (1993) Determination and Contradiction: An Appreciation of and Critique of the Work of Pierre Bourdieu on Language and Education. In: C. Calhoun, E. LiPuma and M. Postone (eds) *Bourdieu: Critical Perspectives* (Chicago: University of Chicago Press), pp. 116–138.

Cowen, M.P. and Shenton, R.W. (1996) *Doctrines of Development* (London: Routledge).

Davydov, V.V. (1988). Problems of Developmental Teaching, parts 1, 2 and 3, *Soviet Education*, 30:8, 15–97, 30:9, 3–83, 30:10, 3–77.

Derry, J. (2008) Technology-Enhanced Learning: A Question of Knowledge, *Journal of Philosophy of Education*, 42:3/4, 505–519.

Forman, E.A., Minick, N. and Stone, C.A. (eds) (1993) *Contexts for Learning: Sociocultural Dynamics in Children's Development* (Oxford: Oxford University Press).

Greeno, J.G. (1997) On Claims that Answer the Wrong Questions, *Educational Researcher*, 27:1, 5–17.

Guile, D. and Young, M. (2003) Transfer and Transition in Vocational Education: Some Theoretical Considerations. In: T. Tuomi-Gröhn and Y. Engeström (eds) *Between School and Work: New Perspectives on Transfer and Boundary Crossing* (Amsterdam: Pergamon), pp. 63–84.

Hatano, G. and Wertsch, J.V. (2001) Sociocultural Approaches to Cognitive Development: The Constitutions of Culture in Mind, *Human Development*, 44, 77–83.

Haugeland, J. (1998) Mind Embodied and Embedded. In: J. Haugeland *Having Thought: Essays in the Metaphysics of Mind* (Cambridge, MA: Harvard University Press), pp. 207–237.

Hedegaard, M. (1998) Situated Learning and Cognition: Theoretical Learning and Cognition, *Mind, Culture and Activity*, 5:2, 114–26.

Hirst, P.H. (2008) In Pursuit of Reason. In: L.J. Waks (ed.) *Leaders in Philosophy of Education: Intellectual Self Portraits* (Rotterdam: Sense), pp. 113–124.

Holquist, M. and Emerson, C. (1981). *The Dialogic Imagination. Four Essays by M. M. Bakhtin* (Austin: University of Texas Press).

Joravsky, D. (1989) *Russian Psychology* (Oxford: Blackwell).

Kirshner, D. and Whitson, J.A. (eds) (1997) *Situated Cognition: Social, Semiotic and Psychological Perspectives* (Mahwah, NJ: Lawrence Erlbaum Associates).

Kozulin, A. (1986) Vygotsky in Context. In: L. Vygotsky *Thought and Language*, A. Kozulin trans. and ed. (Cambridge, MA: MIT Press), pp. xi–lvi.

Lave, J. (1988) *Cognition in Practice: Mind, Mathematics, and Culture in Everyday Life* (Cambridge: Cambridge University Press).

Lave, J. (1996) The Practice of Learning. In: S. Chaiklin and J. Lave (eds) *Understanding Practice: Perspectives on Activity and Context* (Cambridge: Cambridge University Press), pp. 3–32.

Lave, J. (1997) The Culture of Acquisition and the Practice of Understanding. In: D. Kirshner and J.A. Whitson (eds) *Situated Cognition: Social, Semiotic and Psychological Perspectives* (Mahwah, NJ: Lawrence Erlbaum Associates), pp. 17–36.

Lave, J. and Wenger, E. (1991) *Situated Learning: Legitimate Peripheral Participation* (Cambridge: Cambridge University Press).

Lemke, J. (1999) Meaning-Making in the Conversation: Head Spinning, Heart Winning, and Everything in Between, *Human Development*, 42:2, 87–91.

Nardi, B.A. (1997) *Context and Consciousness: Activity Theory and Human–Computer Interaction* (Cambridge, MA: MIT Press).

Ortner, S.B. (1984) Theory in Anthropology Since the Sixties, *Comparative Studies in Society and History*, 26, 126–166.

Robbins, P. and Aydede, M. (2009) A Short Primer on Situated Cognition. In: P. Robbins and M. Aydede (eds) *Cambridge Handbook of Situated Cognition* (Cambridge: Cambridge University Press), pp. 3–10.

Schon, D. (1983) *The Reflective Practitioner* (New York: Basic Books).

Scribner, S. (1985) Vygotsky's Uses of History. In: J.V. Wertsch (ed.) *Culture, Communication and Cognition: Vygotskian Perspectives* (Cambridge: Cambridge University Press), pp. 119–145.

Searle, J.R. (1980) Minds, Brains and Programs, *The Behavioral and Brain Sciences*, 3, 417–424.

Suggate, J., Davis A., and Goulding, M. (2010) *Mathematical Knowledge for Primary Teachers* (London: Routledge).

Taylor, C. (1985) *Human Agency and Language: Philosophical Papers 1* (Cambridge, MA: Harvard University Press).

Tuomi-Gröhn, T. and Engeström, Y. (2003) Conceptualizing Transfer: From Standard Notions to Developmental Perspectives. In: T. Tuomi-Gröhn and Y. Engeström (eds) *Between School and Work: New Perspectives on Transfer and Boundary Crossing* (Amsterdam: Pergamon), pp. 19–38.

Valsiner, J. and Van der Veer, R. (2000) *The Social Mind: Construction of the Idea* (Cambridge: Cambridge University Press).

Van der Veer, R. (ed.) (2000) Criticizing Vygotsky, *Journal of Russian and East European Psychology*, 38:6.

Vygotsky, L.S. (1998) *The Collected Works of L. S. Vygotsky, Volume 5, Child Psychology*, R.W. Reiber ed. (New York: Plenum Press).

Walkerdine, V. (1990) *The Mastery of Reason* (London: Routledge).

Wertsch, J.V. (1992) The Voice of Rationality in a Sociocultural Approach to Mind. In: L.C. Moll (ed.) *Vygotsky and Education: Instructional Implications and Applications of Sociohistorical Theory* (Cambridge: Cambridge University Press), pp. 111–126.

Wertsch, J. (1996) The Role of Abstract Rationality in Vygotsky's Image of Mind. In: A. Tryphon and J.N. Vonèche (eds) *Piaget – Vygotsky: The Social Genesis of Thought* (Hove: Psychology Press), pp. 25–42.

Wertsch, J.V., del Rio, P. and Alvarez, A. (eds) (1995) Sociocultural Studies: History, Action, and Mediation. In: J.V. Wertsch, P. del Rio and A. Alvarez (eds) *Sociocultural Studies of Mind* (Cambridge: Cambridge University Press), pp. 1–34.

Wertsch, J.V., Minick, N. and Arns, F.J. (1984) The Creation of Context in Joint Problem Solving. In: B. Rogoff and J. Lave (eds) *Everyday Cognition: Its Development in Social Contexts* (Cambridge, MA: Harvard University Press), pp. 151–171.

Wertsch, J.V., Tulviste, P. and Hagstrom, F. (1993) A Sociocultural Approach to Agency. In: E.A. Forman, N. Minick and C.A. Stone (eds) *Contexts for Learning: Sociocultural Dynamics in Children's Development* (Oxford: Oxford University Press), pp. 225–256.

Wilson, R. and Clark, A. (2009). How to Situate Cognition: Letting Nature Take Its Course. In: M. Aydede and P. Robbins (eds) *The Cambridge Handbook of Situated Cognition* (Cambridge: Cambridge University Press), pp. 55–77.

Wrong, D. (1969) The Oversocialized Conception of Man in Modern Sociology. In: L.A. Coser and B. Rosenberg (eds) *Sociological Theory: A Book of Readings* (New York: Macmillan), pp. 122–132.

Zinchenko, V.P. (1995) Cultural-Historical Psychology and the Psychological Theory of Activity: Retrospect and Prospect. In: J.V. Wertsch, P. del Rio and A. Alvarez (eds) *Sociocultural Studies of Mind* (Cambridge: Cambridge University Press), pp. 37–55.

P14

3
Constructivism and Schooling

To put the argument about constructivism, schooling and reason that follows in context it is necessary to recall that the central theme of this book is the importance for Vygotsky of the tradition of philosophy that is associated with Spinoza, Hegel and Marx. To neglect this tradition is not only to ignore critical elements in the genesis and development of Vygotsky's thought, but even more importantly it is to subtract from its contemporary relevance and diminish the contribution it can make to current educational questions. It is, of course, possible to abstract certain themes from Vygotsky and assimilate them into a frame of reference that is not his own, and this approach is not to be dismissed out of hand; at the same time the gains made by this approach do not compensate for the losses. The most important of these losses derive directly, or at one remove, from the understanding of reason.

It would be convenient if reason in the philosophic tradition from which Vygotsky drew his inspiration could be characterised as abstract reason and if the position that contemporary commentators adopt could in turn be characterised as rejection of this conception of reason. But as Vygotsky never entertained an idea of abstract reason, and in the light of the fact that his modern commentators do not reject abstract reason out of hand, such a clear demarcation would be wrong on both sides. It is implications, fine distinctions and variations of emphasis that count here. Moreover, the complications are compounded by the fact that the issue with which this book is concerned is not one that directly concerns the authors being considered. These authors touch upon the question of reason, but only in other connections, and the argument here has to rely upon implications and deductions.

Clearly the authors referred to are more aware of the complex issues than the schematisation used above suggests. Referring to Gadamer, Joseph Dunne (1993) stressed the merits of 'conversation' and it is this approach, rather than one of critique, that is attempted here.

Vygotsky Philosophy and Education, First Edition. Jan Derry.

What then is the topic of conversation? What exactly is the issue and why is it important? To get to grips with what exactly is at stake here it is necessary to consider some philosophical background – in particular, that constructivist arguments are generally set in the context of what Brandom calls *a representational paradigm*. So in order to consider them and ensuing debates about schooling, we need to be aware of the impact of this paradigm. If we are to situate Wertsch's criticism of Vygotsky's allegiance to abstract reason, it will be necessary to examine this background, and to do so before we consider the application of constructivist ideas to schooling.

REPRESENTATION AS A PARADIGM

The theme explored here is that of representation as a paradigm and the consequences of this paradigm for the theorisation of sociogenesis.[1] The term 'representation' suggests too many meanings to be immediately clear.[2] My point is that much of post-Vygotskian studies inhabits this representationalist paradigm and that this has theoretical consequences for the treatment of underlying issues including freedom and agency. But to take the idea of a paradigm of representationalism to frame an argument about how sociogenetic explanations might develop is not a straightforward matter. At first sight it would seem that such a paradigm is completely at odds with the position taken by the authors discussed here. Whereas much post-Vygotskian research implicitly takes what Brandom defines as the representationalist paradigm to be a correspondence view of truth (that is, a mirror view of nature or an idea that representations reflect the external world), which they reject out of hand, my argument is concerned with a different aspect of the paradigm, namely its implicit dualism.

What are the most important aspects of the 'representationalist paradigm'? To put the matter simply, it refers to a particular epistemological position involving assumptions about the human condition and the relation of mind to world. The criticism of this paradigm is that it forecloses certain possibilities and that, when adopted without a consideration of philosophical presuppositions, the grounds for this foreclosure appear self-evident.

The representationalist paradigm presents the relation of mind to world as one in which knowledge caused by sense experience is made meaningful by the constructions that are put upon it. The mind is understood to create meaning in a disenchanted world of brute nature or in circumstances where whatever 'reality' there might be is unknowable. This position corresponds to what has been called by Wilfrid Sellars 'the Myth of the Given' (Sellars, 1997) in which experience is understood as something that cannot be a tribunal and yet must also somehow stand in judgement over our thinking. This idea, at the heart of the representational paradigm of the world as independent of mind and made meaningful by the constructions placed on it by mind, is made explicit by Hegel to show that what we take to be the means by which we acquire our knowledge – *the Understanding* – falls far short of explaining how knowledge actually arises. Although it may be thought that an epistemology simply describes how knowledge arises, much more is in fact involved. This becomes clear once we make explicit the additional weight of what has to be carried by the very delimitations that we assume in order to explain how knowledge is possible.

Working in the spirit of Hegel's critique of the Understanding, Robert Brandom and John McDowell develop a different phenomenology in which mindedness and world are not separated as they are in conventional epistemology. Their interests and arguments, now current in philosophy, are far removed from the concerns of post-Vygotskian research.[3] But the philosophical background *is* significant for Vygotsky, and blindness to these arguments has consequences for contemporary post-Vygotskian traditions.

Of particular relevance to this book is the recent work of Robert Brandom, introduced in Chapter 1, and specifically the argument he develops to examine what is distinctive about human knowing, as opposed to a mechanical form of 'knowing'. Since his argument also approaches the matter from a Hegelian direction and since it is the aim of this book to expose some of the Hegelian dimensions of the work of Vygotsky, Brandom's arguments are doubly pertinent.

The previous chapter considered the criticism of abstract rationality levelled at Vygotsky. At the heart of this criticism is a tension between, on the one side, the notion of 'universal abstractions', which are unable to give due credit to local *meaning-making*, and, on the other, the attention to mediational means that is understood to play a role in the genesis of mind. To consider this it is useful first of all to note the compelling case for Vygotsky of conceiving the mind as social. Put briefly, Vygotsky stresses that:

1   what becomes *intra*mental is initially *inter*mental;
2   human beings possess the unique ability to *mediate* their existence and to create stimuli in order to determine their own behaviour;
3   when tools/signs/words are used, the development of their meaning has only just begun; and
4   higher mental functions cannot be understood as originating in lower ones.

The first point above implies a strong position on the sociogenesis of mind by claiming that external activity is internalised not just as a form of knowledge but as a means by which higher mental functions, such as conscious attention and voluntary memory, are formed and come into play. The sociogenetic approach to mind raises a number of problems because so little about the social dimension of mind is settled. Although Vygotsky brought together and studied important ideas bearing upon a sociogenetic approach, the formulation of sociogenesis is also unsettled.

One aspect of the problem of explanation in a sociogenetic account of mind is illustrated by an example, given by Valsiner and Van der Veer, of the role of mediation in a child's learning. They comment: 'It is an interesting question whether mediated processes need to be social in the sense of having an interpersonal origin. Likewise, one might ask whether all cultural transmission requires mediation in the Vygotskian sense' (Valsiner and Van der Veer, 2000, p. 371). They discuss two ways in which a child's external relations with other people can later be used to control its behaviour internally. There is a difference in the examples they use. The first is the well-known example of a baby gesturing meaninglessly. The child's movements are made meaningful by interaction with the adult, who by treating the movement as significant (even though it bears no significance or meaning) responds to it differentially. This is the common example given to illustrate the first development of language for a child. The second example is that of a child crossing the road, whereby the instructions 'look right, then look left' are repeated by the children to themselves, once alone. Though an apparently trivial comparison, Van der Veer and Valsiner's point is that in the former case the mediation of meaning is interpersonal in the sense that the baby's actions are made meaningful externally via intermental activity, whereas in the latter the child simply adopts the same pattern of action as the adult and may have no mediational interpersonal dimension. The actual way in which the intramental becomes intermental is not understood and though various authors have attempted to address 'the internalisation problem', limited empirical examples are available. This book does not deal specifically with the problem of providing an account of sociogenesis but is concerned rather with the implicit philosophical assumptions found in attempts to supply such an account.

A major component of any account of the sociogenesis of mind (whether of higher mental functions or language) is the explanation of meaning. The concept 'representation' plays a key role in accounts of how meaning arises. An initial response is to think of meaning as in some way located within an artefact, sign or mediating tool, which variously stand in place of something in the world and 're-presents' it. Through representation, the same effect occurs as would result from interaction directly with 'natural' objects or phenomena in the world.[4] Of course, representation is generally understood to involve a process far more complex than simply standing in place of, or reproducing, an object already in existence. But it is not clear exactly what this complexity consists in.[5] Brandom remarks that a representationalist paradigm reigns supreme in much contemporary thought, and this, he maintains, delimits the way we think about certain questions.

A central argument of this chapter is that the representationalist paradigm referred to by Brandom underpins much of the discussion of Vygotsky, with consequences for the way in which sociogenesis is theorised. It plays a decisive if undeclared role in the conceptualisation of pedagogy in contemporary schooling and has decisive consequences for the way that constructivist positions are taken in relation to the active participation of learners, both in their learning and also more radically in the constitution of knowledge. This is considered in the latter part of this chapter. The excursion that this book takes into Hegel's philosophy in Chapter 6 provides a basis for comprehending the different philosophical frame that, unlike the one considered here, did actually influence Vygotsky.

The issue of immediate concern here is the influence on schooling and pedagogy that is exercised by the underlying representationalist paradigm. This paradigm, it must be stressed from the start, retains a dualism at odds with the standpoint that Vygotsky developed under the influence of German idealism. Without due regard for the philosophical background of Vygotsky's work and the particular light this sheds on the potential of his contribution, the readings that arise conflict with the position he actually adopted on such crucial issues as reason and instruction. Wertsch's prolific writings since the 1970s have brought the ideas of Vygotsky to a wider audience, and they are a prime example of the reading that finds Vygotsky's use of reason, at certain points, highly problematic. As pointed out in Chapter 2, Wertsch presents Vygotsky as an ambivalent rationalist, oscillating between a caricature of Enlightenment abstract and decontextualised reason, on the one hand, and a more personal, contextually based construction of sense and meaning, on the other.

Two of Wertsch's arguments illustrate how his working within a representationalist paradigm colours the criticisms he makes of Vygotsky. At first sight the suggestion that Wertsch's criticisms inhabit such a paradigm appears unwarranted, for the very point of his criticism of Vygotsky is to take issue with the claim that language, and in particular scientific concepts, *represents* an objective world and is a matter of referential relations between signs and objects. My argument, however, is that Wertsch retains elements of dualism that belong to a representationalist paradigm and as such retains the position he criticises in Vygotsky. To make the point in a different way: once a foundational project of knowledge is found untenable and, with it, the idea that the objectivity of the concepts, words and sentences we use may be explained simply by their representational relation to the world, the common response has been to withdraw to a modest position that restricts knowledge to the individual, local and contextual *meaning-making* of participants. Attention to local meaning-making and withdrawal from an interest in knowledge and meaning transcending the 'context' of production pervade much post-Vygotskian research.[6]

Vygotsky's understanding of reason was not the one ascribed to him by Wertsch, who fails to appreciate its Hegelian provenance. Hegel was as fully aware of the limitations of a foundational project as any contemporary thinker, but he took a line regarding this that is different from much contemporary research. He was aware that this foundational project went hand in hand with the representational paradigm. As a result, he avoided the conclusion to which so much contemporary thought appears drawn – namely, that knowledge itself has no secure basis or, what amounts to the same thing, that it can only ever have local standing. Contemporary thought has shied away from this problem and has thus ended up in a position where the difficulties involved in establishing knowledge are avoided rather than confronted, with the result that the possibility of knowledge itself is called into question. Although Hegel offers a radically different appreciation of 'abstract rationality', this is lost to much contemporary work, owing in part to the alignment of Hegel with Marxism and of Marxism with the failures of Soviet practice. Chapters 5 and 6 consider this issue in more detail. In attempting to complete Kant's project to comprehend the conditions of our knowing, Hegel took a different approach from the one that retained representationalism as a default position.[7] Hegel's work is generative: it works through the assumptions of our claims to knowledge to show that each claim holds more than what is immediately apparent within it.[8] It is significant that while a critique of universal (abstract or decontextualised) rationality is made (by Wertsch and others), the common underpinnings of what is being attacked are internal to the basis from which the attack is made (i.e. there is an implicit dualism retaining a form of the Myth of the Given).

Central to Wertsch's position that Vygotsky was an ambivalent rationalist is the claim that he makes the 'assumption that language and meaning are basically concerned with referential relationships between signs and objects' (Wertsch, 2000, p. 20). This characterisation of Vygotsky's understanding of meaning, and Wertsch's supposed lack of regard for Vygotsky's concern with 'the problem of consciousness', is at odds with the philosophical basis of Vygotsky's work. There is sufficient evidence in Vygotsky's published works to show that he conceived meaning in a more complex way than arising from a word (sign) in reference to an object.[9] Wertsch appears to acknowledge this, but not to the extent that it prevents him from presenting Vygotsky's position as ambivalent.

The philosophical underpinnings of Vygotsky's work can be found implicitly in specific arguments and explicitly in his stated debt to Spinoza and Hegel. Although I am taking issue with the characterisation of Vygotsky by Wertsch and others, my argument is concerned less with the position these commentators take than with the way that the dualism inherent in what they say leads to an under-theorisation of human freedom.[10] It is important to stress the extent to which Wertsch aims to avoid the limitations of Cartesianism in formulating his account of the sociogenesis of mind. But in his attempt to avoid 'methodological individualism' he attributes *agency* to mediational means (including language), and by doing so he remains within a 'representationalist paradigm'.[11] Wertsch draws attention to the dangers of oscillating between, on the one hand, a position that emphasises the tool and, on the other, a conception of the individual as the progenitor of meaning (Wertsch, 1999). However, even though Wertsch and others are predisposed to seeing the formation of knowledge as an organic process, their treatment of mediating means as external objects with causal efficacy introduces an element of Cartesian mechanics into the argument. Or to be more precise, it leaves an element of Cartesian mechanics in their argument that, owing to their lack of attention to the distinction between causes and reasons, remains untransformed. One area of work particularly notorious for its failure to make a distinction between causes and reasons is artificial intelligence, where agency is attributed as easily to a machine as to a human, and it is surely not coincidental that Wertsch concedes that the formulation of mediational means as carrier of agency lends itself to the possibility that machines might properly be conceived as intelligent (Wertsch, Tulviste and Hagstrom, 1993).

ROBERT BRANDOM

We may now turn to Robert Brandom whose work is especially relevant to the distinction between causes and reasons. By 'cause' I mean a relationship in which no conscious purpose on the part of the agent is involved.[12] The agent causes the result without conceptualisation – whether this is a bee building a hive, rain causing corn to grow or an alarm alerting us to a fire. To take this last example, an alarm may be far more effective in *perceiving* the dangers of a fire and sounding the alert than any human being. But when human beings shout 'Fire!' they are always doing more than simply making a warning noise. When a child of five (as opposed to a much younger child whose uttered sounds are only just beginning to operate as language), shouts 'Fire!' the child knows its implications. Five-year-old children appreciate the consequences of the exclamation 'Fire!' and what follows from such an utterance. Brandom uses this example to illustrate his claim that human beings act and communicate *inferentially*. His point, which he derives from Sellars, is that what distinguishes the human form of knowing from the type of knowing we might ascribe to a machine is that knowing, for a human being, consists not merely in expressing a response but in knowing what follows from it – knowing the implications or what Brandom calls the 'giving and asking of reasons' (Brandom, 2000, p. 163). As he puts it, 'even such non-inferential reports must be inferentially articulated', and this point is crucial to any understanding of human intellect:

> One of the most important lessons we learn from Sellars's masterwork, *Empiricism and Philosophy of Mind* (1997) (as from the 'Sense Certainty' section of Hegel's *Phenomenology*), is the inferentialist one that even such non-inferential reports must be inferentially articulated. Without that requirement we cannot tell the difference between non-inferential reporters and automatic machinery such as thermostats and photocells, which also have reliable disposi- tions to respond differentially to stimuli. (Brandom, 2000, pp. 47–48)

I have just mentioned an alarm *perceiving* a fire. This is already an anthropomor- phism, which Brandom takes care to avoid. He talks of machines 'responding differentially to stimulus', by which he means that they respond mechanically to a stimulus. The use of the phrase 'responding differentially', in place of 'perceiving' or 'knowing', is of crucial importance for it introduces a distinction that is hidden by the anthropomorphic use of language. The stimulus in this case – the fire – is a *cause* of their response; in the case of the human being who sounds the alarm, the fire is the *reason* for their response. The human perceives the fire as fire; that is to say that, unlike a machine, it has a concept of fire as part of a system of concepts. For Brandom, making a report as a human being is not merely 'responding differen- tially': it is inferring rather than merely representing, since 'even such non-inferential reports must be inferentially articulated' (Brandom, 2000, p. 47). This emphasis on inference is drawn from Hegel's analysis of what sense certainty entails, and, in keeping with Hegel, Brandom argues that 'in order to master *any* concept, one must master *many* concepts' (Brandom, 2000, p. 49).

For Brandom, the responses that humans make involve an understanding of sig- nificance that is only possible where they already appreciate other concepts. This position may seem to leave us with a 'chicken-and-egg' conundrum: how can you know something before knowing the means of knowing it (in other words, to know one concept you must know many concepts)?[13] Vygotsky deals with this question when he considers the question of method (see Chapter 5 on Spinoza). For the moment it suffices to say that it depends on a holism that rejects dualism. Brandom deals with the issue by explaining that grasping concept use arises from the know- how gained by involvement in social practices. In this he shares with Vygotsky an emphasis on the sociogenesis of meaning. The argument here is the same as that of Vygotsky: 'we must seek the psychological equivalent of the concept not in general representations ... we must seek it in the system of judgements in which the concept is disclosed'[14] (Vygotsky, 1998, p. 55). Brandom contrasts holism about concepts with the atomism that results when concepts are understood only in terms of 'differential responses'.

Wertsch's claim that Vygotsky believed meaning arises from the referential relationship of word to object is coupled to a further claim that for Vygotsky 'the development of meaning is a matter of increasing generalisation and abstraction' (Wertsch, 2000, p. 20). Wertsch finds evidence for both these claims in Vygotsky's *Thinking and Speech*, where the role of the sign in the child's development of both spontaneous and scientific concepts is discussed. Two aspects concern Wertsch: one is the emphasis that Vygotsky places on the relationship of word to object; the second is on what Wertsch describes as decontextualisation.[15] These aspects of Vygotsky's discussion are judged by Wertsch as an extension of Enlightenment traditions of abstract rationality and a commitment to universal reason.

Wertsch has a specific understanding of reference and abstraction in relation to Vygotsky. In support of his argument and to illustrate the one-sidedness of Vygotsky's view, Wertsch draws on Charles Taylor's distinction between *designative* and *expressivist* approaches to meaning. Wertsch presents these as characteristic respectively of the Enlightenment and of Romanticism. He reiterates his representationalist understanding of language when he writes that 'This view of meaning is grounded on the assumption that language functions primarily to *represent* an independent reality' (my italics) and when he quotes Taylor to the effect that:

> We could explain a sign or word having meaning by pointing to what it designates, in a broad sense, that is, what it can be used to refer to in the world, and what it can be used to say about that thing ... we give the meaning of a sign or a word by pointing to the thing or relations that they can be used to talk about. (Wertsch, 2000, p. 26)

Wertsch argues that the relationship between word and object in the designative approach is quite consistent with Vygotsky's account of meaning in relation to scientific concepts. The argument here is that Vygotsky shared this view of the relation of word to world even though his explanation of reference is antithetical to the Hegelianism evident in Vygotsky's writings. The point that Vygotsky stresses when he writes of 'a system of judgements' is that the idea of 'general representations' is inadequate to express what a concept is in thinking:

> According to our hypothesis, we must seek the psychological equivalent of the concept not in general representations, not in absolute perceptions and orthoscopic diagrams, not even in concrete verbal images that replace the general representations – we must seek it in a system of judgements in which the concept is disclosed. (Vygotsky, 1998, p. 55)

Brandom is concerned to develop a theory of meaning that does not take '*representation* as its fundamental concept', and he, like Taylor,[16] explains 'the notion of representational content is most often unpacked in terms of what objects, events or states of affairs actually causally elicited the representation' (Brandom, 2000, p. 25). In common with post-Vygotskian researchers, Brandom argues against a mentalist order of explanation that privileges mind as an original locus. His anti-Cartesianism is common in work that attempts to use Vygotsky's ideas. However, Brandom adds a further dimension by approaching the 'contents of conceptually *explicit* propositions or principles from the direction of what is *implicit* in practices of using expression and acquiring or deploying beliefs' (Brandom, 2000, p. 4). This is a step towards overcoming the dualism that any retention of the representational paradigm maintains. The prioritising of what is implicit in the practice of making explicit is at odds with the characterisation by Wertsch of Vygotsky's use of words: Wertsch takes them as functioning simply as referents to objects without any sense of the inferential background necessary for constituting reference in the first place. Where Wertsch sees the movement in the development of concepts as evidence of Vygotsky's hierarchical idea of knowledge and reason, Vygotsky is actually emphasising the alterations of practices that allow the child to move from operating with concepts as complexes, then as pseudo-concepts and finally as scientific concepts. At each point a concept's character (everyday or scientific) is due to the form of its use. In parallel to Taylor's contrast between the designative and the expressive, Brandom characterises two traditions. He counterposes mind as mirror (Enlightenment) and mind as lamp (Romanticism) to communicate the different ways in which mind and epistemology are understood. He juxtaposes representation and inference, and in criticising representation (and the baggage carried with it) he argues that, in human practices, representations are always underpinned by inferences. This is the case even though we may not be aware of the inferences constituting our use of a particular representation. The point that representation cannot be separated from inference is key to Brandom's concern to distinguish human knowing from any other types of 'knowing'.

The conflation of machine and human intelligence is a crucially important problem relevant to post-Vygotskian research. The attempts to develop an account of mind on the basis of causal explanations fail to distinguish human activity from the behaviour of machines. Representation and inference are not polar opposites but implicated in each other. Wertsch uses Taylor's distinction between the designative and the expressive for a purpose different from what Taylor intended, and this is not just a trivial point. Taylor gives an account of modern philosophy as a precursor to Hegel's synthesis of the tensions between the designative and the expressive, while Wertsch implies a contrast between the authoritarianism of the designative and the greater sensitivity to individuality of the expressive.[17]

THEORISING MEDIATIONAL MEANS WITHIN A REPRESENTATIONALIST PARADIGM

At first sight, it appears counterintuitive to argue that much contemporary Vygotskian research, particularly North American research,[18] works within a representationalist paradigm. Most researchers in the Vygotskian field claim to reject what they see as a representational approach – namely, one that seeks meaning in the relationship between our representations and the world. However, although they have generally objected to a correspondence view of truth or a mirror view of nature, their rejection of the representionalist paradigm supporting these views is incomplete. The rejection of (universal) scheme and (empirical) content (Davidson, 1984) does not lead to a rejection of the relationship itself, and the relation is retained even if the poles are transformed. My argument here is that exactly the same relations pervade explanations that draw on Vygotsky's ideas as those that pervade the classical designatory approach his ideas oppose: that is, explanations in terms of the causal power of tools, signs and discourses ignore the essential element of human agency for any account of sociogenesis, where human agency is understood not merely as another cause in the equation but as inhabiting and acting on a different space – a practice in the space of reasons.[19]

To illustrate this point, here are some examples of the notion of causation that I am describing. I should first acknowledge that in all the attempts to account for meaning below, there is a clear recognition of the contribution of human 'agency'. This agency is, however, insufficiently theorised owing to the representational paradigm in which the ideas are presented. The emphasis is shifted rather to the sociogenetic means or mechanisms. It should be noted, nevertheless, that the Russian/cultural-historical appropriation is somewhat different.

It is important to point out that those concerned with theorising mediational means do not openly embrace the representational paradigm attributed to them here. Indeed they reject it out of hand, and they do not subscribe to the idea that representations stand for external objects or the world. Instead they wish to deny what may be termed *foundational* claims to knowledge,[20] and to concentrate instead on the multiplicity (and even relativity) of meaning-making. But, as I have argued, this position still retains the relation characteristic of a representational paradigm.

The focus of research for commentators rejecting the idea of universal knowledge has shifted to the 'making of meaning' via resources, tools, language and artefacts. And once meaning is understood as something that is made, rather than already present and waiting to be revealed or read off from the real, it is the question of the 'means' of meaning construction that comes to the fore. It is this that is formulated as the key to understanding how meaning arises. Against this, the crucial recognition is that thinking, intellectual activity and learning are not simply the outcome of cognitive process: they are, in the first place, supported by various material means and, in the second, not only sustained but developed by such means. This has implications of paramount importance for education policy at a number of levels.[21]

A number of attempts within education research have been made to account for meaning in different contexts and thereby to inform policy with the aim of making classrooms (or what have more broadly been called 'learning environments') more effective. An influential body of work is devoted to the theorisation of meaning through modes other than language. In recent years there has been a growth of interest in the various modes through which semiosis occurs. This has become an area of interest to many researchers concerned with accounting for meaning by examining the means of its construction. For example, Jewitt and Kress (2002) build on Michael

Halliday's social semiotic approach to communication (e.g. Halliday, 1985) in a multi-modal analysis of representation. The aim is to extend the application of Halliday's social semiotics of written language to all 'modes' of communication,[22] including gesture, visual and bodily movement. They explain Halliday's social semiotic theory as follows:

> He argues that in verbal interactions we have at our disposal networks of options (sets of semiotic alternatives) of the meaning potential of the culture, which are realised in sets of options of formal/material means, the *modes* of our multimodal approach. For him, the semantic system of language (his approach focuses on language) reflects the social function of the utterance as representation, as interaction, and as message, which are realised by the lexico-grammar of the language. The principal assumption is that language is as it is because of the social functions it has evolved to serve: it is organised to serve the interests of those who use it in their social lives. In other words (our 'other words') language can be understood to be the result of constant social/cultural working on or 'shaping' of a *material medium* (sound in the case of language-as-speech) into a resource for representation, which displays regularities as *mode*, the (material yet socially/culturally shaped) resource (as signifier-material) for meaning in the constant new making of signs. (Jewitt and Kress, 2002, p. 279)

This passage has been selected because of its concern with *representation* and the shaping of a 'material medium' into a 'resource for representation'. According to a social semiotic approach, it is in representations that we can discern meaning. To appreciate the power of representation as a concept for dealing with meaning, they argue, it is only necessary to consider the design of advertisements.

I want to take issue with the use of the concept of representation in this context. Although the value of examining the way in which artefacts convey meaning cannot be denied, I want to caution that a dimension of analysis is under-theorised in accounts that start with representation. This dimension is crucial to an understanding of human freedom and how knowledge is conceived. To Halliday's account of language as a material mode for communicating meaning, Kress and Jewitt add a concern with the *motivated* use of signs, where the relation between the form chosen to represent and the meaning intended for communication is not arbitrary. Motivated users of signs choose plausible representational resources to communicate their intent. On this view there is due recognition of the agency or free action of the user, but this is exercised in relation to *choosing* an appropriate representational resource. Agency is assumed. Thus the (Cartesian) individual chooses the *material* sign, and meaning resides or is carried in the mode chosen (whether visual or gestural) (Kress *et al.*, 2001, pp. 1–6).

One difficulty in accounting for agency in research whose aim is to theorise meaning is to determine where meaning is to be located. Jewitt and Kress, and Halliday before them, deal with representational resources as carriers of meaning (i.e. meaning is attached to the representational resource) and credit users with exercising agency in their choice of means. Agency is exercised in the users' choice and in the purposes for which they adopt the representational resource – the resource that in turn is said to transform meaning.

Writing from a sociocultural perspective, Wertsch is concerned to formulate an account of meaning that arises from 'agent-acting-with-mediational-means' (Wertsch, 1998, p. 24) such as artefacts, tools or language. Research into the question of how artefacts, tools or language contribute to thinking is still in its early stages. Wertsch schematises the different ways in which the mediation of mind with tools contributes to thinking.

1   By allowing an activity to be achieved that could not be achieved without the use of a tool (e.g. a technique for multiplication, a map allowing navigation).
2   By enabling a group to perform together an activity that could not be performed by its members acting individually, through offloaded cognitive effort into shared mediating devices (e.g. Hutchins's work on the navigation of ships into port as an illustration of a 'sociotechnical system'[23]).
3   By developing particular ways of functioning mentally.

Again, the direction of research is to comprehend meaning as *representation*.[24] Attempts to theorise the way that mind is sustained and developed by cultural artefacts, whether words or tools, concentrate attention on the *representational* aspect of the tool or word. This supposedly designates its contribution to the development of meaning. The meaning of the tool and the role that it can play are ascribed to the tool itself.

Wertsch sets down some basic claims about 'mediated action and cultural tools'. One is that 'mediated means are associated with power and authority' (Wertsch, 1998, p. 25). 'Mediated means' carry particular 'affordances' of meaning that have consequences for their use. In addition, they express the power of particular interest groups. His claims are an attempt to pin down the way in which tools themselves act. However, one difficulty for any account of how the use of tools realises meaning is that there has to be an understanding of human agency if a judgement is to be made about the contribution that tools make in fashioning the outcome. If the distinctive character of human agency is not appreciated in the creation of meaning, agency can be and is ascribed to anything that appears to exert effect. Although Wertsch intends to account for meaning in a more complex way than by merely ascribing it tools, and although he uses the phrase 'individuals-operating-with-mediational-means' to recognise human engagement in meaning-making, he is in danger of falling prey to the methodological individualism that he claims to avoid. No matter how much he alerts us to the error of explanations that concentrate on either the tool alone or the agent (arguing that such explanations are faced with either methodological individualism or reductionism) (Wertsch, 1999), he is forced to assume that 'mediational means' have agency in their own right (the agency involved in carrying and constraining meaning). His particular conception of meaning and its relationship to representation is crucial to his analysis of Vygotsky, leading to his presentation of Vygotsky's conception of meaning as an issue of ambivalence or, as he puts it, of 'two minds' (Wertsch, 2000).

Where Wertsch tends towards an idea of 'containment' (e.g. affordances that privilege certain activities over others or express specific interests) in his explanation of how tools carry meaning, Gordon Wells takes issue with the idea that an artefact can represent or *contain* knowledge: 'At first sight, it might appear that knowledge is to be found in the artefacts that are the outcome of representational activity,' he writes, referring to texts and other visuographic artefacts, as well as manuals, charts and diagrams, and theoretical papers (Wells, 1999, p. 72). But, he argues, this view of knowledge is untenable on the grounds that a text, for instance, does not 'contain knowledge' unless one can distinguish its script from markings of ink. An interpretive framework is necessary to make sense of a script. Knowledge is not in the texts, he argues, 'but in what writers or readers construct as they use texts as external tools to mediate their own mental activity of representing and knowing' (Wells, 1999, p. 73). Having rejected accounts that place weight on tools as carriers of meaning, Wells responds to the dualism underlying attempts to explain meaning by denying the existence of any knowledge beyond that arising from particular readings. Wells adopts a position that emphasises constructivism and rejects the idea of the existence of knowledge beyond its individual or local construction. He expresses what is involved in specifying the ontological status of knowledge as follows:

> Insofar as the import of talking about knowledge being distributed is to emphasise that the key unit of analysis is not the particular individuals engaged in the activity, still less the representations said to be 'contained' in their minds, but rather multifaceted networks of practices that constitute activity, in which the nonhuman 'actors' are as integral as the human ones, this move constitutes an important corrective to the Cartesian view of knowledge as being located in disembodied individuals (Wertsch, 1998). However, I find it confusing to be told that knowledge is *in* artefacts as, for example, when Cole and Engeström write: 'the cultural environment in which children are born contains the accumulated knowledge of prior generations' (1993, p. 9) – though perhaps 'contains' here is intended to be taken metaphorically. However this is not Pea's intention when he claims that 'tools literally carry intelligence *in* them' and 'knowledge is often carried in artefacts as diverse as tools and notational systems' (1993, pp. 53–4). This seems to me to be hyperbole. (Wells, 1999, p. 75)

While he is comfortable with the idea of 'nonhuman actors', Wells rejects the containment of knowledge or intelligence in artefacts. However, there is an element of inconsistency in the argument. On the one hand, he wishes to maintain that meaning only arises in the 'constitutive activity' of actors and therefore cannot be said to reside in a text, while, on the other, he credits 'nonhuman actors' with an integral role in the constitution of knowledge.

Aaron Sloman, writing from the background of computer science, offers a definition that would not be at odds with the 'containment' argument that Wells rejects but that Wertsch's account of artefacts/tools appears to endorse. Sloman looks for 'a label to cover all the various kinds of information stores, irrespective of what their structures are, or how they are created, or whether we are aware of using them or not' (Sloman, 1996, p. 119). He finds the word 'representation' comes closest to meeting these requirements. Working in the field of artificial intelligence, his aim is to broaden the notion of information beyond one involving conscious use. He suggests as an all-encompassing definition 'that there is a more general notion of representation, which covers all states or structures that store or contain information used to control internal or external behaviour, whether in humans or in other natural or artificial behaving systems' (Sloman, 1996, p. 118). He analyses representations as 'information-bearing control states' (Sloman, 1996, p. 118).

However, by theorising information in this way it is difficult to distinguish human and machine action. Sloman's use of the phrase 'information-bearing control states' to explain representation succinctly expresses an idea central to artificial intelligence (and more specifically to programming),[25] that is, that a certain set of conditions will elicit or cause a predictable set of outcomes. Two points follow from conceiving representations in this way: first, there is an idea of containment – the storing/bearing of information by the representation – implying that meaning is *contained* by the representation; and second, agency is accorded to representations. Even though the power of a representation as 'information control state' is influenced by the context of use, the possibility of an overly deter-minist explanation of human action arises. The possibility of considering the distinctive nature of human utilisation of information (as knowledge) and the necessary involvement of freedom is lost.

Providing a 'mechanics' of mind for post-Vygotskian research is difficult because it raises fundamental questions about the nature of meaning, knowing and agency for which there are no settled answers. But the vacuum this leaves at the heart of the enquiry has not prevented post-Vygotskian researchers from formulating arguments that have definite consequences. The urgent need to answer these ques-tions arises from the key role that schooling is perceived to play in social mobility and social justice, and from the recognition that there is a far greater possibility of *developing* intellect than has so far been appreciated. In contrast to the idea of mind as consisting of innate potential that can be developed only within very limited parameters, the idea implicit in a sociogenetic approach – that mind is not just devel-oped but *created* by social activity – implies a pressing responsibility to understand factors that are key to the development of intellect. Yet, regardless of the fact that these major questions regarding meaning, knowing and agency are unresolved, theoretical positions are blithely adopted that have direct consequences for the practice of schooling, especially regarding knowledge and the role of the teacher.

Both Wertsch and Wells are troubled by school curricula that are based on 'decontexualised rationality', that do not allow learners to make their own meaning and that prioritise instead a particular way of making meaning. Wertsch views the 'privileging' of particular mediational means (ways of solving problems) found in traditional schooling as indicative of an extraordinary authority accorded to abstract rationality since the Middle Ages. He attempts to establish a direct link between his criticism of pedagogical practices that privilege abstract or decontextualised ration-ality and Stephen Toulmin's argument about the received view of modernity.[26] Toulmin refers to Descartes's teachings that the 'demands of rationality impose on philosophy a need to seek out abstract, general ideas and principles, by which particulars can be connected together' (Toulmin, 1992, p. 33), and Wertsch restates Toulmin's summary of the received view that '*abstract axioms were in, concrete diversity was out*' (Wertsch, 1998, p. 67). Wertsch argues that 'the received view is routinely appropriated by people in our sociocultural setting and ... results in viewing certain utterances and arguments as convincing despite the many critiques of this tendency' (Wertsch, 1998, p. 67). Wertsch is interested in the way that individuals make sense of problems that, as he sees things, lead them to privilege abstract rationality over the variety of ways of meaning-making that are available.

CONSTRUCTIVISM

The giving of attention to the process of meaning-making itself, rather than to the outcome of such a process, is often referred to as constructivist theory.[27] Since Piaget and the 'cognitive turn', constructivism has been a major force in educational research. It has succeeded in designating learning as an active process where meaning is acquired through a process of meaning-making rather than through the simple transmission of knowledge or through a behaviourist conditioning of response. Given its emphasis on *genetic epistemology*, constructivism seems ideally suited to a Vygotskian approach to education. Leslie Smith has written authoritatively on the similarities between Vygotsky and Piaget (see Chapter 6). However, Smith does not explore the philosophical differences that distinguish each author so that, although it is possible to find statements suggesting consensus, their different understandings are not revealed. Given the apparent congruency between the two authors, it is not surprising that it is constructivism drawn from Piaget that informs readings of Vygotsky's work. The influence of constructivism and its conception of mind and world pervades both general education literature as well as literature concerned with interpretations of Vygotsky. For this reason it is helpful to contrast the two versions to expose the underlying philosophical assumptions. Constructivism/constructionism and their implicit assumptions have implications for the way that Vygotsky is read.

Some of the extreme polarisations of constructivist positions (see Phillips, 1995) can be viewed as an outcome of the problem of understanding what, within a foundationalist tradition of epistemology, 'objective world' entails.[28] The response to this tradition has consequences for interpretations of Vygotsky. Constructivism as well as constructionism are often counterposed with realism (Parker, 1998; Gergen, 1999). Hence the realism evident in Vygotsky's use of the phrase 'scientific concepts' is seen as evidence of a lack of appreciation on his part of multiple avenues of meaning-making in favour of didactic methods. In summarising Wertsch's account of Vygotsky's description of the development of concepts, Confrey is led to write critically: 'This [Vygotsky's] is a strikingly nonconstructive description and an example of the realist commitment that seems to underlie Vygotskian psychology' (Confrey, 1995, p. 191). Referring to Wertsch, he writes: 'Complexes are "no longer related on the basis of the child's subjective ties or impressions, but on the basis of *objective* connections that actually exist among the objects" (Wertsch, [1985], p. 101)' (Confrey, 1995, p. 191, my italics).

At issue here is the distinction between the constructive power of human beings and the idea of an objective world. A lack of appreciation of the philosophical argument behind these characterisations leads to a limited view of how Vygotsky might have conceived the relation of mind to world.[29] The possibility that a material history involving human 'constructive' activity at some previous point[30] may mediate (i.e. constrain) at a current point is excluded from many applications of situated cognition theory.

The constructivism that frames discussions of Vygotsky is infused with a Cartesianism that restricts *meaning* within observable human activity.[31] The illustration given earlier of the difficulty of accounting for the location of meaning and knowledge operates with undisclosed philosophical assumptions. Implicit assumptions, which are party to a Cartesian position on world and mind, remain despite the apparent rejection of Cartesianism. One such assumption is the characterisation of the world that accompanies an emphasis on constructivism: this is a world devoid of meaning without the contextually sustained activities of participants. For this argument to hold it is necessary to assume the world as a *given* outside and separate from human construction. Of course, this seems the very opposite of the position adopted by many constructivists, that is, that everything is socially constructed. But the argument here is that a correlate of this position, of the 'social construction of everything', is agnosticism in relation to the knowability of such a world or even, in the extreme, to its existence.

The attempt to be agnostic about any idea of world outside human construction does not remove specific assumptions that remain implicit in and key to any argument that is developed. The examples of Kenneth Gergen and Robert Reich illustrate the types of agnostic positions held. In the first case, Gergen takes an explicit epistemological position; in the second, Reich unthinkingly describes an externality in popular imagery. First, Gergen takes up critically the same approach to representation, and to the relation of word to world, as that of Wertsch, considered earlier in this chapter. He deals specifically with the concept of representation insofar as he attacks the relation of signifier to signified, of word to world. However, the position he develops, as a result of his rejection of a representationalist approach, does not take issue with the idea of representation as such – say, in the manner that Hegel does – and he argues instead for an infinite variety of relations (representations). Hence, he remains firmly within the very representationalist paradigm he criticises:

> As we found, however, there is no privileged relationship between world and word. For any situation multiple descriptions are usually possible, and in principle there is no upper limit on our forms of descriptions. Nor did we find any ultimate means for ruling among competing descriptions, of declaring one as corresponding more 'truly' to the nature of reality than another. (Gergen, 1999, p. 34)

This approach to knowledge has practical implications for schooling. Gergen's approach to the question, for example, is representative of influential ideas that, by relativising knowledge, unintentionally undermine it. In discussing progress and science Gergen writes:

> There is no convincing account of how an array of syllables (scientific theory) can increasingly 'capture the contours' of what exists ... there are important advantages in abandoning the view of science as a march to the truth. The claim to vertical movement progress in scientific understanding has no grounds. As we move from Aristotelian physics to Newtonian mechanics and then atomic physics, we come no closer to the truth. We simply move from one domain of meaning to another. (Gergen, 1999, p. 239)

This type of position has a powerful appeal at present. But when it is subjected to detailed philosophic examination, serious flaws in its structure are exposed. Consider Donald Davidson's treatment of truth. In his view, to give up depending on the concept of an uninterpreted reality does not mean relinquishing the notion of truth (Davidson, 1984). On the contrary, given the dualism of scheme and content, what we get, according to Davidson, is truth relative to scheme. Without the dualism of scheme and content – which for Davidson is 'dogma' – relativity goes by the board. The crux of Davidson's argument is that relativism is nothing but an aspect of the dualism of scheme and content, where scheme is understood as distinct from content and is applied to content externally to give it shape. In other words, once a dualism of scheme and content is adopted, according to Davidson, relativism follows virtually automatically since it is the scheme that is posited as the ground for making sense of the world.[32] Davidson also points out that, where the scheme is the context from which the content is constructed, the idea of truth is not avoided but remains, although it remains as relative to scheme. Davidson's (1984) criticism of the dualism of scheme and content is relevant not only to Gergen but also to others like him who question the achievement of truth. What Davidson's argument shows is that the problem of truth is not simply one of final attainment, since similar problems arise when knowledge is produced contextually and validated by local warrants.

It is important to be clear about what appear to be the necessary presuppositions of the type of constructivist argument that Gergen makes, in order to point out their flaws. That is that in the critique of any possibility of representation of an empirically given realm, constructivists continue to hold to a form of the 'Myth of the Given' from which to build their critique and are consequently faced with having to discard notions of rationality, progress and truth. In contrast to Gergen, who is prepared to reject such concepts out of hand, Reich has no such stated intention. As an advisor to the Clinton administration and a former US Secretary of State for Labor, Reich has been influential: indeed Jerome Bruner refers to Reich's book *The Work of Nations* as a text that 'could serve as a policy document in our times' (Bruner, 1996, p. 33). In it Reich popularises the idea of the 'symbolic analyst' as the way of mitigating the declining position of the US economy in an increasingly globalised market. Reich's polemic on the need for education to produce 'symbolic analysts' (learners active in the conceptualisation of the knowledge) depends, in part, on the claim that we are now part of the 'knowledge age' where 'data ... will be available ... at the touch of a computer key' (Reich, 1992, p. 229). Reich uses the contemporary rhetoric concerning new technologies to make his case about the importance of recognising the specific powers of transformation and synthesis possessed by the 'symbolic analyst'. The correlate of this analyst – and it is here that the constructivist elements of Reich's thought become apparent – is a concept of the world as devoid of meaning, bearing no truth apart from that arising from constructive intervention. For when Reich writes, 'Consider first the capacity for abstraction. The real world is nothing but a vast jumble of noises, shapes, colours, smells and textures – essentially meaningless until the human mind imposes some order on them' (Reich, 1992, p. 229), he is giving expression to the same dualism mentioned earlier that Davidson criticises, commonplace in contemporary thought.

To sum up, once one adopts a dualist view of a world that is itself taken to be devoid of the conditions for meaning, responsibility for meaning seems to rest with the human activity of abstraction. The possibility of meaning arising in a historical process, whereby nature is transformed through human activity, simply does not arise. There are two aspects to the implicit philosophy underpinning much post-Vygotskian research: first, a common-sense dualism that the world external to our thoughts and immediate activity is devoid of meaning until the point of meaning-construction – Reich's 'buzzing confusion'; and second, the idea that meaning is limited to the constructive activity of individuals.[33] The first operates with precisely the type of epistemological given that Sellars criticises, while the second operates with a denial of meaning in the world, a meaningfulness that McDowell posits as crucial.

SCHOOLING, CONSTRUCTIVISM AND KNOWLEDGE

Constructivism is influential in the appropriation of Vygotsky, yet at the same time a tension arises as a result of the importance Vygotsky attached to instruction. This tension occurs particularly in the interpretations of the ZPD (zone of proximal development), and hence it has featured prominently in Vygotskian approaches to pedagogy. By introducing the idea of a 'zone' of development, Vygotsky recognised not only that learning did not consist of discrete events within a process, but also that knowledge itself involved a continuing process – that is, it arose in mediation, for nothing is immediate.[34]

One reason for Vygotsky's introduction of this concept was to give emphasis to the developmental aspect of conceptualisation. Although the example he provides barely does justice to the idea of a ZPD, it begins to explain what is at issue. Vygotsky uses the example of two children of the same age performing at the same level in a test (summative assessment) in order to show that a full indication of ability is not provided by this form of assessment.[35] The inadequacy of this form of assessment arises because, at any given point in time, one child may already have reached a higher level of development, but not yet be at the point of making that higher level of 'concept readiness' explicit. The recognition that the acquisition of knowledge and understanding is the subject of a continual process of development, however, does not lead to the conclusion that an infinite variety of ways of knowing are possible, for fundamental to Vygotsky's use of the idea of a ZPD is that the process of 'becoming' (constituent of all knowledge) is not open-ended. What brings a concept to fruition is the intervention of, or interaction with, an abler peer or adult. Hence the idea of a 'zone' recognises the bounded character of knowledge evident in the frame in which it is articulated, in the absence of which knowledge would not be realised.[36] The emphasis on the intervention or instructional frame of an adult gives a weight to instruction not commonly found in constructionist approaches to pedagogy. Thus, while the idea of a ZPD opens the way to viewing knowledge as fluid and constructible, it does not underestimate the importance of the transmission of knowledge between generations.

In contrast to Vygotsky's view of knowledge, the current interest in constructionism and constructivism has led to a focus on knowledge construction, knowledge as a plural ('knowledges') and relativistic approaches to knowledge. The idea of a developmental aspect to meaning in any process of learning introduces the issue of the source of that meaning.

Implicit epistemology has definite policy implications. The aim of diminishing the authority of the teacher and crediting learners with the ability not just to learn through constructing their own meaning, but to make new knowledge, as well as the unproblematised emphasising of 'collaborative communities', are all coupled to particular epistemological assumptions.[37] The works of Hatano, Wells and Jaworski corroborate this claim. Their works are presented here only to illustrate the possibility of a one-sided emphasis on an active constructive aspect of knowledge that by implication avoids consideration of knowledge beyond individual construction. What is said here does not attempt to do justice to their contribution, but merely to attend to the way in which their work can be influential in diverting attention from a focus on knowledge per se.

First, let us consider Hatano, whose argument illustrates issues in the application of a Vygotskian approach to pedagogy. Hatano aims to develop, through Vygotsky's work, a more constructionist approach in applications of Vygotsky's work to schooling in contrast to interpretations of Vygotsky that favour a more 'instructional approach' (cf. Davydov, 1984; Hedegaard, 1996, 1998).[38] The difficulty with arguments pitted against instructional approaches is that the term 'instruction' is used pejoratively, to refer to a transmission model of learning and to the idea that there is a body of knowledge that should be taught to successive generations. The instructional approach is held responsible for the failures of mass schooling, with its transmission approaches and particular stance on knowledge. Hatano argues that a Vygotskian conception of instruction has been interpreted within an empiricist frame in the USA in such a way that it coincides with 'conventional didactic teaching', including 'rote, drill and practice instruction' (Hatano, 1993, p. 154). 'Vygotskians,' he continues, 'have been busy criticizing Piagetians' "romantic child-centered constructivism" without clearly differentiating their conception from transmission' (p. 154). Although Hatano is careful to state that he is offering just *one* interpretation, it is clear that his argument for a more constructivist version depends upon the caricature of the instructional approach that he sets up. This caricature is commonplace, posing constructivism as an alternative to a traditional transmission model of teaching (see Davis, 2010). To make his point clear, Hatano identifies what he admits to be 'the *so-called* Vygotskian conception of knowledge acquisition by instruction … [in] a somewhat caricatured form' (Hatano, 1993, p. 154, italics added). His typification brings to the fore what he sees as a central issue – emphasis on the teacher's authority as knowledge expert rather than the child's own construction of a problem. According to this schematised version of a Vygotskian approach: 'Knowledge to be acquired by the learner (a less mature member of society) is possessed by the teacher (a more mature member) usually in the form of a set of skills or strategies for solving the target problem' (p. 154). It is necessary to bear in mind here that Hatano is aiming to show how, even with an avowedly Vygotskian approach, teachers still perpetuate a form of transmission. He describes the method used as one in which the teacher demonstrates how to solve problems, while the learner takes over steps involved in the solution, with the supporting role of the teacher becoming less and less important.

Although Hatano recognises that this is only one possible interpretation, he still wishes to condemn acquisition by instruction, which he claims has hidden empiricist assumptions. These he details as: (1) the learner's being passive and not needing to understand the meaning of the skills being taught or construct knowledge that goes beyond them; (2) the fact that it is only interaction with the teacher that is understood to allow the acquisition of knowledge; and (3) the assumption that the teacher acts as the only source of information and evaluation. For Hatano, this set of assumptions defines a transmission model. Hatano uses Palinscar and Brown's research on joint problem-solving ('reciprocal teaching', e.g. Palinscar and Brown, 1984) as a method of comprehending a text in order to illustrate his concern that these so-called Vygotskian approaches still place emphasis on the teacher's authority rather than upon the learner's own knowledge construction. With regard to Palinscar and Brown's example of reciprocal teaching, Hatano states that 'if the strategies are acquired *because of the teacher's authority* … rather than to enhance understanding … then "reciprocal teaching" is not based on a constructivist approach' (1993, p. 158, italics added). There are two problems here: first, what Hatano calls the 'authority' of the teacher, and second, the conception of constructivism and its location in contemporary criticisms of abstract knowledge. Both have consequences for how teachers interpret and legitimate their practice.

Hatano's aim is to bring a constructivist dimension to the Vygotskian legacy as he sees it, to revise the 'transmission skills' framework, and so to extend the conception of learning by instruction. He argues that the conception of learners in his caricature of Vygotsky's approach does not fit well with evidence that shows humans as active beneficiaries of interactions with people and with natural and artificial environments. Hatano's response to deficiencies in North American schooling is to provide a 'reinterpretation of Vygotsky's theory as exemplifying "realistic constructivism" … an idea that knowledge is constructed by learners themselves under a variety of sociocultural constraints' and he argues that this 'can legitimately be called a *radical extension* of the Vygotskian conception' (1993, p. 155).

This constructivist reinterpretation illustrates both a widely experienced uneasiness with Vygotsky's position to the effect that there is a body of knowledge that is passed on to the next generation and an equally widely experienced desire to give weight to meaning-making and knowledge construction by learners themselves. But what meaning should be attached to the phrases 'constructed by learners themselves' and 'the teacher's authority'? Such phrases are taken as prescriptions for giving priority to the learner's own construction of knowledge and to the reduction of the role of the teacher to that of 'facilitator' of the child's own constructions (Cobb, 1994).

The opposition of the teacher's authority to learners' meaning-making and knowledge construction also plays a central part in the work of Gordon Wells, although, where Hatano wants to bring about a radical reinterpretation in order to incorporate constructivism, Wells sees Vygotskian theory as already social constructivist (Wells, 1999, p. xii). However, Wells is critical of what he sees as Vygotsky's 'overly optimistic belief in the superiority of scientific rationalism and an unquestioning acceptance of the progressive and benign consequences of schooled instruction' (p. 325). Wells argues against the design of curricula that are independent of the 'needs and aspirations of learners'. This is a tricky area due to the highly politicised nature of what is involved in responding to 'the needs of individual learners' in the current period. On the face of it, any educator can claim to be responding to the needs of learners if they are indeed educated by what the educator does, and it would seem peculiar not to assign the term 'education' to a practice that helped learners to learn. But many commentators attribute covert aims to schooling, seeing these as far removed from education itself.[39] There is indeed a problem over how far 'access' should be interpreted in terms of fulfilling student demands – especially when such demands are not made out of independent interest but in a context in which achievement is measured in a specific way and demand driven by objectives that may not be truly educative. At times Wells's interest in 'inclusion' appears indifferent to the possibility that knowledge (and also the process of education) might be 'counterintuitive' – that is, that they may come into conflict with what learners, at least in the short term, perceive to be their aspirations. To a large extent, the issues at stake in Wells's investigation into an effective pedagogy are a matter of emphasis and depend on the way that they are interpreted by practising teachers.

Certainly Vygotsky would agree with Wells that a learner needs to be fully engaged and actively thinking and constructing if learning is to occur. Vygotsky criticises the way that

> wholly abstract thinking is entirely incomprehensible to the student, and in the Tsarist school produces naked and dry literalism, i.e. an infinite propensity for verbal formulations and for verbal definitions without any effort to penetrate into essentials, and instead of a knowledge of subject matter, there was a knowledge of words. (Vygotsky,1997, p. 173)

However, this did not lead him to conclude that the curriculum should be built around the 'aspirations' of learners. Vygotsky's approach to knowledge was different from that of Wells. For Vygotsky, the issue was to find a way to design curricula so that learners would be in a position to exercise thinking in coming to know a substantial body of knowledge. In this sense the attribute of 'effective practice' was not to work for collaborative meaning-making where meaning is *constructed* by members of the class, but to set up obstacles designed to help thinking to develop in order to foster deeper understanding of existing knowledge.[40]

By contrast, Wells assumes that a 'community' exists in any classroom through which the valuable principles of dialogic pedagogy can be realised, with joint activity working towards shared goals. He argues that there is an automatic link between learning and the development of identity, with the implication that schooling (learning in the ZPD) is responsible for identity development: 'the *whole person* is involved in activity undertaken with others, interaction in the ZPD *necessarily* involves all facets of the personality' (Wells, 1999, p. 331, italics added). The assumption of an immediate link between the 'whole person' and the experience of learning is conflated with a further more sociological claim to the effect that 'because individuals and the social world are mutually constitutive of each other, transformation of the learner also involves transforming the communities of which he or she is a member' (p. 331).

There is an easy slippage in educational practice, from Wells's integration of learning with the development of individual identity to an idea of 'inclusivity' entailing commonly defined values and accepted modes of behaviour, attitude and temperament. Wells's claim that a classroom can be a 'collaborative community', where by implication goals are shared, is contestable. In a later work (Wells and Claxton, 2002, p. 5), Wells recognises that the participants in collaborative activity may not share identical goals or beliefs (though a degree of overlap is necessary for collaboration) and that disagreement is valuable.[41] The appropriation of terms such as 'community', 'collaboration' and 'individual purposes' in the delineation of education practices raises more questions than it answers. Similarly an emphasis on the development of 'the whole person' and 'identity' can be read as entailing the responsibility of educators for the development of individual learners in every aspect of their being. In mass schooling this easily slides into the monitoring of attitudes and behaviour patterns. Walkerdine has made a convincing criticism of the way in which primary classrooms became arenas for increasing social control, under the guise of a more humane and child-centred approach (Walkerdine, 1984). She draws on a Foucauldian perspective to argue that what appear as strategies of freedom – a pedagogic practice that will set children free – are really 'administrative apparatuses for providing techniques of social regulation' (p. 163).

The importance Wells attaches to the value of collaborative activity leads to seeing the teacher as someone who, 'rather than being primarily a dispenser of knowledge and assigner of grades ... sees him or herself as a fellow learner whose prime responsibility is to act as leader of a community committed to the co-construction of knowledge' (Wells, 1999, p. 331). The emphasis is on the construction of values and knowledge, whereby teachers support and guide students as they 'create their own alternative versions of the future' (p. 332). Wells's educational prescriptions and ideals are informed by an explicit rejection of any idea of a *telos* in development;

he shares this with many post-Vygotskian researchers. He outlines three factors since Vygotsky's death that provide 'grounds for challenging what many now consider to be an overly optimistic belief in the universal superiority of scientific rationalism': (1) the criticism of the hegemony of technical rationality; (2) the challenge from cultural anthropologists 'to reject the view that treats the trajectory of European cultural history as the point of reference for evaluating other cultures'; and (3) the idea that 'the influx of immigrants from a range of different cultures has led to a *de facto* multiculturalism that is demanding a re-evaluation of the assumed superiority of white, male, middle-class values and, hence, also the technical-rationality on which it is based' (p. 325). Each of these factors has led to a questioning of knowledge and the directing of attention to the constructive activity of groups of individuals.

Questions of realism and knowledge are fundamental for curricula and institutional design in education. A further example illustrates the part played by epistemology in Wells's theory of education. Wells refers to the use by his colleague Carl Bereiter of Popper's discussion of 'third-world objects' as an illustration of the type of erroneous conceptions of knowledge that educators can subscribe to. Bereiter writes of knowledge objects such as numbers, Newton's second law and Puccini's *Madam Butterfly* as having 'the characteristics of real objects, except for being immaterial. They have origins, histories; they can be described and criticized, compared with others of their kind. They can be found to have properties that their creators or previous generations were unaware of (Bereiter, [1994], p. 22)' (Wells, 1999, p. 73). Incidentally, the idea that knowledge objects may have properties that their creators are unaware of is reiterated, as we shall see, by Ian Hacking. Wells disagrees with Bereiter's claim that knowledge is independent of the construction of individuals at any one point in time. He lays what he perceives to be the error in Bereiter's argument at the door of a particular version of representation. For Wells the flaw in Bereiter's position is his retaining of the idea of representation of 'something' while rejecting the idea that representations match objects in the world:

> The mistake, I think, is in assuming that, because a text or musical score is a representational artefact, there must be an object that exists to be represented; and then, because this object – unlike its representation – does not exist in the material world, in arguing that it must therefore be located in a different world – a World 3. (1999, pp. 73–74)

Here again Wells, in his account of the problem of knowledge in general and schooled knowledge in particular, shows the influence of linguistic discourse analysis and constructivism.

In the following passage, it is the conception of knowledge, rather than the poverty of a representationalist paradigm, that is at issue:

> it may sometimes be convenient to speak as if ideas, theories and concepts had an autonomous and immaterial existence – provided that such terms are recognized

for what they are, that is to say, as *synoptic constructs that function as shorthand expressions in particular genres of theoretical discourse*. In general, however, this way of speaking can be seriously misleading. Serious not simply because it misrepresents the way in which knowledge is constructed and used, but serious also in its consequences for the way in which, in schools and other educational institutions, knowledge, by being reified, becomes a commodity to be transmitted to students and its possession subsequently assessed and quantified. (Wells, 2002, p. 113, italics added)

What Wells is critical of is expressed as follows: 'Separating the "message" from the form in which it is realised, as Popper does, ignores the process by which a theory or any other putative third world object is developed' (p. 113). For Wells, knowledge can be explained only by reference to the discourse and genres through which it is produced. But the nature of the form in the expression 'the form in which it is realised' is not established. Although Wells accepts that knowledge develops over different time scales, his prime concern is to combat an approach to schooling that views knowledge as a product that can be 'transmitted'. So while he mentions that knowledge is constituted over centuries, his aim is to emphasise that all knowledge is constantly reconstituted and transformed by the activity of individuals in definite social contexts. While Wells gives credit to the idea that science develops in history due to a historical process involving the development of technologies and social forces, he would not be in disagreement with Popper, or for that matter with Hacking. However, Wells appears to retain the representational relation criticised by Brandom. Having rejected the idea of an artefact representing a real object, he maintains an ideal–real dualism according to which a theory can only be understood as a relation between one set of signifiers and another:[42]

> However, the fact that we can use the metalinguistic term 'theory' as a way of referring to the current textual end product of this constructive process of synoptic abstraction does not mean that there is a corresponding immaterial object that then exists, independent of the linguistic formulation and argumentation through which it was constructed ... So when Popper argues that the unexpected new problems to which new theories give rise are 'in no sense made by us; rather they are discovered by us; and in this sense they exist, undiscovered, before their discovery' (Popper, 1972, pp. 160–161), I find his claim to be at best hyperbolic, and at worst confusing. (Wells, 2002, p. 114)

Where Bereiter and Popper have a view of knowledge that cannot be reduced to the meaning-making of individuals at specific points in history, Wells finds himself in the position of having to counter his rejection of 'discovery', as opposed to construction, with an argument for the locally situated knowledge construction of the classroom: 'knowledge does not have an existence apart from the situated acts of knowing in which it is constructed, reconstructed and used' (p. 116).

Again the issue of epistemology is crucial in influencing the position adopted by Wells. Arguments concerning appropriate pedagogy are inevitably politicised, and

Wells's position on knowledge is formed in the context of North American schooling where states prescribe educational content in a draconian way, even down to the textbooks used in teaching. Wells's attempt to develop a theoretical framework for handling the idea of knowledge was developed in part as a response to a report on the role of schooling prepared by an educational association in one of Canada's largest provinces. He cautions that his contribution forms part of an ongoing dialogue rather than presenting definitive conclusions (Wells, 1999, p. 52). Wells sees 'the view of knowledge as having an independent existence that can be transmitted through texts of teacher exposition' as 'one of the chief impediments to creating classrooms as "knowledge building communities"' (1999, p. 52). In this situation it is not surprising that once a view of knowledge as the outcome of accurate representations of the world is rejected (the mirror view of nature), the alternative seems to be the continual reconstitution of knowledge via the activity of participants in a particular social context. But the problem with recourse to such a position is the tendency to diminish the role of the teacher as authority or to value texts in their own right.

Some particularly extreme versions of constructivism have the most serious consequences for education. The following anecdote illustrates the extent to which a rejection of the possibility of knowledge existing beyond individual construction is pervasive in schooling. The anecdote was related to Barbara Jaworski by Rita Nolder from her experiences as a mathematics advisory teacher and is used by Jaworski to advocate a particular approach to mathematics education. As the anecdote shows how slippage occurs when epistemological presuppositions are not made clear, it is worth relating in full.

> In a class of 11 year olds working with SMP [School Mathematics Project], the teacher was going around helping students. Rita, feeling redundant, was listening to two boys working with the SMP book on *angle*. They were looking at a diagram of two triangles (i) with angles of 45, 45, 90 and (ii) with angles of 30, 60, 90.

One boy said to the other: 'This one's a triangle [the first], and this one isn't [the second].' The boy speaking seemed to have some image or concept of a triangle which included the first triangle, but not the second. Now, Rita believed that both objects were triangles. The boy made his construction according to his own experience. So did Rita. We might say that the boy was wrong and Rita was right. But this is to make judgements about truth without taking into account the circumstances from which the statements arise. What was the boy's experience which led to his statement? Why did he believe that the second shape was not a triangle?

Jaworski quite rightly goes on to insist that it is necessary to take account of the context in which a statement is made when assessing its validity. However, the term 'context' is under-theorised, resulting in different cases being treated as comparable. In order to illustrate the legitimacy of different conceptions of a triangle, Jaworski relates the boy's 'conception' of a triangle (she resists the use of the term misconception) to the contrast found between different geometries. Contrasting plane geometry with non-Euclidian geometry we may, she suggests, 'be tempted to say that an object with angles adding up to more than 180° could not be a triangle' whereas the sum of the angles of a non-Euclidian triangle on a sphere would exceed 180°. However, this illustration neglects the difference between the case of pupil learning and the case of different geometries. Conceptions of triangles within Euclidian and non-Euclidian geometries are located within a broader field of knowledge, developed over centuries, where systematic relations determine the meaning of particular conceptions. In the case of the boy's 'misconception', reasoning within a systematic field of knowledge has not occurred. The teacher, who does have access to the relevant knowledge field of mathematics, has to elicit from the boy the reasoning that will enable him to revise his misconception and appreciate that both figures are triangles, that is, to understand what a triangle is. Jaworski stresses the benefit of pupil–teacher dialogue that enables teachers:

> to glean a sense of the origins of pupils' ideas and to challenge these in some way if it seems appropriate ... Rita might have asked the boys why the second figure was not a triangle, and could have followed up her question with further examples and situations for the boy to consider, possibly extending his experience and causing him to modify his knowledge. This might be described as 'challenging the student's *misconceptions*', but if there are 'mis'conceptions, what then is a *conception*? Is this some form of knowledge which the 'mis'conception is not? Can a conception be independent of the person or circumstance of the conceiving? (Jaworski, 1993)

These questions raised by Jaworski reveal the degree of conflation of different issues in the understanding of the development of concepts.[43] The interest in working dialogically with the pupils' own conceptions is given priority over any concern to ensure that the pupils are able to distinguish clearly between correct and incorrect knowledge. Indeed, the extract is used by the author to question whether there can be a form of knowledge against which a misconception can be compared. The agnosticism with respect to epistemology at the heart of constructivism is stated explicitly:

> Noddings' response to questions such as this is to recognise that constructivism cannot of its very nature make any statement about the status of knowledge, and so she claims that constructivism is *post*-epistemological. Von Glasersfeld ... accepts Noddings' position and modifies his own language, talking of constructivism as a theory of *knowing* rather than a theory of knowledge. (Jaworski, 1993)

The preceding anecdote is used only to illustrate the sort of discussion arising in mathematics education in the context of constructivist ideas. An understandable concern of educationalists (e.g. Hatano, Wertsch, Jaworski), in the context of the limitations of state schooling, is to redress the poverty of a 'transmission' approach to knowledge by putting in its place a powerful emphasis on the creative dimension involved in any form of understanding. A problem arises when run-of-the-mill responses, achievements and so on are counted as creative. The issue of how

powerful theories with major applications are developed in the minds of particular
individuals is not dealt with by viewing all human activity as creative even though
it may happen that a child (lacking relevant knowledge) may make a comment that
coincides with a major theory – for example, that only triangles in Euclidean geometry have angles that add up to 180 degrees. However, there is far more to the realisation of an original contribution than the coincidence of a critical statement and the
boy's 'experience' mentioned earlier. The idea that an alternative geometry might
validate the boy's conception of the second triangle as 'not a triangle', or prevent
it from being described as a 'misconception', misunderstands what is involved in
knowledge. Because universality is sidelined by the importance of recognising
human activity in a context, well-meaning arguments are led to absurd conclusions.
Cobb comments on 'the "political correctness" that frequently surrounds constructivism in maths and science education' (Cobb, 1994) and argues for the importance
of going beyond purely psychological and individualist constructivism in order to
view learning maths at least in part as enculturation into an intellectual community.
He also makes the point that students construct their own ways of knowing in the
most authoritarian pedagogic situations. The examples of the ability to construct
that are furnished by many proponents of constructivism are typically drawn only
from a conveniently limited range of contexts.

CONCLUSION

The preceding discussion has considered the extent to which attempts to offer an
explanation of the failure of schooling in terms of the transmission of decontextualised rationality have turned to a communitarian constructivism as an alternative.
However, this alternative is not unproblematic, and there are significant points of
difficulty that need to be taken into account. Two points are relevant here: the conflation of the development of individuality and identity with the practice of schooling,
and the subsumption of knowledge to local construction. Richard Sennett offers a
different version of identity, and Ian Hacking a different account of texts and
knowledge.

A different sense of individuality is found in Sennett's conception of public life.
For Sennett a serious problem for contemporary society is the loss of public life, and
the classroom could be taken as an instance of this (although Sennett himself does
not give this example). For Sennett, individuality and personality are enhanced by
the possibility and opportunity of the full development of discrete ways of acting in
discrete circumstances. The ground that sustains these discrete ways of being arises
out of the conventions and rules bounding activity in the public context:

> Convention itself is the single most expressive tool in public life. But in an
> age wherein intimate relations determine what shall be believable, conventions,
> artifices, and rules appear only to get in the way of revealing oneself to another;
> they are obstructions to intimate expression. As the imbalance between public
> and intimate life has grown greater, people have become less expressive. With an
> emphasis on psychological authenticity, people become inartistic in daily life

because they are unable to tap the fundamental creative strength of the actor, the ability to play with and invest external images of self. Thus we arrive at the hypothesis that theatricality has an equally special, friendly relation to a strong public life. (Sennett, 1977, p. 37)

There is a separation 'between public and intimate life' that is assisted by the conventions, artifices and rules that facilitate expressiveness. The idea of identity and activity that underlies Sennett's account of public life is quite different from that implicit in Wells's argument. Sennett's account of identity and activity stands in sharp contrast to the view that identity arises in a community holding shared goals and working towards a common understanding.

Let us turn next to what Ian Hacking has to say about text and knowledge, another aspect of Wells's work. Hacking addresses the question of the relativism that results from an awareness of the different valuations of artefacts and texts in different contexts and periods of history. But unlike Wells, who claims that meaning can only be credited to individuals at a particular point in time, he presents a narrative to illustrate the argument that meaning can be carried beyond the locale of any collection of individuals.

The narrative involves a collection of Chinese porcelain, traded by August der Starke, the Elector of Saxony, in the eighteenth century. This collection was the stunningly beautiful product of techniques of glazing in the style called 'the green family'. Hacking tells how August der Starke's love for his china was so great that he built a palace to house it, but how later the collection was dismissed as of no more value than 'a collection of dolls'. For a century it was left in a crowded cellar. Then, at the end of the nineteenth century, the porcelain was re-exhibited and delighted and amazed scholars before being housed in cellars again during the Second World War and then again returned to an appreciative public gaze (Hacking, 1995, p. 238). For Hacking the adventures of the Chinese porcelain illustrate an argument against both relativism and the idea that a work of art has no intrinsic value. The story of the porcelain can be related as

a human tale of wealth, lust, changes in taste, destruction, survival. Only a sequence of accidents created the Chinese export trade of objects suited to a certain European fashion for *chinoiserie* around the 1700s, and then brought such characteristic examples under one lavish roof, saw the lapse from public taste, witnessed a revival, a firestorm and a return. ... In short there were periods of admiration and times when these pieces were despised, unlit and unloved. (p. 238)

The fact that different periods invest the green family porcelain with a different aura leads to the 'crass' conclusion that '*evidently there is no intrinsic value in this stuff, it goes up and down in the scale of human admiration as the wind blows*' (p. 238).[44] But Hacking argues against this view, preferring, as he says, the empirical claim supported by historical evidence that 'there will be generations that rediscover [the porcelain]. It will time and again *show itself*' (p. 238), even though in order for it to do so, particular conditions must apply. His point is that 'achievements created by humans have a strange persistence that contrasts with fashion' (p. 239).

Hacking makes essentially the same argument in relation to texts when he reports the comments of his undergraduate students about their introductory philosophy course. '"Gee what a great course" was followed by "But you could not help it ... What with all those great books, I mean like Descartes"' (p. 239). Hacking modestly reports that he gives terrible lectures, and he tells his students that he does not understand Descartes but knows that 'it does not matter. Descartes speaks directly to these young people, who know as little about Descartes and his times as I know about the green family and its times. But just as the green family showed itself to me, directly, so Descartes shows himself to them' (p. 239). Even though many of Hacking's students may have thought Descartes and Sartre were contemporaries, 'the value of Descartes to these students is completely anachronistic, out of time ... Descartes, even more than Sartre, can speak directly to them across the seas of time' (p. 239). Hacking also gives the example of Hegel as someone who 'once again shows himself', who speaks 'directly ... after decades of oblivion', even though during his absence he 'dominated the formation of Dewey, and perhaps that of Peirce, and also the young upstarts Moore and Russell who laid waste to him within a few years' (p. 240).

Hacking's appreciation of texts is totally different from that of Wells. For Wells the text is dependent for its meaning on the successive subjective constructions placed upon it,[45] whereas for Hacking the text retains its value, which is to be rediscovered. A text can be read differently from one period to the next, but this different reading does not create new meanings *ex nihilo*. Hegel's text is generative in the sense that it discloses more knowledge with more reading, and also more knowledge is available in the text as history allows it 'to show itself' (Hacking).[46] The different positions taken – on the one side, by Wells, Jaworski and Hatano and, on the other, by Sennett and Hacking – have profound implications for education since they imply quite different positions for educators to adopt towards knowledge and to the role of the teacher as authority or facilitator. The representational paradigm is unable to deal with issues of meaning without oscillating between *either* attributing meaning or agency to artefacts and tools, *or* reducing meaning to the construction of individuals and thereby losing any sense of 'universalising' knowledge.

In his criticism of the pervasiveness of the concept of representation in attempts to deal with meaning, Brandom introduces what should be recognised as an important Hegelian dimension. Hegel exposes the fallacies of a way of thinking that does not recognise the underlying epistemology with which it operates.[47] According to Brandom,

a representational paradigm reigns not only in the whole spectrum of analytically pursued semantics ... but also in structuralism inheriting the broad outline of Saussure's semantics, and even those later continental thinkers whose poststructuralism is still so far mired in the representational paradigm that it can see no other alternative to understanding meaning in terms of signifiers

standing for signifieds than to understand it in terms of signifiers standing for
other signifiers. (Brandom, 2000, p. 10)

His point is that even though a version of the correspondence view of knowledge
according to which a signifier represents an object/event is rejected, the paradigm
is frequently left untouched.[48] It follows, therefore, that the implication of a critique
of the failure of signifiers to represent an external world leads to the relativist position that the knowledge available for human beings arises from the relation between
one signifier and another. Postmodernism has replaced 'signifiers standing for
signified' with 'signifiers standing for signifiers' – but it has not broken decisively
with a representationalist paradigm, that still operates implicitly. Instead of unearthing
the presuppositions of representation, it retains representation as a relation between
representations. In effect it continues the limitations of 'the Understanding', in the
sense that Hegel identifies and exposes to critique, as we shall see in Chapter 6.

The importance of the representational paradigm is not limited to agency, freedom
and the under-theorisation of human activity: it also has an ethical dimension.
Referring to Sellars, Brandom insists that what distinguishes a human from a
nonhuman knower (which only responds differentially) is normativity – the giving
and asking of reasons. This giving and asking of reasons is a necessary element of
human knowing that is always conceptual and, as such, different from nonhuman
knowing, as is apparent in the report of a parrot squawking 'red' in response to a
red object. The normativity immediately locates epistemology in ethics, but not
ethics in the way that it is commonly thought of – as an external code that can be
approved or disapproved, accepted or rejected. To put it another way, values are not
separated from facts. All knowing takes the form of judgements that one *ought* to
make. According to Brandom, following Hegel and before him Kant, human
knowledge and judgement go together, and the Humean distinction between fact
and value is groundless.[49]

In effect, Brandom's interest lies in the priority of inference over reference. This
inversion of the conventional order of explanation gives a different weight to factors
involved in the development of meaning, emphasising human agency and history
rather than artefacts or representational resources. A common-sense understanding
of history is what goes before and has an effect on what comes after, but this understanding leads to problems with the concepts of progress and development of which
writers in the post-Vygotskian research field are wary. This will be discussed further
in Chapter 7. Only one aspect of this very large and complex area needs to be
mentioned here. From Hegel's point of view, history is not a matter of antecedents
to any current state but of a holism that, in contrast to dualism, attributes consequences to activity, but eschews the type of direct causal relation that is commonly
assumed in explanation.[50] My argument is that the dualism implicit in conceptuali-
sations of human meaning-making (semiosis) affects the theorisation of issues that
are crucial to education.

Although the subtleties of philosophical argument needed to unearth the
presuppositions of representationalism are not easily accessible, the work not only
of Sennett and Hacking but also of contemporary philosophers such as Brandom

and McDowell has a bearing on practical questions of education, research and policy. Every position on knowledge, learning and pedagogy makes presuppositions about the nature of knowledge. Approaches to pedagogy are informed by epistemological presupposition as well as empirical research.

When these epistemological presuppositions are not worked through, as in much recent work, there is a tendency to be suspicious of knowledge that is generalised on the grounds that it is decontextualised. Associated with this tendency is the critique of the 'Enlightenment project', interpreted as one of knowing and manipulating the world. This 'project' has been fiercely criticised in several quarters, and the criticisms have been recruited by researchers in education to legitimate a relativist and contextualist approach to knowledge. It has become fashionable to rescind the term 'truth' and to speak of knowledge(s) in the plural. Much criticism of the Enlightenment project is phrased in terms of individual rights, multiculturalism and equality.[51] What education research has lost in the process is the enthusiasm, and the grounds, for examining the political order, which is of far greater importance for education than pedagogic strategy.

It is interesting to note that the ideas discussed above can fit different and even opposed political agendas: Kirshner and Whitson point out that the research on situated cognition has been adopted by advocates of market vouchers, whose views about the funding of public education stand in sharp opposition to those who originally developed these ideas of situated cognition (Kirshner and Whitson, 1997, p. viii).[52] The attack on decontextualised knowledge may be conceived as an attack on authoritarianism and abstraction, but it can easily be construed as grounds for the opportunistic cutting of programmes for formal education or for reducing education to the most narrow programmes of training. Jean Lave has contrasted the success of learning in everyday contexts (as purposeful and motivating) with the inert knowledge of formal schooling. It is possible that the consolidation of such lines of thought may, like Adam Smith's invisible hand, contribute to an end that is no part of their author's intention.

In turning to Hegel, this book signals an alternative position that, while it retains the traditional concept of knowledge, neither ignores nor denies the diversity of routes by which knowledge arrives. For the moment, however, it is not to Hegel alone that we turn, but to Hegel and Kant as reflected through the work of Vygotsky and Piaget.

NOTES

1 I am making use of the work of Brandom when I refer to a 'representionalist paradigm'. Brandom takes care to distinguish the concept of representation from a representationalist paradigm but for the purposes of this book I will treat the terms as synonymous.
2 The discussion of this area in philosophy is extensive and beyond the remit of this book.
3 However, this is not as far removed from post-Vygotskian research as it appears, as David Bakhurst has written on the links between McDowell's work and that of Ilyenkov, a philosopher working in the Vygotskian tradition. It is interesting to note that McDowell supervised Bakhurst's thesis on Soviet philosophy at a time when he was preparing work resulting in his own book *Mind and World*. McDowell and Brandom's work are also connected. McDowell

credits Brandom's writings and conversations with shaping his own thinking and singles out a seminar on Hegel's *Phenomenology of Spirit* that he attended in 1990 relating that 'the effect is pervasive; so much so that I would like to conceive [*Mind and World*] as a prolegomenon to a reading of the *Phenomenology* much as Brandom's forthcoming *Making It Explicit: Reasoning, Representing, and Discursive Commitment*' (McDowell, 1996, p. ix).

4 Or, in the case of Saussurian linguistics, between signifier and signified.

5 A tradition of semiotics and linguistic analysis has been influential in maintaining a representationalist paradigm concerned with this matter.

6 The discussion of the transfer problem in the previous chapter deals with this issue of whether or not knowledge can be understood as transcending the contexts of its production.

7 Evidence of this paradigm is present even in Kant's work where the presupposition of a distinction between the world as we know it and the world in itself sets up problems involving representation. According to Richard Bernstein, when he dealt with 'spontaneity and receptivity, phenomena and noumena' it appears that 'Kant at times, seems to reify these distinctions, to make them into rigid dichotomies that leave us with all sort of aporiai' (Bernstein, 2002, p. 10).

8 In McDowell's sense, Hegel 'exorcises' the questions rather than answering them, but in doing so provides what can stand as an answer (McDowell, 1996, p. xxiii).

9 In fact, René Van der Veer, writing in *Understanding Vygotsky*, suggests that Vygotsky emphasised meaning over the sign and that the claim that 'Vygotsky developed from a period in which he concentrated exclusively on the sign to a more mature understanding of the relevance of word meaning' does not do justice to Vygotsky's position (Van der Veer and Valsiner, 1993, p. 65).

10 Their position is reasonable given the 'representationalist frame' in which the issue of abstract rationality is considered.

11 Wertsch quotes Lukes (1977) for a definition of methodological individualism: 'explanations … couched wholly in terms of facts about individuals' (Wertsch, 1998, p. 19).

12 For a clear account of the issues arising in the equation of reasons with causes and in the reduction of the concept of cause to efficient cause see D'Oro and Sandis (2013). See also Tanney (2009), and Candlish and Damnjanovic (2013).

13 For example, Fodor (1980) and Luntley (2008).

14 This use of the word 'system' has led to the accusation of abstract rationality, that is, the idea that meaning of scientific concepts is determined within a system.

15 The reference here is to schooled knowledge as decontextualised knowledge.

16 Wertsch relies on Charles Taylor's philosophical work in his characterisation of Vygotsky as an Enlightenment abstract rationalist. My argument is that this characterisation of Vygotsky depends upon implicit dualist presuppositions that inform the way that the philosophical tradition is read. It is interesting to note that Taylor's critical reading of McDowell's *Mind and World* retains a form of dualism in that he is concerned that by taking issue with the idea that the content of experience is nonconceptual, McDowell denies the idea of a Heideggerian 'undelimited background'. Taylor wants to recognise the preconceptual or nonconceptual as a form of 'knowing' (Taylor, 2002, p. 111). However, McDowell fields Taylor's criticism by pointing out that: 'Taylor works with a notion of conceptual capacities according to which they are in play only when things come into focus. … Taylor does not emphasise my insistence that actualisations of conceptual capacities must be seen as manifestations of life as opposed to operations of a pure intellect' (McDowell, 2002, p. 283).

17 To some extent the way Wertsch presents the problem is the reaction against a correspondence view of truth. Curiously, although Hegel's critique of epistemology exposes the inadequacy of both correspondence and empiricist view of knowledge, it happens that ultimately Hegel's philosophy subsumes these positions. Within Hegel's philosophy they are quite different from the way they are commonly conceived.

18 It should be noted that while much of the research discussed here is not exclusively North American, equally within North America there is research that does not fit this pattern.

19 Aside from the issue of human freedom, the other major element missing from explanations is history. For Hegel freedom and history are inextricably interconnected.

20 The term *foundational* has different meanings. Here as an object of criticism of those theorising mediational means it signifies claims to knowledge derived from given and certain starting points. For other aspects of this idea see below.

21 The implications are particularly important when research funding is directed specifically to achieving outcomes intended to inform policy. Moreover such funding is commonly aimed at short-term outcomes to respond to election cycles. Systems of education have been constructed on the basis of the expectations of the learner's potential and knowledge of appropriateness of conditions of learning and teaching. The history of education in England can be presented as a narrative of successive conceptions of suitability according to the reigning conception of both ability and possibility within the remits of education funding. Thus the attempt to design contexts for learning that take into account information that will allow the enhancement of educational opportunity and efficiency is important for research concerns, particularly where research funding is determined by policy and the pressure on researchers to deliver amenable accounts is difficult to resist.

22 Mode in this context has a technical meaning developed by Halliday and Kress.

23 Sociotechnical was a term coined by Eric Trist, Ken Bamforth and Fred Emery, consultants at the Tavistock Institute for Social Research in London, to capture the integral interaction between people and technology in workplaces.

24 Dictionary definitions of the word 'mean' and the study of meaning (semantics) both refer to *signification, signify, significance or sign*. This indicates the presence of one thing that stands for another. These dictionary definitions do not indicate the more sophisticated sense that can be derived from Kant's philosophy and that necessarily involves human activity. Of course, we can talk of a sign meaning something, independently of any *judgement* (i.e. the 'giving and asking for reasons' in Brandom's sense) but then the term 'meaning' is being used to express something quite different. An example from nature is of an insect or plant without sting or poison imitating those with sting or poison. The markings act as a sign/signal to predators and have the same result as that of the markings of the genuinely dangerous species. One stands in place of another. In this instance the use of sign is coincident with the stimulus/response of the 'differential response' of a fire alarm referred to by Brandom.

25 Sloman includes in his catch-all use of the term 'representation' 'information states of simple homeostatic devices, like thermostats' and 'more complex representations ... involved in the control of internal or external behaviour in a human brain ... such as those encoding information about the grammar of our language' (Sloman, 1996, p. 118).

26 This argument is developed in *Cosmopolis* (Toulmin, 1992).

27 Although there are important differences between the terms *constructivism* and *constructionism*, they are used interchangeably here as both terms appear in this book only in so far as they represent the dualism under consideration. Gergen comments on their interchangeable usage: '[Constructivism] is a tradition ... represented in recent psychology by such figures as Jean Piaget, George Kelly, and Ernst von Glasersfeld. Constructivists propose that each individual mentally constructs the world of experience. In this sense the mind is not a mirror of the world as it is, but functions to create the world as we know it. From this perspective there could be as many realities as there are minds to conceptualise or construe. ... the constructivist perspective is similar to the constructionist in the emphasis it places on human construction of what we take to be "the real". It is largely for this reason that many scholars will use the words "constructivism" and "constructionism" interchangeably ... for constructivists the process of world construction is psychological; it takes place "in the head". In contrast, for social constructionists what we take to be real is the outcome of social relationships' (Gergen, 1999, pp. 236–237).

28 By using the shorthand 'foundationalist tradition' here I mean to capture the tradition that Hegel criticises in the *Phenomenology* – both dualism and representationalism are necessary elements in a foundational approach to knowledge.

29 For example, Ilyenkov's work on the question of the ideal sheds a different light on the question of subjective and objective and ideal and real.

30 For example, the technologies developed through long periods of history framing certain questions, problems and results (Hutchins, 1995).

31 The problem of meaning is to locate how meaning arises, where it is located, what process provides meaning. A simple realist solution is the correspondence theory of truth, that is, that our representations reflect an independent world that is real. Once this position is undermined the question of meaning comes to the fore. A postmodern position on this issue is to maintain that there are an infinite variety of ways of 'making meaning' with no one taking precedence over another.

32 By utilising Davidson's argument here, I do not mean to imply that 'scheme' is restricted to the use that Davidson makes of it. The relation of scheme and content could still hold even where scheme involves nontextual forms of meaning-making.

33 This would seem to suggest an emphasis on human freedom, as the individual is viewed as the ground of meaning. This might appear to contradict what I am claiming, that is, that human freedom is neglected. However, the point that I am making views freedom as historical and as such neither a matter of a Cartesian will or of causal effect from an epistemological given.

34 It is difficult to do justice in a few sentences to what mediation means. See entry in Inwood (1995, pp. 183–186).

35 For a full consideration of assessment and its importance as a tool for developing learning rather than only assessing learning, see Black and Wiliam (1998a, 1998b).

36 Unless, that is, it were realised by the 'boundedness' of a dualist world that provided sense data – a *given*.

37 This would seem to be at odds with the claims of writers who aim to be agnostic on epistemology. However, their lack of commentary on epistemology does not prevent their having an implied position by default.

38 A difficulty here is the meaning of 'instructional' and the extent to which this refers only to a passive caricature of a learner or to an approach that emphasises a core body of knowledge.

39 For instance, Braverman's (1974) characterisation of education as limited to basic skills, conformity to the rules of society and obedience, in contrast to Pippin's (2000) claim that liberal education is one in which learners, in acquiring knowledge, also understand the *reasons* for holding such knowledge.

40 Vygotsky's approach does not deny that learners are active in coming to know, but holds that learners are not *creating* knowledge.

41 The activity theory of Engeström makes conflict key to development, albeit at an early stage of a process of DWR (developmental work research). For Engeström, the 'double bind' generating an impasse in activity provides the focal point for 'expansive learning'.

42 Wells states that he is using the form of dialogue to develop a theory of knowledge and implies that his words are provisional and exploratory.

43 In this development no conception of history is present.

44 The term 'crass' is actually used by Hacking to describe his own statement, but in fact he believes the statement does justice to the relativist position.

45 Wells is normally referring to texts that bear no comparison to the texts that Hacking has in mind (school classroom texts as against Descartes's *Meditations*).

46 Similarly a scientific theory or mathematical formula is generative beyond its original value and purpose.

47 Hegel's exposure of what is involved in our way of grasping the world compels consideration of human freedom. Thought and freedom are thus inextricably linked. For Spinoza the development of intellect and freedom are one and the same.

48 The correspondence view of truth presupposes that representations map isomorphically on to the world.

49 However, advocates of a fact–value distinction are not completely mistaken in their attempt to keep values separate from facts. The argument that values intricately combine with facts does not necessarily entail that the values are ones that individuals have added consciously (actively). The values are implicit in the very process of thinking: to perceive something is to distinguish it as significant and to relate it to other concepts – place it in a space of reasons. This is quite different from the position that most provokes negative response from those who advocate a fact–value distinction in popular discussion; for example, when an individual labels a particular scientific theory as subscribing to a particular set of moral or immoral positions.

50 The argument made by Bakhurst (1991) that Vygotsky's view of higher mental functions could not be reduced to their primitive antecedents is a case in point. An account of higher mental functions (intellect) cannot be made simply from neurophysiology, developmental biology or child development.

51 The 'Science wars' and the 'Culture wars' have been a part of a continuing debate that has influenced approaches to curricula and, at a deeper level, shaped ideas about knowing and knowledge.

52 '… situated cognition theory … has served as a powerful platform for analysing the pressing problems and possibilities of schooling and schools … But such research has subsequently been co-opted to argue for literal apprenticeships in the United States … and to advocate market-driven vouchers as a way to eliminate public education' (Kirshner and Whitson, 1997, p. viii).

REFERENCES

Bakhurst, D. (1991) *Consciousness and Revolution in Soviet Philosophy: From the Bolsheviks to Evald Ilyenkov* (Cambridge: Cambridge University Press).

Bereiter, C. (1994) Constructivism, Socioculturalism, and Popper's World 3, *Educational Researcher*, 23:7, 21–23.

Bernstein, R.J. (2002) McDowell's Domesticated Hegelianism. In: N.H. Smith (ed.) *Reading McDowell on Mind and World* (London: Routledge), pp. 9–24.

Black, P. and Wiliam, D. (1998a) Assessment and Classroom Learning, *Assessment in Education*, 5:1, 7–73.

Black, P. and Wiliam, D. (1998b) *Inside the Black Box: Raising Standards Through Classroom Assessment* (London: School of Education, King's College).

Brandom, R. (2000) *Articulating Reasons: An Introduction to Inferentialism* (Cambridge, MA: Harvard University Press).

Braverman, H. (1974) *Labor and Monopoly Capital: The Degradation of Work in the Twentieth Century* (New York: Monthly Review Press).

Bruner, J.S. (1996) *The Culture of Education* (Cambridge, MA: Harvard University Press).

Candlish, S. and Damnjanovic, N. (2013) Reason, Action and the Will: The Fall and Rise of Causalism. In: M. Beaney (ed.) *The Oxford Handbook of the History of Analytic Philosophy* (Oxford: Oxford University Press).

Cobb, P. (1994) Constructivism in Mathematics and Science Education, *Educational Researcher*, 23:7, 4.

Cole, M. and Engeström, Y. (1993) A Cultural-Historical Approach to Distributed Cognition. In: G. Salomon (ed.) *Distributed Cognitions: Psychological and Educational Considerations* (Cambridge, UK: Cambridge University Press), pp. 1–46.

Confrey, J. (1995) How Compatible Are Radical Constructivism, Sociocultural Approaches, and Social Constructivism? In: L.P. Steffe and J. Gale (eds) *Constructivism in Education* (Hillsdale, NJ: Lawrence Erlbaum Associates), pp. 185–226.

Davidson, D. (1984) Essay 13 – On the Very Idea of a Conceptual Scheme. In D. Davidson (ed.) *Inquiries into Truth and Interpretation* (Oxford: Clarendon Press), pp. 186–222.

66   *Vygotsky Philosophy and Education*

Davis, A. (2010) Learning. In R. Bailey, R. Barrow, D. Carr and C. MacCarthy (eds) *Sage Handbook of Philosophy of Education* (London: Sage), pp. 323–336.

Davydov, V.V. (1984) Substantial Generalization and the Dialectical-Materialist Theory of Thinking. In: M. Hedegaard, P. Hakkarainen, and Y. Engeström (eds) *Learning and Teaching on a Scientific Basis: Methodological and Epistemological Aspects of the Activity Theory of Learning and Teaching* (Aarhus: Aarhus University).

D'Oro, G. and Sandis, C. (eds) (2013) From Anti-Causalism to Causalism and Back: A History of the Reasons/Causes Debate. In G. D'Oro and C. Sandis (eds) *Reasons and Causes: Causalism and Anti-Causalism in the Philosophy of Action* (Basingstoke, UK: Palgrave Macmillan).

Dunne, J. (1993) *Back to the Rough Ground: 'Phronesis' and 'Techne' in Modern Philosophy and in Aristotle* (Notre Dame, IN: University of Notre Dame Press).

Fodor, J. (1980) On the Impossibility of Acquiring 'More Powerful' Structures. In: M. Piattelli-Palmarini (ed.) *Language and Learning: The Debate Between Jean Piaget and Noam Chomsky* (London: Routledge), pp. 142–162.

Gergen, K.J. (1999) *An Invitation to Social Construction* (London: Sage).

Hacking, I. (1995) Three Parables. In: R.B. Goodman (ed.) *Pragmatism: A Contemporary Reader* (London: Routledge), pp. 237–249.

Halliday, M.A.K. (1985) *Introduction to Functional Grammar* (London: Edward Arnold).

Hatano, G. (1993) Time to Merge Vygotskian and Constructivist Conceptions of Knowledge Acquisition. In: E.A. Forman, N. Minick and C.A. Stone (eds) *Contexts for Learning: Sociocultural Dynamics in Children's Development* (New York: Oxford University Press), pp. 153–156.

Hedegaard, M. (1996) How Instruction Influences Children's Concepts of Evolution, *Mind Culture and Activity*, 3:1,11–24.

Hedegaard, M. (1998) Situated Learning and Cognition: Theoretical Learning and Cognition, *Mind, Culture and Activity*, 5:2,114–26.

Hutchins, E. (1995) *Cognition in the Wild* (Cambridge, MA: MIT Press).

Inwood, M. (1995) *A Hegel Dictionary* (Oxford: Blackwell).

Jaworski, B. (1993) Constructivism and Teaching – The Socio-Cultural Context, http://www.grout.demon.co.uk/Barbara/chreods.htm (accessed 16 May 2013).

Jewitt, C. and Kress, G. (2002) Multimodal Research in Education. In: S. Goodman, T. Lillis, J. Maybin and N. Mercer (eds) *Language, Literacy and Education: A Reader* (Stoke-on-Trent: Trentham Books/Open University), pp. 277–292.

Kirshner, D. and Whitson, J.A. (eds) (1997) *Situated Cognition: Social, Semiotic and Psychological Perspectives* (Mahwah, NJ: Lawrence Erlbaum Associates).

Kress, G., Jewitt, C., Ogborn, J. and Tsatsarelis, C. (2001) *Multimodal Teaching and Learning: The Rhetorics of the Science Classroom* (London: Continuum).

Lukes, S. (1977) Methodological Individualism Reconsidered. In: S. Lukes (ed.) *Essays in Social Theory* (New York: Columbia University Press), pp. 177–186.

Luntley, M. (2008) Conceptual Development and the Paradox of Learning, *Journal of Philosophy of Education*, 42:1, 1–14.

McDowell, J. (1996) *Mind and World* (Cambridge, MA: Harvard University Press).

McDowell, J. (2002) Responses. In: N.H. Smith (ed.) *Reading McDowell on Mind and World* (London: Routledge), pp. 269–305.

Palinscar, A.S. and Brown, A.L. (1984) Reciprocal Teaching of Comprehension Fostering and Comprehension Monitoring. *Cognition and Instruction*, 1:2, 117–175.

Parker, I. (ed.) (1998) *Social Constructionism, Discourse and Realism* (London: Sage).

Pea, R.D. (1993) Practices of Distributed Intelligence and Designs for Education. In: G. Salomon (ed.) *Distributed Cognitions: Psychological and Educational Considerations* (Cambridge: Cambridge University Press), pp. 47–87.

Phillips, D.C. (1995) The Good, the Bad and the Ugly: The Many Faces of Constructivism, *Educational Researcher*, 24:7, 5–12.

Pippin, R. (2000) *Liberation and the Liberal Arts*, annual talk at the University of Chicago, http://www.ditext.com/pippin/aims2000.html (accessed 16 May 2013).

Popper, K.R. (1972) *Objective Knowledge: An Evolutionary Approach* (New York: Oxford University Press).

Reich, R. (1992) *The Work of Nations: Preparing Ourselves for 21st Century Capitalism* (New York: Vintage Books).

Sellars, W. (1997) *Empiricism and the Philosophy of Mind* (Cambridge, MA: Harvard University Press).

Sennett, R. (1977) *The Fall of Public Man* (London: Faber and Faber).

Sloman, A. (1996) Towards a General Theory of Representations. In: D. Peterson (ed.) *Forms of Representation* (Exeter: Intellect Books), pp. 118–140.

Tanney, J. (2009) Reasons as Non-Causal Context-Placing Explanations. In: C. Sandis (ed.) *New Essays on the Explanation of Action* (Basingstoke: Palgrave Macmillan), pp. 94–111.

Taylor, C. (2002) Foundationalism and the Inner–Outer Distinction. In: N.H. Smith (ed.) *Reading McDowell on Mind and World* (London: Routledge), pp. 106–120.

Toulmin, S. (1992) *Cosmopolis: The Hidden Agenda of Modernity* (Chicago: University of Chicago Press).

Valsiner, J. and Van der Veer, R. (2000) *The Social Mind: Construction of the Idea* (Cambridge: Cambridge University Press).

Van der Veer, R. and Valsiner, J. (1993) *Understanding Vygotsky: A Quest for Synthesis* (Oxford: Blackwell).

von Glasersfeld, E. (1990) An Exposition of Constructivism: Why Some Like It Radical. In: R. Davis, C. Maher and N. Noddings (eds) *Constructivist Views on the Teaching and Learning of Mathematics* (Reston, VA: NCTM), pp. 19–29.

Vygotsky, L.S. (1997) *Educational Psychology*, R. Silvermann trans. (Boca Raton, FL: St. Lucie Press).

Vygotsky, L.S. (1998) *The Collected Works of L. S. Vygotsky, Vol. 5, Child Psychology*, R.W. Reiber ed. (New York: Plenum Press).

Walkerdine, V. (1984) Developmental Psychology and the Child-Centred Pedagogy: The Insertion of Piaget into Early Education. In: J. Henriques *et al.* (eds) *Changing the Subject: Psychology, Social Regulation and Subjectivity* (London: Routledge), pp. 153–202.

Wells, G. (1999) *Dialogic Inquiry: Towards a Sociocultural Practice and Theory of Education* (Cambridge: Cambridge University Press).

Wells, G. (2002) Dialogue about Knowledge Building. In: B. Smith (ed.) *Liberal Education in a Knowledge Society* (Chicago: Open Court), pp. 111–138.

Wells, G. and Claxton, G. (eds) (2002) *Learning for Life in the 21st Century: Sociocultural Perspectives on the Future of Education* (Oxford: Wiley-Blackwell).

Wertsch, J.V. (1985) *Vygotsky and the Social Formation of Mind* (Cambridge, MA: Harvard University Press).

Wertsch, J.V. (1998) *Mind as Action* (New York: Oxford University Press).

Wertsch, J.V. (1999) Mediated Action. In: W. Bechtel and G. Graham (eds) *A Companion to Cognitive Science* (Oxford: Blackwell), pp. 518–532.

Wertsch, J.V. (2000) Vygotsky's Two Minds on the Nature of Meaning. In: C.D. Lee and P. Smargorinsky (eds) *Vygotskian Perspectives on Literacy Research* (Cambridge: Cambridge University Press), pp. 19–30.

Wertsch, J.V., Tulviste, P., and Hagstrom, F. (1993) A Sociocultural Approach to Agency. In: E.A. Forman, N. Minick and C.A. Stone (eds) *Contexts for Learning: Sociocultural Dynamics in Children's Development* (Oxford: Oxford University Press), pp. 225–256.

4

Vygotsky and Piaget

A Case of Different Philosophies

INTRODUCTION TO THE PHILOSOPHIC BACKGROUND

The preceding chapter set out the problem of decontextualisation as it is posed in relation to Vygotsky's work. It took issue with the way in which causality is assigned to context in the formation of mind and attempted to show that too many of the terms used in this area are taken as unproblematic. This chapter and the next continue the argument, concentrating on the philosophic tradition informing Vygotsky's work. Their aim is to make explicit in Vygotsky's work what many commentaries leave unsaid: namely, that it has a definite philosophic provenance that conditions and shapes its arguments.

It is often difficult to attribute to an author the clear influence of any particular philosophy, but this was not the case with Vygotsky as he actually named his sources. They earned him no credit in the Soviet Union, where Stalinism imposed a narrow caricature of Marxism as the criterion of theory. Van der Veer and Valsiner (1993) have contributed to an excavation of the influences on Vygotsky, and although their work has established his debt to Hegel and Spinoza, there is little to explain in detail exactly what this debt comprises (Van der Veer, 1984; Kozulin, 1990; Bakhurst, 1991; Brockmeier, 1996; Bronckart, 1996; Robbins, 2001; Blunden, 2011).

In this chapter features of Vygotsky's and Piaget's work are compared as a way to reveal the significance of different philosophic approaches for educational theory. Both writers are concerned with the genesis of intellect. Piaget adopted an approach that attempts to understand the development of knowledge as following the same course as the development of faculties. As Piaget put it: 'The fundamental hypothesis of genetic epistemology is that there is a parallelism between the progress made in the logical and rational organisation of knowledge and the corresponding formative psychological processes' (Piaget, 1970, p. 13). Piaget believed that parallelism plays an important role for any understanding of the

Vygotsky Philosophy and Education, First Edition. Jan Derry.
© 2013 Jan Derry. Editorial organisation © Philosophy of Education Society of Great Britain.
Published 2013 by John Wiley & Sons, Ltd.

growth of knowledge. Vygotsky, in line with the importance he attached to the social, emphasised the sociogenetic development of faculties and knowledge. For Piaget, 'the flow of construction is from one's interactions with one's nonhuman environment toward an exchange with others. In Vygotsky, the flow of conceptual development is reversed' (Confrey, 1995, p. 202). Comparisons of Vygotsky and Piaget are commonly made from the point of view of psychology, but attention here is directed to the less well-aired, but no less important, philosophic differences between them. This chapter and the next two put these differences in context by considering parts of the philosophy of Hegel and Spinoza that are relevant for Vygotsky's conception of mind and world and its differences from that of Piaget. As was noted in Chapter 1, commentaries on Vygotsky have not always been attentive to the distinctive features of his work that arise from these philosophic concerns.

The importance of the philosophic background to Vygotsky's work cannot be underestimated. The contrast between Piagetian and Vygotskian positions, which is presented in many discussions as an internal dispute within educational research about learning, is also of *philosophic* significance. Discussion within education research about scientific concepts, the nature of knowledge, the process by which knowledge can be learned and the nature of rationality mimics issues that have been examined over centuries of philosophic dispute (see e.g. Dunne, 1993).

The issues involved here are philosophic but this does not preclude them from having important practical implications. Differences in the conceptualisation of consciousness have implications for the understanding of constructivism and universal knowledge, and hence for pedagogy. The philosophic dimensions of the differences between Vygotsky and the early Piaget, in particular those involving egocentrism and concept development, have not yet been fully explored in educational theory.

Due to his early death, Vygotsky was able to engage only with the earlier part of Piaget's work. Although many of his criticisms would have required tempering by Piaget's later acceptance of the significance of social influences, the philosophic differences remain. His comments on Piaget's early work help us to see how Vygotsky himself perceived the influence of their different approaches. Piaget later expressed regret at not coming to read Vygotsky's work until much later and conceded some of the points raised by Vygotsky, while other elements of his thought remained unchanged. Asking himself whether or not his work 'confirms or invalidates Vygotsky's criticisms', he responded: 'The answer is both yes and no: on certain points I find myself more in agreement with Vygotsky than I would have been in 1934, while on other issues I now have better arguments for answering him than would previously have been the case' (Piaget, 2000, p. 241).

Contrasting the two major exponents of philosophic psychology in the twentieth century runs the risk of constructing an artificial divide. However, since there is already an established literature considering both differences and similarities in their psychological work, there can be good grounds for believing that their philosophic presuppositions require examination. Both thinkers were fully aware of the philosophic suppositions of their work. Brockmeier, who has pointed out how

'Piaget never lost sight of the philosophic dimension of psychology' (Brockmeier, 1996, p. 125), comments on Piaget's retreat from the metaphysical issues of his youth, which were largely Bergsonian,[1] and 'the emergence ... of the omnipresence of reference to Kant ... [For Piaget] the main issue ... is nothing other than the construction of the categories of understanding in *The critique of pure reason*'[2] (Bronckart, 1996, pp. 92–93). Rather than merely resting with epistemology's concern to show only how knowledge is possible, Piaget took over the term 'genetic epistemology' from J. M. Baldwin to show how the acquisition and growth of knowledge is possible.

An ancient version of genetic epistemology can be found in the last chapter of Aristotle's *Posterior Analytics* (Book 2, Chapter 19, 99b 15–100a 8), which deals with Plato's argument in the *Meno* that learning and the acquisition of new knowledge are impossible because all learning presupposes knowledge. Known as 'the learning paradox' (Bereiter, 1991) in modern times, it raises the question of the identity of thought and being – how mind and world can in any way be connected. At a time when educational research is predominately concerned with the details of policy for immediate implementation, the fact that every position necessarily involves philosophic issues of relevance beyond education is pushed aside as lacking practical urgency. This is what makes Vygotsky's debate with Piaget significant: it shows that by opening or foreclosing avenues of enquiry, the philosophic traditions underlying apparently straightforward positions have the greatest possible practical significance. Vygotsky's confrontation with Piaget not only exemplifies his involvement in a particular philosophic tradition but also helps to reveal the innovative and original nature of his work. Comprehension of the philosophic influences on his work also enables a defence of his interest in what has come to be mistermed 'abstract' or 'decontexualised rationality'.

VYGOTSKY AND PIAGET: SCIENTIFIC/EVERYDAY CONCEPTS

Vygotsky introduces his comments on Piaget's work in Chapter 6 of *Thinking and Speech* as an aside to his discussion of the nature and development of 'scientific concepts'. He notes that his distinction between everyday and scientific concepts is initially a heuristic device and that a task of research is to clarify the differences between these types of concepts as they develop in the process of concept-formation (Vygotsky, 1987, p. 172).

Vygotsky refers to Tolstoy's discussion of the learning of word meanings (concepts) in order to illustrate the general weakness of thinking about concept development in children and then to raise the issue of learning scientific concepts.[3] Endorsing Tolstoy's position that concepts cannot be taught directly, he argues that the learning of concepts entails a 'complex and delicate' developmental process. Although he accepts Tolstoy's argument that crude and direct interference damages the delicate process, as if one were trying to build the full flower from the petals extracted from the bud, he argues that 'a complex, more direct method of instruction will lead to development to higher levels' (p. 171). For Vygotsky, Tolstoy's belief in naturalist development 'underestimates the potential for direct influence' and 'exaggerates the distance between instruction and development' (p. 171).

Two conclusions relevant to modern education theory can be found in this area of Vygotsky's work: (1) formal intervention has productive and unique consequences for development; (2) the process of concept formation is of greater complexity and subtlety than is often imagined by a conventional empiricist epistemology.

Vygotsky uses Tolstoy's commentary on a child's learning to develop his argument concerning concept development. He makes the distinction between everyday and scientific concepts, defining everyday concepts as what Tolstoy had in mind: 'because they emerged from the child's everyday life experience, we will refer to the latter as "everyday"' (Vygotsky, 1987, p. 172). Vygotsky comments that a distinction between everyday and scientific concepts is often ignored, even though it is possible to make a variety of distinctions – between the heuristic, the theoretical and the empirical. In Piaget's case a distinction is made between different types of concepts, but although Vygotsky acknowledges this, he remains critical of Piaget's account of how a child learns concepts. He finds errors and contradictions in Piaget's argument, in particular his limited explanation of consciousness. It is these errors and contradictions that Vygotsky points to in Piaget's work that expose the radically different philosophic approaches that underpin their work.

Three examples are used here to illustrate the philosophic difference between Vygotsky's and Piaget's approaches to the relation between everyday and scientific concepts: both the meaning and the place of inner speech and the idea of development. All these matters are interlinked. The argument here is that certain characteristics of Piaget's explanation can be understood as a reflection of a presumed Kantian framework that contains the following elements: opposition as distinct and separate; the separation of different processes from one another; and concentration on an autonomous individualist model of development, albeit one that recognises the social. It should be noted here that this presumed Kantian framework should not be taken as a valid statement of Kant's work. Like other great philosophers, Kant is open to a variety of readings, some of which fail to capture the richness and depth of his work.

Vygotsky takes issue with Piaget's assumptions about children's use of concepts. Piaget is concerned with the way in which children's thought differs from that of adults. Vygotsky comments that Piaget inclines towards asserting that only the child's *spontaneous* concepts (Vygotsky assumes Piaget's term to have the same referent as his own) reflect the character of the child's thought. René Van der Veer and Jaan Valsiner note that by spontaneous concepts Vygotsky meant those 'that are acquired by the child outside of the context of specific instruction' (Van der Veer and Valsiner, 1993, p. 270). As they are mostly taken from adults, but are not introduced in a systematic fashion, Vygotsky preferred to call them 'everyday' rather than 'spontaneous' since this usage avoided the impression that the child acquired them spontaneously. It is important to note, however, that Vygotsky's conception of everyday concepts is that, although arising without systematic instruction, they do not develop as a 'natural' process but within the context of the culture of human practices and activities that the child inhabits (Hedegaard, 2007,

p. 247). This conception of everyday concepts is significant for an understanding not only of the differences but also of the coincidences in the concept of knowing between Vygotsky and Piaget, of which we shall see more below.

Piaget emphasised the autonomy of reason and the constructive power of the individual to develop their capacities in interaction with their environment, but he did not attend to the social nature of that environment. He resisted any 'reduction of intellectual processes to cultural transmission', seeing thought as 'an *individual* issue that only gradually becomes socialised' (Perret-Clermont, 1997, p. 80). Intellectual processes could be understood as an extension of biological development and more akin to 'a kind of "biological reason"' (p. 80). In his book *Biology and Knowledge* Piaget states:

> If truth is not a copy, then it is an organization of the real world. But an organization due to what subject? If this subject is merely a human one, then we shall be in danger of extending ego-centrism into a sort of anthropo- or even socio-centrism with minimal gain … what we must try to do here is not get away from nature … but to penetrate it gradually with the aid of science … if the true is an organization of the real, then we first need to know how such an organization is organized, which is a biological question … as the epistemological problem is to know how science is possible, then what we must do, before having recourse to a transcendental organization, is to fathom all the resources of the immanent organization … the very nature of life is constantly overtaking itself, and if we seek the explanation of rational organization within the living organization *including its overtakings*, we are attempting to interpret knowledge in terms of its own construction, which is no longer an absurd method since knowledge is *essentially construction*. (Piaget, 1971, pp. 361–362)

The individual's adaptive behaviour in an environment is the source of the development of cognitive capacities, and there is no sense here that this behaviour is already situated in a social environment, an environment that involves not merely passive learning but active teaching. Shayer also notes that 'Piaget's own model of adaption, being the result of the dialectic of assimilation and accommodation, does seem to contain implicitly the notion that it is only the child's own efforts which are the process of accommodation' (Shayer, 1997, p. 35). Perret-Clermont comments on Piaget's 'lack of interest in social factors influencing development' and suggests that his resistance to their influence was possibly due to 'the ideological climate in which he lived, where authority was generally perceived as something extraneous, repressive – at best as a protection – and where local institutions had been forced to negotiate a relative autonomy with foreign powers' (Perret-Clermont, 1997, p. 86).

Unlike Vygotsky, who placed such great importance on the social environment in which the child's first responses develop and saw instruction as playing a crucial role in *leading* development, Piaget resisted the idea that transmission from one generation to the next could form the basis of understanding: 'because transmission is organised by an authority principle that precludes autonomy of thought' (Perret-Clermont, 1997, p. 78).[4]

Central to the idea of the construction of knowledge through the exercise of our faculties is the Kantian idea of receptivity.[5] This is the idea that at one level concepts develop merely by the mind interacting with the world.[6] For Vygotsky, who rejected the stark dualism of mind and world, all knowing occurs within what later philosophers call the *space of reasons*, which develops historically through human activity. Development entails learning not only at the more passive level, involving what Kant has called 'receptivity', but also at a deeper level where a more conscious construction takes place.

Vygotsky's conception of scientific concepts includes a strong sense of the primacy of the social as existing prior to the development of the child's cognitive capacities. The child's acquisition of scientific concepts arises within a rich social environment. However, scientific concepts or non-spontaneous concepts are constituted by the nature of their logical relation to other concepts which makes them different from concepts derived from everyday experience. Despite their different form, everyday and scientific concepts are, for Vygotsky, interconnected: 'the weakness of the everyday concept lies in its incapacity for abstraction, in the child's incapacity to operate on it in a voluntary manner', whereas the potential weakness of the scientific concept lies in its '"*verbalism*", in its insufficient saturation with the concrete' (Vygotsky, 1987, p. 169). There is an interplay between both forms of concept. In the case of Piaget, Vygotsky argues, different conditions hold for everyday or nonspontaneous concepts: 'Once it is accepted that non-spontaneous concepts do not reflect the child's thought, and that these characteristics are contained only in the child's spontaneous concepts, we are obliged to accept the notion that between the child's spontaneous and non-spontaneous concepts there exists an impassable, solid, external barrier that excludes any mutual influence' (p. 174). Vygotsky argues that 'Piaget contradicts his own argument that the child reworks the concept in learning it' (p. 174): Piaget fails to appreciate fully that it is a child's own characteristics of thought that are expressed in non-spontaneous concepts as well as in spontaneous concepts. Here the significant point is that, for Vygotsky, non-spontaneous concepts (the concepts of science and abstract thought) still express the characteristics of an individual's own thought in their development in that they arise dialogically, building on the form of thinking that exists for the individual at that current point in time. There is no break in the way in which an individual grasps new concepts.

In effect, Vygotsky attacks the dualism characteristic of the monological approach to reason at the base of Piaget's thinking. His approach presupposes the dialogic origin of scientific concepts. The issue of whether Vygotsky entertained a logocentric and monologic conception of reason has been commented upon by various authors (Wertsch, 1991, 1992, 1996, 2000; Lemke, 1999; Wegerif, 1999; Wells, 1999; and see Chapter 2 above). Commentaries on his *Thinking and Speech* (included in Vygotsky 1987) make the case that while Chapter 5 does not work with a dialogic notion of concept development, Chapter 6 does seem to entertain this (Minick, 1987). To commentators like Wertsch and Lemke, this appears simply as ambivalence rather than as the result of the philosophic frame in which he was working.

Piaget's concept of opposition, expressed as part of his argument about the development of scientific concepts, requires seeing the elements of the opposition as distinct and separate, and not as distinct and mutually dependent at the same time. By contrast, Vygotsky posits the formation (determination) of one concept as the negation of another. He remarks on how Piaget 'sees only the break, not the connection. As a consequence he [Piaget] views the development of concepts as a mechanical combination of two separate processes which have nothing in common and move as it were along two completely isolated or separate channels' (Vygotsky, 1987, p. 174). Vygotsky argues that, as a consequence of this approach adopted by Piaget,

> the process involved in socialization of thought that we find in instruction (among the most important processes in the child's development) turns out to be entirely independent of the child's own internal processes of intellectual development ... [And reciprocally] the socialisation of the child's thought [via instruction] is represented as unconnected with the internal development of the child's representations and concepts. (Vygotsky, 1987, p. 174)

Of importance here is the way in which different philosophic positions encourage different views of the development of intellectual faculties. Moreover, these views, adopted on the basis of different philosophic positions, have practical implications. The limitations of Piaget's Kantian position have real-world implications: an emphasis upon the 'child's own internal process of intellectual development' is not without consequences when used to inform educational practices. For instance, it was the Piagetian emphasis on the individual spontaneity of the child that had consequences for the implementation of the computer environment by the name of 'Logo', developed by Seymour Papert and his team (Papert, 1993). By producing a physical image of instructions that the child had input into a computer, Logo was expected to provide extensive opportunities for a child's intellectual development: it supplied a means to model thinking. The idea was to create an environment that, in keeping with Piaget's ideas, would enable children to build their own intellectual structure via activity in the simulated Logo world. Papert's confidence in the children's spontaneous ability to learn from a creatively constructed environment was drawn from Piaget's Kantian understanding of a child's spontaneous development and maturation in a rich environment.[7] Subsequent research examining the successes and failures in the use of Logo has supported Vygotsky's emphasis on the role of instruction by highlighting 'the crucial influence of the teacher in the learning of Logo' (Hoyles and Sutherland, 1992, p. 141). Papert's project entails a particular notion of constructivism – 'constructionism'.[8] With a different concept of development in mind, Vygotsky takes issue with the way that 'Piaget represents the child's mental development as a process where the characteristics of the child's thought die out'. He goes on to explain that, for Piaget,

> The developmental process is not represented as the continual emergence of new characteristics of thought of higher, more complex and more developed

forms of thought on the foundations of more elementary and primary forms of thought. Rather development is portrayed as a process through which one form of thought is gradually and continually being forced out by another. (Vygotsky, 1987, p. 175)

And he continues:

What is new to development arises from without. The child's characteristics have no constructive, positive, progressive or formative role in the history of his mental development. ... it became clear that the relationship between instruction and development is presented as one of antagonism in the process of formation of the child's concepts ... the child's thinking is placed in opposition to the adult's thought. One does not arise from the other; one excludes the other ... One must be done away with so that the other can take its place. (1987, p. 175)

The notion of one form of thought ending and another beginning without the two coexisting and interpenetrating is exactly the type of dualism that Vygotsky resists. It is clear that Vygotsky has a different understanding of opposition/negation from the one he attributed to Piaget: his bears the hallmark of Hegel's concept of *Aufhebung*.

It is necessary at this point to make a brief detour to signal one of the main concepts of Spinoza and Hegel, leading proponents of a definite and distinct tradition of Western thinking that stands apart from the empirical tradition. In the passages cited above the concept 'opposition' has a different meaning in the two traditions. When Vygotsky wrote of opposition, he drew from the Hegelian tradition where a clash of opposites results, not in a disappearance of one but a transcendence to which both contribute, that is, *Aufhebung*. The concept (*Aufhebung*) has a more complex meaning than distinct elements clashing as externalities. Inwood explains that Hegel uses the term *Aufhebung* in all three senses of its meaning at once – 'to raise, to hold, lift up', 'to annul, abolish, destroy, cancel, suspend' and 'to keep, save, preserve' (Inwood, 1995, p. 283). According to Inwood, '*Aufhebung* is similar to determinate [negation] that has a positive result. What results from the sublation of something, e.g. the whole in which both it and its opposite survive as moments, is invariably higher than, or the [truth] of, the item(s) sublated' (p. 284). Blanck notes that the related term '*supersede* ... is commonly translated into Russian with the aid of the word *skhoronit* which has both a negative and positive meaning: *liquidation* and *conservation*' (Blanck, 1992, p. 46). It is in this Hegelian sense that Vygotsky understands the term 'opposition', as moments preserved in any subsequent development, rather than as distinct and separate, in the manner implied in his discussion of Piaget.

If we return to the relation of everyday to scientific concepts, we can see that, for Vygotsky, this is not a relation of separation but rather a *repositioning* that arises when a child uses a word for a different purpose and, as a result, in a new sense. However, as the old meaning is retained in the new, the new is, therefore, not entirely novel. Consequently, what is involved is not only a merely different understanding of a new concept but also crucially a new element of conscious awareness – an ability to act in the world in a new way. Vygotsky drew from Zh. I. Shif's research, which showed that there is a higher level of conscious awareness in the use of scientific concepts than in the use of everyday ones. In the child the weakness of an everyday concept is the child's inability to operate with it in a voluntary manner; its strength is its saturation with the immediate perceptual experience. For instance, the concept *brother* can be used appropriately as a term of reference, but the child may not automatically be in a position to understand it as part of a system of other concepts that give it meaning. According to Vygotsky: 'The child formulates Archimedes' law better than he formulates his definition of what a brother is' (Vygotsky, 1987, p. 178). In this example Vygotsky argues that the concept *brother* and the concepts involved in Archimedes' law are learned in different ways. The concept *brother* has already completed much of its developmental path and is saturated with the child's rich personal experience before the child has need to use the term in a scientific way (by defining it). In the case of Archimedes' law, the concept has barely begun such saturation with content when the teacher starts to introduce it as a scientific concept. For the school-age child 'the weakness of the *everyday* concept lies in its *incapacity for abstraction*, in the child's inability to operate on it in a voluntary manner … In contrast, the weakness of the scientific concept lies in its *verbalism*, in its insufficient saturation with the concrete' (p. 169).

The distinction between Vygotsky's and Piaget's notion of different kinds of concepts parallels the distinction between their philosophic approaches. As already noted, it was Vygotsky's view that Piaget separated the different kinds of concepts more starkly than he did and in a way that was at odds with his emphasis on their co-dependence.

Piaget's Kantianism has quite different educational implications from the Hegelianism of Vygotsky. Kant's elaboration of the process of how knowledge is possible has the potential to leave terms separate and unrelated. Faculties of mind, spontaneity and receptivity, of concept and intuition, are distinguished in order to comprehend their different functions in thought. Each in its own turn explains a different mode in which knowing arises and distinguishes conscious knowing, in the case of spontaneity, from the passive reception of information, in the case of receptivity:

> Our knowledge springs from two fundamental sources of the mind; the first is the capacity of receiving representations (receptivity of impressions), the second is the power of knowing an object through these representations (spontaneity [in the production] of concepts). Through the first an object is *given* to us, through the second the object is thought in relation to that [given] representation (which is mere determination of the mind). Intuition and concepts constitute, therefore, the elements of all our knowledge, so neither concepts without an intuition in some way corresponding to them, nor intuition without concepts, can yield knowledge. (Kant, *Critique* A50/B74)

It is to be noted that, in Vygotsky's discussion of everyday and scientific concepts, the child's 'incapacity of abstraction' of everyday concepts and 'insufficient saturation of the concrete' of scientific concepts is seen to raise exactly the same issues for him as they do for Kant. Kant addresses the problem of overcoming the gap between mind and world arising from dualism with his often quoted reference to a dove in flight: the dove wishes the air was removed so that it could fly with less resistance, not appreciating that it is the very resistance of the air that sustains its flight.[9] The reference is to the limitations of a common understanding of thought as completely separate from and bearing no relation to the world that it represents. But, for Vygotsky, the inadequacy of 'thought without content' and 'intuitions without concepts' is resolved not by the assumption of common modes of understanding inherent in human nature but by social development. Although Vygotsky's discussion of the different modes of knowing specifically concerns the school-age child, and although the location of that discussion in a consideration of Piaget's views appears to restrict it to children, the underlying argument has wider application to thought in general. In particular, once the idea of a concept is understood dynamically rather than as a static representation of the world (that is, as a tool that is modified according to context of development and application), then what is initially posed as an issue for child development becomes relevant to the use of concepts by adults.

An issue at the heart of the discussion of scientific and everyday concepts is the way in which concepts (and words) are understood. The creation of scientific concepts, that is, their systematicity, plays a direct role in the formation and development of spontaneous concepts since these are not formed in a void but deployed in the already existing space of reasons that the practices and activities of human beings constitute. Van der Veer notes that when Vygotsky speaks of everyday or spontaneous concepts, he is thinking of children being inducted into usage by adults. The adult draws on a different conceptual structure and positioning from that of the child. Thus while children may have their own position within a space of reasons in which to use the concept and within which the concept has meaning for them, they are drawing on a term that has meanings and locations of which they are not yet aware.[10] Consequently, they move within a domain (a space of reasons) that is not yet fully their own.

A 'historical' approach is evident throughout Vygotsky's writing. In his discussion of scientific concepts he criticises the view that scientific concepts may be learned in a completed form, and emphasises that, on such a view, 'scientific concepts do not have their own internal history' (Vygotsky, 1987, p. 169). He notes that the development of scientific concepts is not accomplished simply by teaching them to the child and by the child's learning them. He argues from research that it is known that the concept is not just a set of associative connections but a 'complex and true act of thinking' (p. 169). Although educational researchers and practitioners may ostensibly take account of this point, it is difficult to avoid the assumption that a concept has been taught if pupils claim that they have understood it. Not only is it difficult to take account of the development of taught concepts in a system of monitorable results,[11] it is also possible that where such a system exists, with results sometimes being monitored even on an hourly basis, no development can take place at all. Pupils' apparent failures are attributed to an inability to develop concepts rather than to a lack of opportunity for concept development. By 'the development of concepts' what is meant here is not only a formal understanding of the concept but the ability to situate it within a system of concepts.

A crucial point for Vygotsky is that the understanding of word meaning is a process of development, irrespective of age.[12] When a child learns the meaning of a word, the development of the understanding of its meaning, rather than being completed, has only just begun. Moreover, its meaning is not learned as a result of the direct transmission of a concept as an empty verbal form, to be committed to memory but without thought. Understanding meaning involves the development of a series of functions: voluntary attention, logical memory, abstraction, comparison and differentiation. Such complex mental processes, Vygotsky stresses, cannot simply be learned, since the word acts within a system as a tool and performs more than merely a representational function.

The tendency to abstract the concept of *thinking* from the world in which it takes place and the forms through which it is expressed finds its origin in Descartes's dualism. Vygotsky continually attempts to explain mind (thinking) and world in a different way from this. He uses the Hegelian terminology of *becoming* in an attempt to retain the complexity of what is easily misunderstood as a simple relation of representation between thought and word: 'thought is not expressed in the word, but is completed in the word. One might therefore speak of the becoming (the unity of being and non-being) of thought and word' (Vygotsky, cited in Van der Veer and Valsiner, 1993, p. 370). As Valsiner and and Van der Veer stress, Vygotsky maintained that 'the relation between words and thoughts is not a thing but a process' (1993, p. 370).

CONSCIOUSNESS

Vygotsky's discussion of scientific concepts and their relation to everyday concepts cannot be separated from the deeper questions of consciousness and will. Consciousness is a problematic concept, and it is understood in a variety of ways, extending from simply having the capacity to pay attention, at the one extreme, to metacognition, at the other.[13] For Vygotsky, consciousnesses remained an unsettled question and one on which researchers and commentators were still working, and this continues to be the case. But one thing we can say here is that in keeping with his rejection of Cartesian dualism, Vygotsky does not see consciousness as a state of mind apart from the objects and activities of consciousness. For Vygotsky, to be conscious is to be conscious of something, whether of an object or of an activity. As part of the issue of consciousness Vygotsky is particularly concerned with 'conscious awareness'. This is a level of consciousness that comes about as a simple natural attribute but arises as a distinct aspect of consciousness as an activity: 'Conscious awareness is an act of consciousness whose object is the activity of consciousness itself' (Vygotsky, 1987, p. 190). Vygotsky links conscious awareness to scientific concepts:

> Scientific concepts have a unique relationship to the object. This relationship
> is mediated through other concepts that themselves have internal hierarchical

systems of interrelationships. It is apparently in the domain of scientific concepts that conscious awareness of concepts or the generalization and mastery of concepts emerges for the first time ...Thus conscious awareness enters through the gate opened up by the scientific concept. (1987, p. 191)

By changing the relation to the object, new possibilities for action arise: 'To perceive something in a different way means to acquire new potentials for acting with respect to it. At the chess board to see differently is to play differently' (p. 190).[14] Vygotsky remarks that, in Piaget's thought, it is not possible to find 'the thought that "spontaneous" is a synonym for "lack of conscious awareness"' when referring to concepts. He continues: 'Only within a system can the concept acquire conscious awareness and a voluntary nature. Conscious awareness and the presence of a system are synonyms when we are speaking of concepts, just as spontaneity, lack of conscious awareness, and the absence of system are three different words for designating the nature of the child's concept' (p. 191). Conscious awareness is totally different from being merely aware: it is the capacity to reflect on the process of reflection. Ilyenkov (1977, pp. 38–39) discusses the capacity not just to experience the rays of the sun on our eyeballs, but to have a concept of the sun projecting its rays. In other words, we can conceive the sun apart from the effect it has on the rods and cones at the back of our eyes and thus see the sun as more than what would simply be the experience of a biochemical process.

For Vygotsky, 'at one and the same time, generalization implies the conscious awareness and the systematisation of concepts' (Vygotsky, 1987, p. 191). Vygotsky argues that what Piaget failed to see was that the empirical laws and regularities, which he drew from his work with children, applied only within the domain of children's unsystematised thought. Piaget had not appreciated the possibility that the child's lack of systematisation was dependent on the conceptual location of the child's thinking activity and was not a quality of the child's thought as such. Vygotsky argued that 'the capacity for deduction is only possible within a definite system of relationships among concepts' (1987, p. 192). It was within a system that, for example, sensitivity to contradiction was possible.

Margaret Donaldson and her colleagues' replication of Piaget's experiments (regarding conservation ability and the egocentrism of the child) achieved different results from Piaget because they introduced into the test what was in effect systematic meaning. However, this was not exactly the way in which they interpreted the success of their results. In *Children's Minds*, Donaldson explains the success of Martin Hughes's redesign of the 'mountain task' in terms of the fact that it 'requires the child to act in ways which are in line with certain very basic purposes and intentions (escape and pursuit)' (Donaldson, 1978, p. 24). She saw it as introducing the motives and intentions of the characters involved in the task. It could, however, equally be argued that Hughes's replication introduced not merely a context that provided purposes and intentions but also the systematicity necessary to allow the child to make decisions according to a meaningful system of relations. If Brandom's point about the inferential character of any representation is taken seriously (i.e. in Vygotskian terms, its location in a system of concepts), then what the children were offered in Hughes's task was a visibility of the 'reasons that follow from' and the 'reasons that are implied by' the task's events. The evidence in the Hughes experiment indicated that the vast majority of children were able to 'de-centre', unlike the 'egocentric' children evident in Piaget's experimental results.

Piaget's category of egocentrism is so closely involved with a dualism as to be unacceptable to Vygotsky. Vygotsky's critique of Piaget's designation of egocentrism as evidence of a child's incapacity to think abstractly is based on the argument that conscious awareness is sustained by the location of concepts in meaningful relations to one another. In the case of scientific concepts, meaning is developed by the location of concepts to one another rather than solely by direct reference to the world.

As we have seen, Vygotsky used the systemic relation of concepts and the possibility of conscious awareness (reflection on the way in which thinking proceeds) to criticise Piaget's understanding of the relation between egocentrism and thought in the child: 'We found the source of the lack of conscious awareness of concepts not in egocentrism but in the absence of system in the child's spontaneous concepts' (Vygotsky, 1987, p. 193). Human capacities come into being as a result of development that necessarily involves social interaction. They are not built on any pregiven foundation. As Davydov puts it, human mental functions are not given at the time of birth but arise only cultural-historically (Davydov, 1997, p. xxix). Vygotsky came to the conclusion that the study of children's behaviour needed radical review in order to show that even the most elementary functions were mediated from birth: 'even the most elementary functions, even those that arise at the earliest stage of man's life, possess a mediative, i.e. specifically human, structure' (1997, p. xxviii). Vygotsky's appreciation of what Hegel called 'the Understanding' (a matter that will be dealt with later) alerted him to all the difficulties of this approach:

> The social nature of each higher mental function has thus far escaped the attention of investigators who did not think to represent the development of logical memory or voluntary activity as part of the social formation of the child because in its biological beginning and in the end of mental development, this function appears as an individual function; only genetic analysis discloses the path that unites the beginning and end points. (Vygotsky, 1999, p. 41)

The actual movement through which higher mental functions are determined by social genesis is little more understood today than it was in Vygotsky's lifetime. In part this is because these functions in their completed forms present themselves as individualistic and natural; and, even more to the point, they are almost compelled to present themselves in this way because of the social conditions of modern society. Vygotsky was well aware of the significant change in the direction of research that was needed to address this area: 'The internalization of socially rooted and historically developed activities is the distinguishing feature of human psychology, the basis of the qualitative leap from animal to human psychology. As yet the barest outline of this process is known' (Vygotsky, 1978, p. 57). In taking this completed form, in which higher mental functions present themselves as the object of analysis, social science, including psychology, tends to remain implicitly Cartesian despite the exponential increase of interest over the last 30 years in Vygotsky's ideas and in externalist accounts of mind.

CONCLUSION

At the end of the earlier section on consciousness, it was said that in order to grasp Vygotsky's understanding of consciousness it was necessary also to understand his ideas of science and development. These ideas, together with that of free will, have already been raised in this chapter. The point we need to stress now is that none of these concepts – consciousness, free will, science and development – can be understood, on Vygotsky's account, as apart from one another. Each one is related to the other three. For example, when consciousness is stimulated by externalities, our responses are not passive: our actions involve concepts that have a systematic relation to one another. Systematically related concepts of this type are characteristic of science. The possibility of acting, rather than merely behaving, arises through the human capacity to formulate scientific concepts – or, to put it another way, to develop what Spinoza called adequate ideas. This is a matter for the following chapter, where the concepts of activity and passivity will be more fully considered.

In drawing this chapter to a close, it is important to underline how Vygotsky's criticism of Piaget brings to light the differences of philosophic approach employed. On the one side, there is the Kantianism of Piaget; on the other, the influence of Spinoza and Hegel. From the standpoint of the latter, the dualism that stems from Descartes and orders common intuition today is rejected out of hand and with it many issues that appear self-evident in contemporary research. We may mention just one of these here as it has particular significance for the interpretation of Vygotsky. This is the idea, first, that there was a homogeneous body of thought from the mid-seventeenth century to the end of the eighteenth century that can be classed as Enlightenment thought and, second, that this body of thought was committed to abstract rationality. No stronger critics of the concept of abstract rationality can be found than Spinoza and Hegel, the very philosophers from whom Vygotsky drew his inspiration and under whose influence he shaped his theories.

NOTES

1 'Reading Bergson was a revelation ... I was overwhelmed by the certitude that God was life in the shape of this *élan vital* or vital force of which my interest in biology allowed me to study a small section. ... I would dedicate my life to philosophy, and my main purpose would be to reconcile science and religious values' (Piaget, in Perret-Clermont, 1997, p. 76).

2 Piaget occupied the Chair of Philosophy of Science at Neuchâtel.

3 Vygotsky remarks that Tolstoy 'had an extraordinary understanding of the nature of the word and its meaning [and] saw with both clarity and precision the futility of attempting to transmit concepts directly from teacher to student' (Vygotsky, 1987, p. 170).

4 So much hangs on what is understood by the term 'transmission' here. Transmission may be understood as the most impoverished form of didacticism or as a rich engagement with the learner where activity is central, as in the case of Vygotsky's conception of the zone of proximal development.

5 For an introduction to the concept of receptivity, see Caygill: 'Receptivity involves the "capacity" [of the subject] to be affected by objects ([*Critique of Pure Reason*] A 26/B 42). It forms one of two sources of knowledge … namely the "capacity for receiving representations (receptivity for impressions)", which is accompanied by the "spontaneity of concepts" (A 50/B 74) … in combination with spontaneity it allows the generation of knowledge' (Caygill, 1995, p. 350).

6 For Piaget, 'knowledge develops in children through their interaction with the environment, in the course of which they first come to co-ordinate their own actions and then to abstract more general operations from these co-ordinations' (Duveen, 1996, pp. 52–53).

7 Bruner writes that 'Too often, human learning has been depicted in the paradigm of a lone organism pitted against nature … in the Piagetian model where a lone child struggles single-handed to strike equilibrium between assimilating the world to himself or himself to the world' (Bruner 1985, p. 25). Although Bruner's view has been disputed by Leslie Smith (1995, p. 6), my point remains that Papert retained an overall individualist emphasis, holding to the view that children could, through activity, develop their own cognitive structure independently.

8 Constructivism is a widely used concept within education research, taking a variety of forms. Steffe and Gale (1995), in a reader entitled *Constructivism in Education,* dealt with no fewer than six different versions of it: social constructivism, radical constructivism, social constructionism, information-processing constructivism, cybernetic systems and sociocultural approaches to mediated action

9 'The light dove, cleaving the air in her free flight, might imagine that its flight would be easier in empty space. It was thus that Plato left the world of the senses, as setting too narrow limits to the understanding, and ventured out beyond it on the wings of the ideas, in the empty space of the pure understanding … It is indeed the common fate of human reason to complete its speculative structures as speedily as may be, and only afterwards to enquire whether the foundations are reliable' (Kant, *Critique*, A5/B9).

10 In Brandom's terms, to use a concept (word) is to be involved in 'the game of giving and asking of reasons' (Brandom, 2000, p. 192). That is not necessarily in a formal and explicit sense: the space of reasons is present regardless of conscious awareness. In Vygotskian terms the child's utterance (as soon as it is more than noise) participates in the game of giving and asking for reasons, insofar as the utterance is meaningful. It is meaningful to the extent that the child has reasons for the use of the 'noise' or utterance by virtue of having a sense of what follows from and what supports the utterance.

11 A system of monitorable results refers to the restrictive and excessive summative assessment conditions in which much formal education takes place.

12 '… word meaning develops. The discovery that word meaning changes and develops is our new and fundamental contribution to the theory of thinking and speech' (Vygotsky, 1987, p. 245).

13 It can also be understood as the opposite of unconsciousness, though Vygotsky makes it clear that when he speaks of conscious awareness he is not using the term this way. He notes that 'Freud's research establishes that the unconscious – which is carved out from consciousness emerges comparatively late' (Vygotsky, 1987, p. 190). For Freud unconsciousness arises symbiotically with consciousness, and does not exist simply in opposition.

14 Vygotsky is influenced by Spinoza's argument in the *Ethics*. Spinoza discusses how our common-sense Cartesian understanding of freedom affects the ideas we have, leading us to experience greater pain or sadness than is necessary. By repositioning elements involved in an affect (e.g. by reassigning what we link together) the strength of affect may be altered. Proposition 48 states: 'Love or hate – say, of Peter – is destroyed if the sadness the hate involves, or the joy the love involves, is attached to the idea of another cause, and each is diminished to the extent that we imagine that Peter was not its only cause' (Spinoza, 1993, p. 114).

REFERENCES

Bakhurst, D. (1991) *Consciousness and Revolution in Soviet Philosophy: From the Bolsheviks to Evald Ilyenkov* (Cambridge: Cambridge University Press).

Bereiter, C. (1991) Confronting the Learning Paradox: Commentary, *Human Development*, 34:5, 294–298.

Blanck, G. (1992) Vygotsky: The Man and His Cause. In: L.C. Moll (ed.) *Vygotsky and Education: Instructional Implications and Applications of Sociohistorical Theory* (Cambridge: Cambridge University Press), pp. 31–58.

Blunden, A. (2011) *Concepts: A Critical Approach* (Leiden: Brill Academic).

Brandom, R. (2000) *Articulating Reasons: An Introduction to Inferentialism* (Cambridge, MA: Harvard University Press).

Brockmeier, J. (1996) Construction and Interpretation: Exploring a Joint Perspective on Piaget and Vygotsky. In: A. Tryphon and J.N. Vonèche (eds) *Piaget – Vygotsky: The Social Genesis of Thought* (Hove: Psychology Press), pp. 125–143.

Bronckart, J. (1996) Units of Analysis in Psychology and Their Interpretation: Social Interactionism or Logical Interactionism? In: A. Tryphon and J.N. Vonèche (eds) *Piaget – Vygotsky: The Social Genesis of Thought* (Hove: Psychology Press), pp. 85–106.

Bruner, J. (1985) Vygotsky: A Historical and Conceptual Perspective. In: J.V. Wertsch (ed.) *Culture, Communication and Cognition: Vygotskian Perspectives* (Cambridge: Cambridge University Press), pp. 21–34.

Caygill, H. (1995) *A Kant Dictionary* (Oxford: Blackwell).

Confrey, J. (1995) How Compatible Are Radical Constructivism, Sociocultural Approaches, and Social Constructivism? In: L.P. Steffe and J. Gale (eds) *Constructivism in Education* (Hillsdale, NJ: Lawrence Erlbaum Associates), pp. 185–226.

Davydov, V.V. (1997) Introduction: Lev Vygotsky and Educational Psychology. In: L. Vygotsky *Educational Psychology* (Boca Raton, FL: St. Lucie Press), pp. xxi-xxxix.

Donaldson, M. (1978) *Children's Minds* (London: Fontana).

Dunne, J. (1993) *Back to the Rough Ground: 'Phronesis' and 'Techne' in Modern Philosophy and in Aristotle* (Notre Dame, IN: University of Notre Dame Press).

Duveen, G. (1997) Psychological Development as a Social Process. In: L. Smith, J. Dockrell and P. Tomlinson (eds) *Piaget, Vygotsky and Beyond: Future Issues for Developmental Psychology and Education* (New York: Routledge), pp. 52–69.

Hedegaard, M. (2007) The Development of Children's Conceptual Relation to the World, with Focus on Concept Formation in Preschool Children's Activity. In: H. Daniels, M. Cole and J.V. Wertsch (eds) *The Cambridge Companion to Vygotsky* (Cambridge: Cambridge University Press), pp. 246–275.

Hoyles, C. and Sutherland, R. (1992) *Logo Mathematics in the Classroom* (London: Routledge).

Ilyenkov, E.V. (1977) *Dialectical Logic: Essays on Its History and Theory* (Moscow: Progress Publishers).

Inwood, M. (1995) *A Hegel Dictionary* (Oxford: Blackwell).

Kozulin, A. (1990) *Vygotsky's Psychology: A Biography of Ideas* (Brighton: Harvester Wheatsheaf).

Lemke, J. (1999) Meaning-Making in the Conversation: Head Spinning, Heart Winning, and Everything in Between, *Human Development*, 42:2, 87–91.

Minick, N. (1987) The Development of Vygotsky's Thought: An Introduction. In: L.S. Vygotsky *The Collected Works of L. S. Vygotsky, Volume 1 – Problems of General Psychology*, N. Minick trans., R.W. Reiber and A.S. Carton eds (New York: Plenum Press), pp. 17–36.

Papert, S. (1993) *Mindstorms: Children, Computers, and Powerful Ideas* (New York: Basic Books).

Perret-Clermont, A. (1997) Revisiting Young Piaget in Neuchâtel Among His Partners in Learning. In: L. Smith, J. Dockrell and P. Tomlinson (eds) *Piaget, Vygotsky and Beyond: Future Issues for Developmental Psychology and Education* (New York: Routledge), pp. 70–91.

Piaget, J. (1970) *Genetic Epistemology* (New York: Columbia University Press).

84   *Vygotsky Philosophy and Education*

Piaget, J. (1971) *Biology and Knowledge: An Essay on the Relations Between Organic Regulations and Cognitive Processes* (Chicago: University of Chicago Press).

Piaget, J. (2000) Commentary on Vygotsky's Criticisms of Language and Thought of the Child and Judgement and Reasoning in the Child, L. Smith trans., *New Ideas in Psychology*, 18, 241–259.

Robbins, D. (2001) *Vygotsky's Psychology-Philosophy: A Metaphor for Language Theory and Learning* (New York: Kluwer Academic/Plenum Publishers).

Shayer, S. (1997) Piaget and Vygotsky: A Necessary Marriage for Effective Educational Intervention. In: L. Smith, J. Dockrell and P. Tomlinson (eds) *Piaget, Vygotsky and Beyond: Future Issues for Developmental Psychology and Education* (New York: Routledge), pp. 36–59.

Spinoza, B. (1993) *Ethics and Treatise on the Correction of the Intellect*, A. Boyle trans. (London: Everyman).

Smith, L. (1995) Introduction to Piaget's *Sociological Studies*. In J. Piaget *Sociological Studies* (London: Routledge), pp. 1–21.

Steffe, L.P. and Gale, J. (eds) (1995) *Constructivism in Education* (Hillsdale, NJ: Lawrence Erlbaum Associates).

Van der Veer, R. (1984) Early Periods in the Work of L.S. Vygotsky: The Influence of Spinoza. In: M. Hedegaard, P. Hakkarainen and Y. Engeström (eds) *Learning and Teaching on a Scientific Basis: Methodological and Epistemological Aspects of the Activity Theory of Learning and Teaching* (Aarhus: Aarhus University), pp. 87–98.

Van der Veer, R. and Valsiner, J. (1993) *Understanding Vygotsky: A Quest for Synthesis* (Oxford: Blackwell).

Vygotsky, L.S. (1978) *Mind in Society: The Development of Higher Psychological Processes*, M. Cole *et al.* eds (Cambridge, MA: Harvard University Press).

Vygotsky, L.S. (1987) *The Collected Works of L. S. Vygotsky, Vol. 1, Problems of General Psychology*, N. Minick trans. R.W. Reiber and A.S. Carton eds (New York: Plenum Press).

Vygotsky, L.S. (1999) *The Collected Works of L. S. Vygotsky, Vol. 6, Scientific Legacy*, M.J. Hall trans., R.W. Reiber ed. (New York: Kluwer Academic/Plenum Publishers).

Wegerif, R. (1999) Two Models of Reason in Education, *The School Field*, 9:3–4, 77–107.

Wells, G. (1999) *Dialogic Inquiry: Towards a Sociocultural Practice and Theory of Education* (Cambridge: Cambridge University Press).

Wertsch, J. V. (1991) *Voices of the Mind: A Sociocultural Approach to Mediated Action* (London: Wheatsheaf).

Wertsch, J.V. (1992) The Voice of Rationality in a Sociocultural Approach to Mind. In: L.C. Moll (ed.) *Vygotsky and Education: Instructional Implications and Applications of Sociohistorical Theory* (Cambridge: Cambridge University Press), pp. 111–126.

Wertsch, J. (1996) The Role of Abstract Rationality in Vygotsky's Image of Mind. In: A. Tryphon and J.N. Vonèche (eds) *Piaget – Vygotsky: The Social Genesis of Thought* (Hove: Psychology Press), pp. 25–42.

Wertsch, J.V. (2000) Vygotsky's Two Minds on the Nature of Meaning. In: C.D. Lee and P. Smargorinsky (eds) *Vygotskian Perspectives on Literacy Research* (Cambridge: Cambridge University Press), pp. 19–30.

5
Spinoza and Free Will

FREEDOM

The social character of thought, discussed in Chapter 4, raises the question of free will. Vygotsky's understanding of free will derives from Spinoza. His work is peppered with references to Spinoza and, according to his childhood friend Semyon Dobkin, Spinoza was his favourite philosopher. In the preface to *The Psychology of Art*, submitted as his doctoral thesis, Vygotsky noted his debt: 'My intellect has been shaped under the sign of Spinoza's words, and it has tried not to be astounded, not to laugh, not to cry, but to understand' (Vygotsky, [1925] 1971). In volume 6 of his collected works, in the section 'The Teaching about Emotions, Historical Psychological Studies', there is an extended discussion of the difference between Spinoza and Descartes, highlighting the elements of Spinoza's philosophy found most relevant to Vygotsky. The present chapter develops three themes involving the issue of free will necessary to an understanding of Vygotsky's work. They are: (1) his distinctive idea of freedom understood as self-determination; (2) the distinction between this idea of freedom and a common-sense concept of free will; and (3) arising from these, the issue of determinism and determinist readings of Marx.

Free will, in Spinoza's conception, cannot be separated from his idea of truth; Vygotsky owes so much to Spinoza that his epistemology cannot be properly grasped without appreciating this. For Spinoza, truth is necessary to freedom and the two are inextricably linked. Free will depends upon whether the thought that drives an action is adequate. Adequacy, whose sense will be considered shortly, is also a key concept for Spinoza. Spinoza's conception of freedom is a deeper, more ontologically embedded notion than the simplistic idea that the possibility of free action depends upon sufficient knowledge. The link between adequate ideas and free will is crucial for Vygotsky as well, and is inextricably related to his argument that in the development

Vygotsky Philosophy and Education, First Edition. Jan Derry.
© 2013 Jan Derry. Editorial organisation © Philosophy of Education Society of Great Britain.
Published 2013 by John Wiley & Sons, Ltd.

of intellect is the possibility of theorising freedom in a way that is quite different from the one entrenched in our common-sense view of how we act in the world.

According to Vygotsky 'the development of *freedom of action* is directly functionally dependent on the use of signs' (Vygotsky, 1999, p. 65). Vygotsky mentions Wolfgang Köhler's research with chimpanzees and his observation that 'monkeys are slaves of the visual field to a much greater extent than adult humans'. For Vygotsky it is important to distinguish activity that is the product of biological evolution from activity that arises 'in the process of the historical development of man'. He describes how human labour created 'the higher mental functions that mark man as man' and that in 'using a stick, primitive man masters from outside, with the help of a sign, processes of his own behaviour and subordinates his actions to a goal, making external objects serve his activity – tools, soil, rice'(Vygotsky, 1999, p. 64). On the question of free will he wrote:

> The philosophical perspective opens before us at this point of our study. For the first time in the process of psychological studies we can resolve essentially purely philosophical problems by means of a psychological experiment and demonstrate empirically the origin of the freedom of the will ... We cannot help but note that we have come to the same understanding of freedom and control as Spinoza developed in his 'Ethics'. (Vygotsky, 1997b, p. 219)

The phrase in this passage 'for the first time' is particularly significant as it implies that there is something in the modern period that gives the issues discussed under the remit of philosophy a practical character that they have not had previously. In other words philosophy in the modern period has become practical knowledge. On the matter of freedom, also a specifically modern matter, Vygotsky turned to Engels' argument about the implacability of necessity: 'Engels places in one order the control of nature and the control of self.[1] Freedom of will with respect to one and the other is, for him as for Hegel, understanding necessity' (Vygotsky, 1997b, p. 218).

The common conception of will as 'freedom from restraint' seems completely at odds with the idea of necessity. However, as intellect is a key aspect of will for Vygotsky, and intellect is by its nature restrained (what in the Vygotskian literature is known as 'embedded'), its coexistence with freedom is not a problem. Freedom and necessity are at the heart of Vygotsky's account of how mindedness is formed and sustained by mediation with artefacts in a social domain. Spinoza opposed the idea of the mind as a metaphysical entity (a soul) free to act on the world at will. Spinoza was particularly important for Vygotsky on this question of freedom. As Errol Harris puts this: '[Spinoza] believed that human freedom was not, as was commonly held, indeterminacy of choice, but was self-determination, entirely by one's own nature, free from external compulsion. This for him was action proper, while determination by extraneous causes was passion, the subjection to which he called bondage' (Harris, 1992, p. 6). In the process of grappling to establish a distinction between human beings and animals that would do justice to the higher ability of humans (of the kind that theological explanations of the soul attempt to capture), Spinoza develops a framework that has the potential to be read as determinist. This issue of determinism was referred to in Chapter 3 in connection with recent research in artificial intelligence that draws on the idea that the mind is developed externally: this research easily leads to a causally reductive notion of consciousness and agency. However, Vygotsky was well aware of the danger presented by a determinist account of free will that would fail to do justice to the fullness of our mental lives:

> In the final analysis, the question is: does what is higher in man, his free and rational will and his control over his passions, allow a natural explanation that does not reduce the higher to the lower, the rational to the automatic, the free to the mechanical, but preserves all the meaning of this higher aspect of our mental life in its fullness, or to explain the higher, do we inevitably have to resort to rejecting the laws of nature, to introducing a theological and spiritualistic principle of absolute freewill not subject to natural necessity? In other words, the question is: is scientific knowledge of higher forms of conscious activity possible or impossible, is human psychology as a science, not as applied metaphysics as it is in all consistent idealists, beginning with Descartes, continuing with Lotze, and ending with Bergson, possible or impossible? (Vygotsky,1999, p. 173)

FREE WILL

The concept of freedom has different meanings in different traditions of thought. The sense in which we commonly think of ourselves as free actors owes much to Descartes's modernist separation of mind and world. To understand the sense of free will that informs Vygotsky's work, by contrast, it is necessary to get to grips with the sense that derives from Spinoza and Hegel. This is not easy to grasp, since it seems counterintuitive and goes against our sense of our activities as resulting directly from the exertion of will.[2] Moreover, we inhabit a world whose social institutions and structures are premised on an implicit Cartesian notion of will (Gergen, 1999; Ilyenkov, 2009). In our common-sense conception, will presents itself to us as a capacity, a power vested within ourselves which, located in the soul, can operate on the world as an independent force, set apart from the world of matter upon which we act. Coupled to this everyday common-sense conception of freedom is the idea that free will is the unencumbered pursuit of the objects of desires and wants – that I am free to consume what I like. What this presupposes is a certain conception of what I am and of what I desire as if my identity were an outcome of my consumption patterns. No thought is given to the possibility that my desires may not be genuinely my own in the sense that they determine me externally.[3] As Spinoza remarks: 'we are in many ways driven about by external causes ... like waves of the sea driven by contrary winds we toss to and fro unwitting of the issue and of our fate' (*Ethics*, Part III, scholium to Proposition 59). So even though I may be aware of my desires I may not appreciate what determines them in the first place.

Spinoza's conception of freedom is so different from the common-sense notion that some commentators, from the perspective of this notion, have viewed him as a mechanical determinist without any concept of freedom at all. In order to comprehend that he does indeed have a concept of freedom and thus to understand how it differs from the common-sense notion, it is necessary to understand a number of elements of Spinoza's philosophy which may not seem immediately relevant. These include his accounts of thought and extension as attributes of one substance, *causa sui* (cause of itself), adequate as opposed to inadequate ideas and the distinction between passions and affects.

Let us consider the central idea underlying Spinoza's philosophy that everything that exists is one substance – God or Nature (*Deus sive natura*) – of which all entities are modes or modifications.[4] Spinoza's treatment of theological questions led him to reject a dualist worldview. This central idea of Spinoza was reached through a lengthy argument that concluded that God or Nature, the one substance, consisted of an infinite number of attributes of which thought and extension are parts. As God is infinite, he argued, he must also be totally self-determined (*causa sui*) as infinity, by definition, excludes anything external: 'By God I understand a being absolutely infinite, i.e., a substance consisting of an infinity of attributes … There is only one substance in the universe; it is God; and everything else that is, is in God' (*Ethics*, Part I, Definition 6). Only God or Nature has total self-determination; everything else in the universe has lesser degrees of it, human beings having the highest degree possible after God or Nature. It is in self-determination that human beings exhibit freedom. A free agent is not one whose actions are undetermined, but one whose actions are self-determined; and self-determination arises only when we are not driven by our passions. By 'passion' Spinoza means an affect produced by external causes rather than by our own power.[5] When we are not controlled by our passions, we understand the reasons of our actions.[6] Perhaps because of this, Spinoza is often placed alongside the Stoics (DeBrabander, 2007). Certainly he shares with them a sense of human existence not troubled by the anxiety of what the modern conception understands as free choice. The Stoics accept events that are unavoidable. Spinoza's conception of freedom does not deny the necessity of the Stoics but rather understands freedom as arising in self-determination: 'That thing is said to be FREE (libera) which exists by the mere necessity of its own nature, and is determined to act by itself alone' (Spinoza, 1993, p. 4).

In response to Descartes's notion of freedom as lack of compulsion by external cause, Spinoza writes:

> if by a man who is compelled he means one who acts against his will, I admit that in certain matters we are in no way compelled and *in this respect we have free will*. But if by compelled he means one who, although he does not act against his will, yet acts necessarily, then I deny that we are free in anything. (quoted in Kashap, 1987, p. 168)

This is an unfamiliar notion of free will, but it is a notion of freedom nonetheless. Freedom arises here because of necessity, not in spite of it.

Spinoza continually disputes the Cartesian conception of will grounded in a dualism comprising a material world on the one hand and a wilful mind capable of free action in relation to it on the other. He ridicules the common-sense notion of free will based on the conviction 'that the body is moved by mere command of the mind, or is kept at rest, and that it performs many things which merely depend on will or ingenuity of the mind' (Spinoza, 1993, p. 86). Also he denies its existence: 'The body cannot determine the mind to think, nor the mind the body to motion, nor to rest, nor to any other state (if there be any other)' (1993, p. 85). The belief that we have the power to act in the world free from any material restraint of our circumstance is caricatured by Spinoza as a metaphysical faith in will.[7] Vygotsky cites Spinoza on this:

> Spinoza most acutely contrasts his thought with Descartes. Spinoza claims that Descartes ... significantly promotes the false opinion that affects depend absolutely on our will and that we can control them infinitely. Spinoza says that he cannot 'be surprised enough that a philosopher, having strictly held to reaching conclusions only on the basis of sources that are certain of themselves and claiming only what he recognises clearly and definitely, and so frequently reproving the scholastics for thinking to explain dark things by hidden properties, how this philosopher accepts a hypothesis that is darker than any dark property'. (Vygotsky, 1999, p. 126)

In contrast to Descartes, who assumed free will without accounting for the source of its power, Spinoza provided an argument to the effect that free will arises in the development of intellect. This is an insight from which Vygotsky benefits. As previously noted, however, Vygotsky appreciated that any explanation of will that attempts to remove metaphysical or theological assumptions risks determinism. Kashap points out that 'Descartes takes "the will" and "the understanding" to be distinct; for Spinoza the two are one and the same ... the will and the intellect are nothing but the individual volitions and the ideas themselves. But the individual volition and the idea are one and the same' (Kashap, 1987, p. 103). Kashap argues that, because of the theory of what has been described as 'parallelism',[8] commentators such as H. H. Joachim have been led to remark that Spinoza makes 'the last vestiges of the popular conception of free will disappear' (Kashap, 1987, p. 106). Joachim is concerned that, although Spinoza admits conscious desires, he denies the reality of purposive action. Kashap remarks, however, that Spinoza repudiates the charge that he reduces human beings to the level of plants or stones. Indeed, the central concern of the *Ethics* is purposiveness, and Spinoza made his concern with improvement through understanding quite explicit. Kashap, discussing Joachim's view, says that what 'Spinoza discredits and contemptuously rejects, is action towards "ideals not yet real, but yet to be realized", or "action with a view to the attainment of an unpossessed 'better'"' (Kashap, 1987, pp. 107–108). The point here, which also relates to the possibilities of policy for development, is that change can only be brought about in conjunction with the potential for development. Development cannot be imposed according to an abstract *ratio* whose 'ideals [are] not yet real, but yet to be realized'.

Kashap offers an explanation of how Spinoza was able to hold the two seemingly incompatible views that, on the one hand, every particular thing 'must involve reference to determining conditions outside its own nature' and that, on the other, human beings as finite things can be said to direct their efforts 'purposefully towards an end of which they are conscious' (Kashap, 1987, p. 109). He suggests that the understanding of explanatory conditions does not, for Spinoza, preclude purposive and intentional action. By taking over an essentially similar rejection of a mind–body dualism, Vygotsky was able to frame his work in a context that allowed him to work with a notion of human agency that lies within a realm of determination but has the possibility of freedom.

For Vygotsky, the 'mastery' of external determinations is crucial, just as for Spinoza an entity is free only to the extent that it is the cause of itself, to the extent it is self-determined. Vygotsky, like Spinoza before him, understands that self-determination is not possible through a pure act of will and to illustrate how the problem of free will may be overcome, he turns to the philosophical anecdote of Buridan's ass in which the animal, being unable to choose between the stimulus of two equal bales of hay, starves and dies. Vygotsky remarks that this anecdote 'is usually used to illustrate that our will is determined by our motives and [that] when the motives are equal, selection between them becomes impossible and our will is paralysed.' Like a piece of paper that is pulled with equal force at both sides, it remains in the same position. He refers to Spinoza's discussion of the anecdote and notes that if a man were to find himself in the same position, then he would be an unthinking being and more of an ass than the animal. According to Vygotsky this comment of Spinoza touches on the 'most important element that distinguishes the will of man from the will of the animal' (Vygotsky, 1997b, p. 209).

In this connection he describes an experiment where two kinds of activities are presented to a child but where, through a balancing of motives, the child's selection is complicated by an emotional impediment similar to the 'Buridan situation'. To resolve the situation, the child introduces a new neutral stimulus, a die, but ascribes to the die a motive that if it lands on one side, the first choice will be made and if on the other side, the second. This has the effect of introducing an auxiliary motive into the situation. Vygotsky asks: Would we call the child's action free or unfree?

> On the one hand, it was not free at all but strictly determined ... [but on] the other hand, in themselves the black and white sides of the die do not to any degree compel the child to take one action or the other. The child himself ascribed to it the force of a motive in advance and he himself linked one action to the white side and the other to the black side of the die ... Thus we have maximum freedom and a completely voluntary animal. (Vygotsky, 1997b, p. 210)

Vygotsky goes on to say: 'The experiment tells us that freedom of the will is not freedom from motives ... [the child's] freedom is the recognition of necessity' (1997b, p. 210). Vygotsky uses the example to assert the possibility of freedom in human activity through the use of mediating artefacts. In the simple case of an inability to decide, a human may toss a coin. No matter that the point appears trivial, the human has an additional means of interaction with external determination which the ass lacks (Vygotsky, 1997b, p. 46). By attributing to the die a significance that it does not possess in itself, the child acquires positive potential for action without which the question of freedom would not arise in the first place. According to Vygotsky, artificial devices allow us to master our own mental processes. Psychological tools direct the mind and behaviour just as technical tools transform the object: 'Psychological tools are artificial formations ... They are directed toward the mastery of [mental] processes – one's own or someone else's – just as technical devices are directed towards the mastery of processes of nature.' Vygotsky gives the following examples of psychological tools (Vygotsky, 1997a, p. 85): 'numeration and counting, mnemotechnic techniques, algebraic symbolism, works of art, writing, schemes, diagrams, maps, blueprints, and all sorts of conventional signs'. It is through the use of such tools that children first learn to master their own behaviour. Behaviour is moved not by an innate metaphysical power – Descartes's will – but from reflexive interaction in the world.

Vygotsky follows Spinoza in taking the basis of freedom to be the human ability to separate ourselves from our passions, from the contingencies of nature, and to make for ourselves a space within which we can determine our actions. Such actions are determined not by causes that are completely external but by ones that lie within our sphere of efficacy. The concept of freedom can be discerned, for instance, in the contrast between Vygotsky and Piaget discussed in Chapter 4. Vygotsky discusses the sense in which consciousness is just *assumed* by Piaget. Whereas, for Piaget, consciousness occurs in children once the bankruptcy of their own thinking is evident, for Vygotsky consciousness arises as a result of the subject's changing location in relation to external forms of determination.

A further aspect of Vygotsky's disagreement with Piaget's Kantianism concerns existence. For Spinoza and also Hegel, in order to explain the existence of a thing it is also necessary to explain its genesis. A thing cannot be apprehended merely as it appears in existence. In Chapter 6, which discusses Hegel's critique of the Understanding, I shall consider genesis and the importance of history in more detail. Vygotsky looks to the unfolding of consciousness rather than merely positing its realisation in response to the bankruptcy of egocentric thought. Vygotsky finds the genesis of consciousness in the development of scientific concepts. This is the argument, noted earlier, that Vygotsky used in order to criticise Piaget's failure to understand that children's lack of conscious awareness is affected by their position in relation to what they are asked to understand, rather than by any conflict between their own childish concepts and those that give them access to reality.

To reiterate, human behaviour according to Vygotsky is neither controlled nor directed by immediate means on the basis of pure acts of will, but is moved indirectly through the use of signs and tools. Modification of the world by human activity creates an artificiality (or 'artefactuality') of conditions. Within such artificial conditions volition, as illustrated by the example of Buridan's ass, is directed or mediated, but in these circumstances the cause of an action arises through our own creations or artefacts and not in response to external determinations beyond our control. This provides for human beings the possibility of a universality not available to animals which do no more than respond directly to environmental stimuli, that is, without conscious mediation or reflection.

Bakhurst links this aspect of Vygotsky's work to that of Ilyenkov. Ilyenkov captures the creative moment of human activity when he claims that 'The capacity to think is just the capacity to inhabit an idealized environment' (Bakhurst, 1991, p. 244). Ilyenkov also draws on Spinoza: '[As Spinoza correctly believed,] Thought prior to and outside of its spatial [external] expression in appropriate material forms simply does not exist' (Ilyenkov, cited by Bakhurst, 1991, p. 245). We think that we 'will' the world into existence, when we do not. Ilyenkov captures thought's embedded (or better – embodied) yet universal character, when he states that it is:

> the mode of action of the thinking body ... the genuine, specific form of the action of the thinking body is its *universality* ... *Man – the thinking body – builds his movements according to the form of any other body.* He does not wait until the insurmountable opposition of other bodies forces him to swerve from his path; the thinking body freely negotiates any obstacle of the most complex form. *The ability actively to build one's action according to the form of any other body*, actively to make the form of a spatial movement agree with the form and disposition of all other bodies, Spinoza considers the distinguishing feature of the thinking body, the specific mark of those actions that are called 'thought,' 'reason'.[9] (Ilyenkov, cited by Bakhurst, 1991, pp. 250–251)

As Bakhurst puts it: 'It is this ability to conform to the dictates of no particular situation, but of any, that Ilyenkov calls thought's *universality* ... Thought embodies the permanent possibility of transcendence; it may always go beyond what it took to be its own limits' (Bakhurst, 1991, p. 251).

While this bodily dimension of thought is absent from Piaget's characterisation of a contemplative mind, it is central to Vygotsky's theory:

> Consciousness arises out of life and forms only one of its features. But once awakened, thought itself defines life. Or more accurately, a thinking life defines itself through consciousness. As soon as we separate thought from life, from dynamics, and from necessity, we have deprived it of all reality; we have put off all paths to the clarification and explanation of the traits and chief purposes of thought: to define lifestyle and behaviour, to change our actions, to direct them, and to free them from the power of concrete circumstances. (Vygotsky, 1993, p. 237)

Following Spinoza, a crucial question for Vygotsky is how to free ourselves from our concrete circumstances, from our passions; how to be free, not determined by external causes but to be a cause of ourselves (*causa sui*). According to Spinoza we are not able to control ourselves directly through a will that is not tied to matter; we can only achieve freedom by altering our position in relation to external determinations, or, as Vygotsky put it, by creating extrinsic stimuli.

Let us consider Spinoza's account. How does this self-determination arise? What are its conditions? For Spinoza we can only be said to be free when we are guided by adequate knowledge rather than when we are moved by external causes. To be guided by adequate rather than inadequate knowledge is to be free from external determination. To repeat Ilyenkov, our freedom is expressed in our ability to inhabit an idealised environment, or as Bakhurst and McDowell might put it, to be responsive to reasons. For instance, when the child uses a die to facilitate his response he has attributed reason to it. The die itself tells him nothing of what to do; it is only the significance that the child himself has attached to it that allows the choice to be made.

It is important to remember that Spinoza's argument about self-determination depends upon the underlying belief that thought and extension are attributes of one substance. From the standpoint of this position, he takes 'the will and the intellect [to be]... one and the same'. It is as though the shape of intellect at any one point in time is the same as the degree of will since Spinoza sees a parallel between 'the order and connection of ideas' and 'the order and connection of things' (they are the same) (*Ethics*, Part II, Proposition 7). A particular volition is nothing but a particular idea. But the question still remains as to how we can account for our degree of self-determination. Here, Spinoza's distinction between adequate and inadequate ideas comes to the fore. The more our actions are formed by adequate ideas, that is, ideas where the genetic connections are understood explicitly, the more we are determinate of our own actions and we are said to be active. The more we act according to inadequate ideas (ones whose full connections are unknown),[10] the more we can be said to be passive and in consequence of this our actions are not free: 'The physical and mental behaviour of a human being ... may be active or passive to various degrees. The more it stems distinctively or creatively from its own conatus, the more active it is; the more it is merely acted on by external things, the more passive it is' (Sprigge, 1995, p. 848). Spinoza calls the active behaviour of the mind 'adequate ideas', the passive behaviour 'inadequate ideas'. Adequate ideas necessarily constitute more genuine knowledge:

> Spinoza regards us in bondage so far as we are under the control of external things (in a sense which includes especially mental processes of our own that we do not properly understand) and as free to the extent that we meet life with creative understanding of what will best serve the purposes that adequate ideas will determine in us. (Sprigge, 1995, p. 848)

Spinoza's conception of freedom gained by the holding of adequate ideas relates to a notion of truth totally different from the one to which we commonly hold, where truth is opposed to falsity and taken to refer directly to something in its presentation, rather than to the 'order and connection of ideas' that constitute that presentation. Let us consider this more directly.

SPINOZA AND TRUTH

Spinoza insists that:

> error is always the privation of knowledge; to say that an idea or proposition is false is to say that it is relatively incomplete and fragmentary, and is therefore to

say something about its lack of logical relation with other ideas; the falsity is corrected as soon as the idea is placed in connexion with other ideas in a larger system of knowledge. (Hampshire, 1992, p. 87)

In other words, false belief is not opposed to truth but rather is a matter of incomplete knowledge (Hampshire, 1992).

Returning to a guiding argument in this book, it should be clear that the notion of truth in Spinoza and Vygotsky is fundamentally different from that which is expressed in terms of propositional knowledge, yet it is the assumption that, when Vygotsky talks of scientific concepts, he is referring to propositional knowledge that leads commentators, such as Wertsch, to criticise him for advocating a decontextualised form of rationality. Propositional knowledge is often taken to involve statements that correspond to, or picture, truths of the world. But when the dualist conception of mind and world is replaced by the idea of different attributes of the same substance, the question of the relation of thought to the world takes a different form. Truth is no longer something that can be ascribed to isolated propositions.

Spinoza's idea of truth is taken up by Hardt in a discussion of Deleuze. Hardt argues that, 'Along with Thomas Mark, a perceptive American commentator, Deleuze shows that Spinoza's theory of truth is an ontological theory of truth' (Hardt, 1993, p. 90). He continues: 'Mark explains that the traditional approach of Anglo-American and analytical interpreters of Spinoza (Joachim, Stuart Hampshire, Alasdair MacIntyre) counterposes Spinoza to a correspondence theory of truth and in line with a "coherence theory" where truth is defined as coherence within the orderly system that constitutes reality' (Hardt, 1993, p. 131). (This reading of Spinoza still sees thought as operating only within a realm of contemplation, rather than as a material activity.) Hardt explains Mark's argument that, in contrast to American and analytical interpretations, 'Spinoza is better situated in the much older epistemological tradition of truth as being. "If we wish to see Spinoza's theory of truth in its historical setting we must contrast the correspondence view of truth not with coherence, but rather with theories of 'truth of being' or 'truth of things' [i.e. as] ontological truth"' (Hardt, 1993, p. 131). Hardt argues that Mark does not take this line of argument far enough when he takes it as sufficient to situate Spinoza within the 'Platonic tradition'. Once truth is understood as ontological, Hardt continues, then an inextricable relationship exists between truth and power, and Spinoza's rightful place is, as Deleuze places him, in a line of thought that subsequently runs through Nietzsche (Hardt, 1993). Foucault draws from this tradition when he argues that something is true because it is powerful, not powerful because it is true.

Spinoza's argument that ideas are true by virtue of their adequacy calls for attention to the structure and genesis of thought, as Hardt explains:

> Adequate ideas are expressive, and inadequate ideas are mute. In other words, the distinctive character of an adequate idea is that it tells us something about the structure and connections of being (or at least the attribute of thought) through a direct expression of its efficient and formal causes. From an ontological perspective,

the inadequate idea tells us nothing because we cannot recognise its place in the productive structure of thought.[11] (Hardt, 1993, p. 90)

Spinoza introduced a material and 'historical' element into Descartes's requirement of clear and distinct ideas (and in doing so paved the way for Hegel's historical concept of mind):

> A given idea of a circle may be clear and distinct, but it remains inadequate unless it explains the path of its own production. An adequate idea of a circle might, for example, involve the idea of a fixed radius rotated around a central point; it expresses its cause ... An adequate idea of justice would have to express the means by which we produce or construct such an idea; it would involve a genealogy of ideas that result in this idea. (Hardt, 1993, p. 132)

The description of a circle as a figure where all straight lines drawn from the centre to the circumference are equal would be inadequate since it expresses only one of its properties but not how the circle is produced and/or how its essence can only be captured by expressing the elements intrinsic to its formation. For Spinoza the adequate idea of the circle is, as Kashap puts this, of 'a figure described by a straight line wherein one end is fixed and the other is free. This clearly comprehends the proximate cause and states how the figure is brought about, and hence constitutes a proper definition' (Kashap, 1987, p. 6):

> Spinoza suggests that if the thing to be defined is a dependent or a created thing then its definition must specify the conditions or factors which explain how it comes to be (i.e. its immediate or proximate cause). The innermost essence of a thing that depends for its existence on conditions external to itself consists precisely in those conditions without which it could not be produced, or come to be what it is. ... once the essential conditions for its production have been specified then it would be possible to infer all the characteristics or properties of a thing from such a definition. This ... clearly involves an unfolding of the very nature of the thing that is being defined. (Kashap, 1987, p. 5)

This conception of truth is different from the everyday one and supports a reading of Vygotsky, different from some Western commentators'. For instance, Brockmeier argues that Vygotsky shared the same Kantian starting point as Piaget, with the assumption that 'there is no absolute and objective cognition of the world as it really is' (Brockmeier, 1996, p. 140). Thus Brockmeier's interpretation of Vygotsky, which presupposes a mind–world dualism, is simply not sustainable when thought and extension are understood as attributes of one substance. To the extent that Vygotsky follows Spinoza, his interpretation is open to doubt since the Spinozan idea of truth points in precisely the opposite direction, that is, towards the idea that objective cognition of the world is possible.

Kashap points out that, for Descartes, error depends on two factors in combination: the power of understanding and the power of will. Understanding allows us to apprehend ideas, but it does not affirm or deny them. Citing Descartes, Kashap notes the emphasis on free choice: 'The faculty of will consists solely in our having the power of choosing to do a thing or choosing not to do a thing' (Kashap, 1987, p. 99). Spinoza, by contrast, rejects the notion of liberty that Descartes imagines the mind to possess: liberty cannot be distinct from necessity. Hence free action is not a matter of choice or volition but of the mind's activity as opposed to its passivity.

Activity concerns the quality of activity rather than its merely taking place: that is, the mind is active when its ideas are adequate, and passive when its ideas are inadequate. We *act* when we are the adequate cause of our actions, when the ideas on which our actions are based are adequate ideas. This is a sense of action totally different from the common one, in which no such profound distinction is made. So many of the actions that we feel ourselves to be engaged in would, if we accept Spinoza's line of argument, be understood merely as vain repetition. Often such repetition perpetuates what it is intended to change. This, of course, is a standard psychotherapeutic position: an action that is claimed by a patient to be effective is revealed in fact to be preserving the situation that the patient wishes to change. For Spinoza such activity, though it comprises concrete actions, is not really activity at all; or, to be precise, because it is driven by inadequate ideas, it is in fact passivity. Here again freedom, truth and goodness are matters of ontology rather than representations, and existence depends on aspect and activity rather than an *assigned* essence.

The 'Learning Paradox' provides a helpful means by which to illustrate the way in which Spinoza's influence on Vygotsky has a bearing on contemporary educational concerns. For Spinoza it is the particular connection of one idea to another which constitutes its adequacy. Vygotsky appreciates this point, seeing that to educate involves the 'relocation' of ideas. This is different both from what are termed child-centred approaches and traditional didactic approaches. The attempt to grow a higher understanding exclusively from children's experiences fails as completely as attempts to implant a higher understanding without regard to these experiences. The former overestimates the child's capacity to learn without teaching and the latter underestimates the conditions for learning. The point is relevant to Plato's dialogue of the *Meno* where it is argued that knowledge is already present in the child and that the actualisation of the knowledge is neither a reduction to nor an ignoring of the particularities of the child.[12] Understanding pedagogy as a process of adjusting the connection of ideas already known but connected differently is quite different from a familiar conception of pedagogy as an approach consisting of techniques and style. Vygotsky makes the point that two people can appear to have the same level of knowledge but in fact differ widely. This is because if we make a summative assessment of an individual's knowledge we may not immediately have access to the way that their ideas are connected and more than this, ideas are always in a process of development and come to fruition in the context in which they are used. Through dialogue with a teacher, the learner's ideas come to fruition: they are *actualised* in the relevant set of connected ideas (what Bruner describes as induction into particular cultural practices). Vygotsky describes the assessment of the mental development of children of the same chronological age, who perhaps are revealed to have a similar mental age. He states:

> If I stop at this point, people would imagine that the subsequent course of development and of school learning of these children will be the same, because it depends on their intellect ... Now imagine that I do not terminate my study at this point, but only begin it ... Suppose I show ... [that these children] have various ways of dealing with a task ... that the children solve the problem with my assistance. Under these circumstances it turns out that the first child can deal with the problems up to a twelve-year-old's level, the second up to a nine-year-old's level. Now, are these children mentally the same? (Vygotsky, 1978, pp. 85–86)

Bruner considers what he describes as Vygotsky's 'stunning concept' of the zone of proximal development (ZPD) in a discussion of Plato's account of knowledge in the *Meno*. One of Bruner's arguments stresses that as novice learners we already know a great deal. The idea that we can only know what we already know, that is, we cannot know anything new, is referred to as the Learning Paradox: that is, how is it possible to know when knowledge already presupposes the means of knowing? Bruner explains that the idea of ZPD rests on 'the brute fact, perhaps first celebrated by Plato in the *Meno* where he discusses the young slave's apparent "knowledge" of geometry while being questioned appropriately by Socrates, that ignorant learners can do better in understanding a matter when prompted or "scaffolded" by an expert than they can do on their own' (Bruner, 1987, p. 4). In a later work he argues: 'In some deeper sense, grasping something abstractly is a start toward appreciating that seemingly complicated knowledge can often be derivationally reduced to simpler forms of knowledge that you already possess' (Bruner, 1996, p. 51). To illustrate his point Bruner gives the example of a mystery story with a note inserted in the text saying that the reader already holds all the knowledge necessary to solve the crime. He makes the point that an educator can lead children

> to recognise that they know far more than they thought they ever knew, but that they have to 'think about it' in order to really know what they know [to actualise the knowing]. And that, after all, was what the Renaissance and the Age of Reason were all about! But to teach and learn that way means you have to adopt a new theory of mind. (Bruner, 1996, p. 52)

DETERMINISM AND DEVELOPMENT

The preceding discussion has attempted to illuminate elements of Spinoza's philosophy relevant to Vygotsky's approach to mind. In doing so it has raised the issue of determinism, which is a continuing theme of this book. In Chapter 2 it appeared in relation to attempts to provide 'a mechanics of mind'. In this chapter it is addressed in relation to attempts to provide a causal account of mind and will.

How is freedom to be located in relation to determinism? The freedom and determinism debate has a long and distinguished history in philosophy. Once a theological conception of freedom is rejected, a conception that is based on an understanding of mind as of some different substance from the world and thus able to transcend that world and the mechanical causes by which the world moves, then the alternative scientistic position appears only to offer an explanatory base in efficient causes. But if a causal explanation appears to offer the alternative to a metaphysical or mystical conception of freedom, this comes at the price of reducing human action to the mechanical and determined, thus leaving no space for freedom, nor, it may be added, any means for assigning responsibility. The difficulty of subscribing to causal explanations of agency as an alternative to a theological position is that, in attempting to explain human sociogenesis, it tends to attribute the causes of what a human being is entirely to the environment, such that it becomes the determining factor. If this were the case then the development of humanity would be a viable project for policy based on scientific data. Given the commitment to 'the construction of socialist man' in the context in which Vygotsky was working, his thought was vulnerable to assimilation in such scientistic terms. The dangers of such misinterpretation persist as policy makers still believe that it is possible to see different outcomes as the result of factors about which precise information can be captured.

These problems of determinist explanations arise in a similar way in interpretations of Marx. The idea of economic determinism is fostered by a crude reading of Marx, where a determinate relation is taken to exist in what became known as the base and superstructure model. The temptation is then to see human beings simply as a product of their circumstances. This determinism plagued Vygotskians: it was precisely this that provoked the rift with Leontiev and the Kharkov group because they could not accept Vygotsky's insistence on the existence of a plane that was not explicable in terms of tool use in an environment. Glassman provides an illustration of the typical case of a commentator on Vygotsky who misreads Marx and in doing so produces a particular interpretation of Vygotsky. But there is a problem with his account also, specifically in respect of the idea of progress. In discussing Leontiev and Vygotsky, Glassman argues that their work contains the idea of the progressive evolution of social systems championed by Spencer as well as of the social philosophy of Marx and Engels: 'Marx and Engels seem to have partially embraced Spencerism along with Darwinism ... the difference for Marx and Engels was that, rather than seeing progress as driving activity, progress emerged out of activity' (Glassman, 1996, p. 311). Reading Marx in this way influences interpretations of Vygotsky's work. The common conflation of Marx's work with the practice of Soviet Marxism imposes reductive notions of progress and development that are then transferred to readings of Vygotsky. On many occasions Marx himself found the need to refute crude conceptions of his interest in Darwin's work. It was Spencer who used the phrase 'struggle for survival', often wrongly attributed to Darwin, who, like Marx, did not hold the conception of progressive development that is often read into their work.[13]

Bruner notes that Vygotsky 'did *not* subscribe to the Soviet Marxist dogma that then viewed man as a mere "product" of history and circumstance' (Bruner, 1987, p. 2). He also recognises the possibility in Vygotsky's work of conceiving freedom differently when he states: 'In the end Vygotsky flirts with the idea that the use of language creates consciousness and even free will' (Bruner, 1987, p. 2). Bruner suggests that Vygotsky's interest in the place of consciousness in mental life put him at odds with Stalinist ideologues, and he accounts for this as follows. The 'battle of consciousness' became central to Soviet psychology only after the Stalinist suppression was lifted. Vygotsky's followers were lined up against the Pavlovians. An improvement of relations between the two sides could arise, however, only when Vygotskian theory was restated in the language of the second signal system of Pavlov. The second signal system incorporates the notion that language and concepts mediate human existence as a second signal rather than as a first signal where stimuli act on the nervous system directly. This model of signalling has, however, overly determinate implications, and it remains in question if this alternative can do justice to the sense of freedom in Vygotsky, especially given his interest in the 'transcendent' quality of art.

The issue of determinism infuses much work in the Vygotskian field, and it was there right from the start. When Leontiev and other members of the Kharkov group split with Vygotsky, its was precisely this that was the issue. The split has been presented as a contrast between Vygotsky's emphasis on semiotic mediation and the focus Leontiev wanted on social activity. In his obituary of Vygotsky, Leontiev wrote that Vygotsky's ideas belonged to the past and that there must be a move away from semiotic mediation: the Kharkov group must distance itself from those ideas (Van der Veer and Valsiner, 1993). In 1939 Zinchenko wrote an article in which he argued that the priority Vygotsky gave to semiotic mediation should be abandoned (Kozulin, 1990). Yet, as we shall see in Chapter 7, the issue of semiotic mediation was more than a matter of the idealism of the sign versus the materialism of the tool.

CONCLUSION

To bring this chapter to a conclusion let us turn our attention to two further issues concerning determinism: the first concerns explanations of freedom framed exclusively in terms of causation; the second involves the question of normativity. Both of these issues are critical in appropriations of Spinoza and hence, at one remove, in the understanding of Vygotsky as well.

The problem of determinism arises when explanations of freedom are addressed solely in terms of causes. Although Spinoza has suffered from being understood as a determinist, his working through of ideas offers the possibility, as we have seen, of theorising freedom in a radically different way.

The situating of freedom in terms of the free will–determinism polarity has led those commentators who understand freedom as freedom from necessity to conclude that Spinoza has no notion of free will at all. Martin Jay sees Spinoza as a determinist who argues that free will is an illusion, which 'an understanding of logical necessity would dispel' (Jay, 1984, p. 29). Georgi Plekhanov's reading of Spinoza and the interpretation of his work by Soviet Marxism support

Jay's interpretation. Although a first reading of Spinoza may indeed suggest a determinist and mechanical approach, it is nevertheless possible to see a clear notion of freedom in his working out of certain fundamental questions. While Spinoza's use of geometric exposition supports the impression that the argument is determinist in its conception, his approach can be understood heuristically: it can be taken as a demonstration that he is as systematic as Descartes even though the argument does not start from a Cartesian point of certainty. Thus Spinoza's 'anti-foundationalist foundationalism' is opposed to Descartes's foundationalism. Stuart Hampshire comments that Spinoza's 'metaphysics of the mind, which provides his scheme or outline of science of psychology, was certainly not simply mechanical or behaviouristic' (Hampshire, 1988, p. 70). This judgement is shared by many other Spinoza scholars. Errol Harris points out that Spinoza denies that his theory subjects humanity to fate, arguing that he is not a mechanical determinist (Harris, 1992, p. 31).

Ilyenkov argues that the geometric structure of Spinoza's argument should not be misread as proof of a determinist position:

> It is not so easy, however, to bring these brilliant principles out because they are decked out in the solid armour of the constructions of formal logic and deductive mathematics that constitute the 'shell' of Spinoza's system, its (so to say) defensive coat of mail. In other words, the real logic of Spinoza's thinking by no means coincides with the formal logic of the movement of his 'axioms', 'theorems', 'scholia', and their proofs. 'Even with philosophers who gave their work a systematic form, e.g. Spinoza, the real inner structure of their system is quite distinct from the form in which they consciously presented it,' Karl Marx wrote to Ferdinand Lassalle. (Ilyenkov, 1977, p. 29)

What is important here is not so much whether Spinoza was a mechanical determinist, or even whether Vygotsky was party to the determinist tendencies of post-revolutionary Russia's attempt to implement policies for rapid development, but the extent to which a particular way of working through certain questions opens up new possibilities. Ilyenkov denies the reductive reading of Spinoza's idea; indeed the whole impetus of dealing with thought as an attribute of one substance prevents any reduction of thought to neurons or causal mechanisms in physiology.

Where, on Descartes's view, the will, and therefore freedom, have neither cause nor explanation, Spinoza has a definite conception of freedom based on self-determination. To be free for Spinoza is to be a cause of oneself. Will is not separate from intellect, or from the adequacy, or inadequacy, of ideas. Freedom is found in necessity but in a necessity that human beings mediate as their own rather than one that remains uncompromisingly external. The idea of freedom untouched by necessity is impossible. Vygotsky grasps this point as a way to understand freedom through mediation. Bruner recognises the beginnings of a theory of freedom in Vygotsky but also that he was unable to complete this task. The task is not even addressed within contemporary psychology.

A further difficulty facing attempts to theorise freedom (and, in tandem, intellect) stems from the Cartesian dualism of mind and world. Linked to the problem of consciousness and the question of human agency is the question of ethics. In the Cartesian model, ethics is relativised by the separation. In parallel to the gap between mind and matter, a distinction is implied between evaluative and descriptive use of language. Hume asserts that there is an unbridgeable gap between fact and value – the impossibility of deducing an *ought* from an *is*. Dualism entails a separation of the normative from the positive and a complementary separation of reason from the passions. The critique of rationality, or more specifically abstract rationality, depends upon the assumption of the separation of a reason (dealing with the facts of the world) from the passions (entwined with values and intentions).[14]

Here then is one of the crucial claims of this book: namely, that the critique of Vygotsky on the grounds of abstract rationality fails to recognise the philosophical tradition within which Vygotsky was working. It is hoped that the discussion of Spinoza above, brief though this inevitably is in the context of this book, is sufficient to show that the claims made by those who criticise Vygotsky for abstract rationality fail to do justice to the complexity of the issues involved.

The argument here complements the argument of the preceding chapter since it shows that for Vygotsky, following Spinoza, the question of the intellect and the problem of freedom are part and parcel of one another. Recent philosophy, it is important to acknowledge, has laid the grounds for overcoming the separation of the positive and the normative that stems from Hume. An important instance is McDowell's use of Sellars's critique of the 'Myth of the Given' to formulate a position where reasons are to be understood as in the world, laid down by our intentional activity:

> Thought can bear on empirical reality only because to be a thinker at all is to be at home in the space of reasons. And being at home in the space of reasons involves not just a collection of propensities to shift one's psychological stance in response to this or that, but the standing potential for a reflective stance at which the question arises whether one ought to find this or that persuasive. (McDowell, 1996, p. 125)

The phrase 'the space of reasons' contains complicated ideas about the character of our knowing, but it has an important bearing on our understanding of Vygotsky's interest in the semiotic. For, as we shall shortly see, Vygotsky was influenced not only by Spinoza but also by Hegel. It is to the nature of this influence that must now turn.

NOTES

1 Vygotsky went beyond Engels to criticise Descartes who 'cannot always make a clear distinction between passions of the soul and passions of a soulless machine' (Vygotsky, 1999, p. 176).

2 'Traditionally the will was taken to be a mental faculty responsible for acts of volition such as choosing, deciding, and initiating motion. This faculty of the soul or mind was taken as one of the most important, separating us from animals and inanimate objects' (Weatherford, 1995, p. 910).

3 Conceptions of freedom inform education practices. They can be understood as forming part of the 'folk psychologies' (Bruner, 1996) underlying pedagogic practices. For instance, some practices of 'child-centred education' emphasising the 'rights' of children (another problematic area) to follow their own interests/desires/wants are premised upon it.

4 This account of Spinoza's ideas does not consider his work directly but rather through the perspective of Vygotsky and therefore he is read backwards through Marx and Hegel rather than attempting to capture the fact that he was on the cusp of modernity, combining an enchanted medievalism with the concepts of modernity.

5 The passions were a major preoccupation of seventeenth- and eighteenth-century thinkers (James, 1997).

6 On this matter, Freud has a debt to Spinoza for his practice of therapy. In discussing Spinoza, Moreau refers to Freud who, he writes: 'in one of his interjections ... asserts that he [Freud] has always lived "in a Spinozist environment"'. Moreau goes on to argue that 'a certain number of Freudian motifs recall the great themes of the *Ethics* without ever repeating them: first of all, the idea that the psychological does not reduce to the conscious, and that events occurring in the psychological realm manifest themselves in the body' (Moreau, 1996, p. 428).

7 Indeed the very conception of a mind free from substance perpetuates this position.

8 Parallelism is the term used to used to describe the simultaneous existence of the human mind and human body, without one being the cause of changes in the other. Kashap suggest that Spinoza's statement: 'The body cannot determine the mind to thought, neither the body to motion or rest' (*Ethics*, Part III, Proposition 2) 'is the first of its kind in so-called modern philosophy which suggests a distinction between causes and reasons of human behaviour' (Kashap, 1987, p. 117).

9 Bakhurst notes that Ilyenkov's 'conception of thought largely emerges during his treatments of Spinoza' (Bakhurst, 1991, p. 251).

10 See Chapter 3 note 14.

11 This relates directly to pedagogical approaches which attempt to make the development of any concept explicit to the learner.

12 'These opinions were somewhere in him ... This knowledge will not come from teaching but from questioning. He will recover it for himself' (Plato, 1956, p. 138).

13 Marx writes in a letter to Ludwig Kugelmann, 27 June 1870: 'Mr. Lange has made a great discovery. The whole of history can be brought under a single great law. This natural law is the *phrase* (in this application Darwin's expression becomes nothing but a phrase) "struggle for life", and the content of this phrase is the Malthusian law of population or, rather, overpopulation. Thus instead of analysing the "struggle for life" as represented historically in various definite forms of society, all that is done is to translate every concrete struggle into the phrase "struggle for life", and this phrase itself into the Malthusian "population fantasy". One must admit that this is a very impressive method – for swaggering, sham-scientific, bombastic ignorance and intellectual laziness' (Marx and Engels, 1934, p. 20).

14 Curiously this is the exact opposite of the intended goal of those critiquing abstract rationality. Their purpose is to show that emotions or the affective dimension of thought is central to thinking. As a result there is a need to reject what they take (mistakenly) to epitomise abstract reason – thought devoid of affect. It can be argued that the separation of affect and reason which they criticise is a supposition of their own making.

REFERENCES

Bakhurst, D. (1991) *Consciousness and Revolution in Soviet Philosophy: From the Bolsheviks to Evald Ilyenkov* (Cambridge: Cambridge University Press).
Brockmeier, J. (1996) Construction and Interpretation: Exploring a Joint Perspective on Piaget and Vygotsky. In: A. Tryphon and J.N. Vonèche (eds) *Piaget – Vygotsky: The Social Genesis of Thought* (Hove: Psychology Press), pp. 125–143.
Bruner, J. (1987) Prologue to the English Edition. In *The Collected Works of L. S. Vygotsky, Volume 1, Problems of General Psychology*, N. Minick trans., R.W. Reiber and A.S. Carton eds (New York: Plenum Press), pp. 1–16.
Bruner, J.S. (1996) *The Culture of Education* (Cambridge, MA: Harvard University Press).
DeBrabander, F. (2007) *Spinoza and the Stoics* (London: Continuum).
Gergen, K.J. (1999) *An Invitation to Social Construction* (London: Sage).
Glassman, M. (1996) Understanding Vygotsky's Motive and Goal: An Exploration of the Work of A. N. Leontiev, *Human Development*, 39, 309–327.
Hampshire, S. (1988) *Spinoza and Spinozism* (Oxford: Oxford University Press).
Hampshire, S. (1992) *Spinoza: An Introduction to his Philosophical Thought* (London: Penguin Books).
Hardt, M. (1993) *Gilles Deleuze: An Apprenticeship in Philosophy* (London: University College London Press).
Harris, E.E. (1992) *Spinoza's Philosophy: An Outline* (Atlantic Highlands, NJ: Humanities Press).
Ilyenkov, E.V. (1977) *Dialectical Logic: Essays on its History and Theory* (Moscow: Progress Publishers).
Ilyenkov, E.V. (2009) *The Ideal in Human Activity* (Pacifica, CA: Marxist Internet Archive Publications).
James. S (1997) *Passion and Action: The Emotions in Seventeenth-Century Philosophy* (New York: Oxford University Press).
Jay, M. (1984) *Marxism and Totality: The Adventure of a Concept from Lukács to Habermas* (Berkley: University of California Press).
Kashap, S.P. (1987) *Spinoza and Moral Freedom* (New York: State University of New York Press).
Kozulin, A. (1990) *Vygotsky's Psychology: A Biography of Ideas* (Brighton: Harvester Wheatsheaf).
Marx, K. and Engels, F. (1934) *Marx and Engels Selected Correspondence, 1841–1895* (London: Lawrence and Wishart).
McDowell, J. (1996) *Mind and World* (Cambridge, MA: Harvard University Press).
Moreau, P. (1996) Spinoza's Reception and Influence. In: D. Garrett (ed.) *The Cambridge Companion to Spinoza* (Cambridge: Cambridge University Press), pp. 408–433.
Plato (1956) *Protagoras and Meno*, W.K.C. Guthrie trans. (London: Penguin Books).
Spinoza, B. (1993) *Ethics and Treatise on the Correction of the Intellect*, A. Boyle trans. (London: Everyman).
Sprigge, T.L.S. (1995) Spinoza. In: T. Honderich (ed.) *The Oxford Companion to Philosophy* (Oxford: Oxford University Press), pp. 845–848.
Van der Veer, R. and Valsiner, J. (1993) *Understanding Vygotsky: A Quest for Synthesis* (Oxford: Blackwell).
Vygotsky L.S. ([1925]1971) *The Psychology of Art* 'Preface', http://www.marxists.org/archive/vygotsky/works/1925/preface.htm (accessed 22 May 2013).
Vygotsky, L.S. (1978) *Mind in Society: The Development of Higher Psychological Processes*, M. Cole *et al.* eds (Cambridge, MA: Harvard University Press).
Vygotsky, L.S. (1993) *The Collected Works of L. S. Vygotsky, Volume 2, The Fundamentals of Defectology (Abnormal Psychology and Learning Disabilities)*, J. Knox, trans., R.W. Reiber and A.S. Carton eds (London: Plenum Publishers).

Vygotsky, L.S. (1997a) *The Collected Works of L. S. Vygotsky, Volume 3, Problems of the Theory and History of Psychology*, R. Van der Veer trans., R.W. Reiber and J. Wollock eds (New York: Plenum Press).

Vygotsky, L.S. (1997b) *The Collected Works of L. S. Vygotsky, Volume 4, The History and Development of Higher Mental Functions*, M.J. Hall trans., R.W. Reiber ed. (New York: Plenum Press).

Vygotsky, L.S. (1999) *The Collected Works of L. S. Vygotsky, Volume 6, Scientific Legacy*, M.J. Hall trans., R.W. Reiber ed. (New York: Kluwer Academic/Plenum Publishers).

Weatherford, R.C. (1995) Will. In: T. Honderich (ed.) *The Oxford Companion to Philosophy* (Oxford: Oxford University Press), pp. 910–911.

6
Vygotsky, Hegel and the Critique of Abstract Reason

To grasp the extent to which Vygotsky's ideas go beyond a limited concept of abstraction and decontextualisation, it is necessary to understand the different philosophical frame and presuppositions in which his thought was developed. The preceding chapter set out elements of the ideas informing his work through an examination of aspects of Spinoza's thought, especially that concerning free will, determination and truth. This chapter continues with a discussion of the most significant philosopher for Vygotsky – Hegel.

Hegel's philosophy is not readily accessible. As Stephen Houlgate remarks, 'there is no short cut ... There is nothing but the long and difficult, at times tortuous, at times exhilarating path through the details' (Houlgate, 1998, p. 19). Simplistic guides to Hegel rarely achieve much and often falsify his thought completely (Pinkard, 2000). Hence it goes without saying that it is not a straightforward task to summarise his contribution to philosophy. The aim of this chapter, then, is limited to providing illustrations of the link between his work and Vygotsky's and in particular to see how this shows that the argument that Vygotsky employed an abstract decontextualised form of reason is groundless.

KANT AND DUALISM

A difficulty with the interpretation of Vygotsky's idea of scientific concepts and abstraction is that it has tended to accept the presupposition of a dualism of mind and world, even, it would sometimes seem, the same dualism that goes back to Descartes. Questions of dualism were a major theoretical issue in the seventeenth and eighteenth centuries from Descartes to Hume, and from Hume the issue was taken up by Kant and then by Hegel.

One aspect of this dualism is the traditional epistemological problem of how subjective mind and objective world are connected in such a way as to make knowledge

Vygotsky Philosophy and Education, First Edition. Jan Derry.
© 2013 Jan Derry. Editorial organisation © Philosophy of Education Society of Great Britain.
Published 2013 by John Wiley & Sons, Ltd.

of the world possible, together with a related concern that any account should respect the freedom of spontaneity, that is, the exercise of judgement. Kant responded to this philosophical dilemma, which had dogmatism at one pole and scepticism at the other (Bird, 1996), with a transcendental account of the conditions of our knowing. This account has been the subject of numerous readings, many of which (Pippin, 1997; Pinkard, 2000; Sedgwick, 2012) see the precursor of Hegel's thought and draw attention to Hegel's appreciation of the transcendental deduction. At the same time Hegel believed that Kant did not heed its full implications (Sedgwick, 1997). If Hegel's reading is right, this could explain why later writers have found an ambivalence in Kant between the 'dark side' of his metaphysics where receptivity and spontaneity can be considered as separable (Bird, 1996) and a more insightful side where he deduces that receptivity and spontaneity make an inseparable contribution to knowledge (McDowell, 1996).

In the light of the predisposition of educational theories to favour the effectual separability of spontaneity and receptivity it is hardly surprising to find that the influence of Kant on education has been to continue the dualisms which haunt his work rather than to follow the most progressive elements of his thought. Thus the contrast with Hegel below does no more than capture the more common characterisations of his work. Three contrasts between Kant and Hegel can be noted:

1 Kant's idea of a realm that cannot be known as opposed to Hegel's position that everything is knowable;[1]
2 Kant's argument that the mind already has within it the means to construct the world in a particular way as opposed to Hegel's argument that the mind does not exist a priori but emerges in social activity;[2]
3 Kant's emphasis on representations as providing a correspondence to the world that we have knowledge of,[3] as opposed to Hegel's emphasis on meaning arising inferentially within a system.[4]

It must be stressed that this contrast between Kant and Hegel is related especially to the importance for educational thought of popular understandings of their work. As a result it stops short of a scholarly treatment of their philosophies. These contrasts are indispensable for locating abstract rationality as a theme in a particular history of philosophy that gives Kant pride of place and more or less ignores Hegel. While the literature on Vygotsky does not appear overtly to have taken this history as a basis of its understanding, its use of concepts such as representation, reality and constructivism, as discussed in Chapter 3 above, is consistent with its terms.

The impact of Kant on education research is of course clearly evident in the extensive work directly influenced by Piaget. Jens Brockmeier notes the contrast between the approaches of Piaget and Vygotsky in terms of the 'unsolved relation between the *constructivist* emphasis of the great Geneva scholar and the *interpretative* approach that has developed out of the Russian psychologist, semiotician, and cultural theorist' (Brockmeier, 1996, p. 127). With regard to constructivism, Leslie Smith argues that Vygotsky's approach involves a social Platonism and that this precludes its being a component of his thinking: 'Social Platonism and constructivism are incompatible and so an exclusive choice would have to be made between them. Evidently, Piaget ([1995], pp. 71, 208) denies all commitments to Platonism, whereas the Platonist commitments of Vygotskyan accounts have been insufficiently realised' (Smith, 1996, p. 117). The constructivist assumption of the separation of world and mind leads Smith to the conclusion that social Platonism – in which logic is enculturated in a social space – and constructivism are incompatible.[5] To the extent that Piaget was influenced by Kant, his understanding of how children acquire knowledge depends upon his implicit conception of engagement with the world as a process that brings out the veracity of transcendental idealism. The mind is able to intuit because it is equipped with the categories of understanding characteristic of any human mind. It is these categories of understanding that account for the universality and necessity of particular forms of knowledge.

It is Smith's concern with the question of how new knowledge is possible that motivates his critique of Vygotsky. Smith has recourse to these categories when, in relation to the question of how new knowledge is possible, he champions Piaget against Vygotsky. The Kantian position, he claims, offers a way out of the learning paradox as the conditions of knowing are in the mind prior to any actual knowledge. In Kantian terms, my ability to know geometry depends upon an innate conceptual capacity; for Piaget this capacity necessarily requires maturation. Kant sets out to resolve the dualism of world and mind by positing the categories of understanding. His goal was to establish the possibility of synthetic a priori knowledge.[6] This was crucial for overcoming two problems: first, the idea that knowledge is dependent on experience; and second, the rationalist alternative that knowledge is simply the internal relation of concepts to one another.

Hume held that a priori knowledge could be found only in analytic propositions, that is, in propositions that are true by definition, where there is nothing contained in the subject that is not already present in the predicate – for example, 'all bachelors are unmarried men' or 'the angles of a Euclidean triangle equal 180 degrees'. Part of what had to be resolved was how our experience of the world becomes knowledge for us. What, Kant asked, are the conditions of the possibility of our knowing?[7] That is, how can our thoughts have the content they do? He showed how it is possible to have knowledge that is due *both* to our experience and to the way in which, as human beings, we are capable of understanding. Kant's transcendental idealism implied that synthetic a priori knowledge of objects of experience is possible because objects must conform to the conditions under which they can become objects for us in the first place. Incidentally, this is the philosophy underlying constructivism and work within educational theory concerned with perspectivism – the idea that no knowledge exists beyond the means by which that knowledge is realised. The difficulty here of course is specifying what is to be understood by the expression 'the means by which the knowledge is realised'. Might this be the individual discourse of a classroom teacher? Or the biographies of individual students? Or the *space of reasons* within which any propositional statement is made (thus giving the proposition an inferential rather than representational form)? Or is it the historical forms of what Hegel called *Geist*?

It is relevant to note here that the Humean claims that prompted Kant to deal with these questions in a new way were characteristic of the modern period. Greek philosophy, to which Hegel returned, dealt with the question of mind and world in a fundamentally different way from the dualist approaches that came to prominence in the seventeenth century. According to Caygill, by the time that Kant came to the problem, Aristotle's account of the abstraction of sensible and intelligible forms had 'become narrowed by the focus upon the problem of conception or the abstraction of ideas and notions from sensible experience. The human subject was divided into faculties of sensibility and intellect. The problem of how to bring together sense data and ideas was solved either rationalistically or empirically' (Caygill, 1995, p. 119). Kant's 'Copernican revolution',[8] Caygill continues, involved reversing the idea that cognition conforms to objects, putting in its place the idea that the thought of objects conforms to our ways of knowing.[9] This way of thinking became known as transcendental idealism – transcendental in the sense that knowledge transcends experience, ideal in the sense that objects are only knowable to the extent that they conform to the conditions of our knowing.

Kant reunited what seventeenth- and eighteenth-century philosophers had separated and made distinct. In the process, he exposed the limits of both rationalism and empiricism, and saw that some way of synthesising the two was necessary to ground the possibility of knowledge. The logic of his argument compelled him to confront the perennial question of the relation between theory and practice, and, following from this, the relation between the necessary and the contingent. By asserting the inadequacy of both empiricism and rationalism he was drawn to the conclusion, famously captured in the following words, that 'Thoughts without content are empty, intuitions without concepts are blind. ... The understanding can intuit nothing, the senses can think nothing' (Kant, 1973, B75, A51).[10]

In rejecting the rationalist belief in mathematics as abstract reason able to operate independently of experience, Kant wrote: 'Misled by such a proof of the power of reason, the demand for extension of knowledge recognises no limits. The light dove, cleaving the air in her free flight and feeling its resistance, might imagine that its flight would be easier still in empty space' (Kant, 1973, A5, B9). Where Kant posits the relation between intuitions and concepts as inextricable (even though they retain their distinct characters), Vygotsky, working within a Hegelian frame, argued that the possibilities of what we receive and what we reflect upon are linked to one another genetically, that is, historically. In fact, ways of knowing have an actual, practical symbiotic, historical relation, and forms of knowing are in fact developed from activity rather than by linking the categories of understanding (by our nature, as Kant assumes). Hence Vygotsky follows a Hegelian rather than Kantian approach to the problem of consciousness. Like Hegel he has a science of consciousness.[11]

The issue of abstract rationality appears problematic only when it is conceived in terms of a dualist understanding of a mind and world, separated from each other by a void. Within the framework of dualist theory, the void between the subject and the object of knowledge can only be overcome either by the imposition of a rationality with imperial pretensions or by emphasising, to the exclusion of all else, the specificity and situatedness of human values, understandings and forms of knowledge.

Kant remained dualist in so far as he assumed certain categories of the mind and limited the domain of our knowing. Our knowledge of the world was understood to arise through the different components of how we come to know – *spontaneity* (the way the mind makes sense of the world) and *receptivity* (the way the world is given to a subject) remained separate. Andrew Bowie (1998) explains how once spontaneity and receptivity are understood as not fully separated, it is no longer viable to think of the subject and the world in terms of a dualism. Significantly, this is the case for Vygotsky.

To repeat a point made earlier, in keeping with readings of Kant's work, regarding his ambivalence, it is possible to detect the remnants of a dualism which led Kant to conceive of receptivity and spontaneity as isolable and their contributions to knowledge as separate. At the same time he had the insight that we should 'marvel', according to McDowell (1996, p. 97), that 'reality is not located outside a boundary that encloses the conceptual' (1996, p. 41); it remained for Hegel to express this insight in a phenomenology of cognition.

Bowie refers to Schleiermacher, the originator of modern hermeneutics, when he spells out these issues. But – a point of particular relevance here – he also notes parallels in some strains of modern analytical philosophy, such as in McDowell's *Mind and World*. Robert Brandom addresses the same questions, also from within the analytic tradition. It is surely not by chance that McDowell states that both his own work *Mind and World* (1996), and Robert Brandom's *Making it Explicit* (1994),[12] can be considered prolegomenas to a reading of Hegel's *Phenomenology* (McDowell, 1996). It is also significant that contemporary analytical philosophy, though steeped in the dualist frame of thought, is making a move from Kantian dualism to a Hegelian rethinking of the questions of mind and world. In his introduction to Wilfrid Sellars's *Empiricism and the Philosophy of Mind*, Rorty remarks:

> Philosophers in non-anglophone countries typically think quite hard about Hegel, whereas the rather skimpy training in the history of philosophy which most analytical philosophers receive often tempts them to skip straight from Kant to Frege. It is agreeable to imagine a future in which the tiresome 'analytical–Continental split' is looked back upon as an unfortunate, temporary breakdown of communication … . (Rorty, 1997, p. 12)

It is interesting to note that consideration of the mind of the kind that Vygotskians were undertaking was happening at the same time as this move in analytical philosophy was taking place.

Bowie lists as problems of the dualist framework of mind (subject) and world (object): (1) the 'incoherent separation of knowable "appearances"' and (2) the unknowability of 'things in themselves'. There is also the question of 'how we gain an accurate "re-presentation" of a "ready-made" world of pre-existing objects: this would require a complete account of the difference between what is passively received from the "outside" and what is actively generated by the "inside" mind' (Bowie, 1998, p. x). The dualism underlying accounts of mind and cognition is continually referred to. Either the dualism appears resistant to attempts to eradicate it from the form of explanation, or it is accepted as defining the human condition. The major point to Bowie's book, however, is that dualism still underlies some forms of explanation that attempt to incorporate anti-dualist conceptions of mind (see, for example, Lemke and Wertsch). Prawat makes the point that the attempts by Vygotskians to deal with the issue of individual mentalist descriptions of mind repeat the problems that they attempt to evade. As it stands, Prawat argues, 'strategy-based Vygotskian theory is subject to the *same* dualist afflictions that plague head fitting cognitive psychology. Chief among these is the problem of accounting for how a mind separated from the world can truthfully represent the world' (Prawat, 1999, p. 61). Even though attempts to move away from a mentalist conception of mind place emphasis on the role of 'socially developed cultural tools as mediators of intra- and intermental functioning' (Prawat, 1999, p. 61), there still remains either the same epistemological problem or a collapse into relativism with no stance on knowledge at all.

In many respects, then, dualism survived Hegel's critique: even though the claim is made that 'we are all anti-dualist now', it still provides a widely held common-sense understanding. It is particularly influential in the social sciences. So how are we to place Hegel in this story?

HEGEL AND DUALISM

The problem of knowledge in a dualist world throws up the old antinomies. German philosophy has a long tradition of working through this question, and it reached one of its critical moments in Kant's attempt to show how empirical knowledge is possible when it requires a universality not found in experience. And although Kant's later work moved towards overcoming the rigid separation of concept and intuition and of spontaneity from receptivity, dualism remained (Pinkard, 2000, p. 339). But Kant's position provoked a massive controversy in which Hegel played a decisive role. Hegel dealt with it from a radically different standpoint, and this transformed the terms in which it can be posed. In contrast to Kant, he rejected the categorical separation of subject and object, thereby opening a philosophical space within which the antinomies of dualism could be transcended. For Hegel (like Vygotsky) cognition is a historical process (the phenomenology of spirit),[13] and philosophy inhabits a totality of all that there is without the need for an external or posited foundation. Philosophy has no privileged starting point, nor does mind, for mind does not stand free from the matter of which it is part. Hegel started from Spinoza's conception of totality as one substance (God or Nature) of which every-thing is part, and these Spinozist roots of Hegel's philosophy were important for Vygotsky. But Hegel recognised the difficulties that the deep entrenchment of dualism created for this approach – similar to those caused by attempting to under-stand quantum mechanics within a Newtonian paradigm. He argued that it was impossible to grasp Spinoza without a conscious effort. According to Hegel: 'When one begins to philosophise one must first be a Spinozist. The soul must bathe in the aether of this single substance, in which everything one has held for true is submerged' (Hegel, cited in Beiser, 1995, p. 5). Hegel is often associated with a kind of postmodernist caricature of an abstract, hierarchical, decontextualised reason, but this is far from the truth. When Hegel referred to Spinoza's single substance, he was not alluding to a mystical idea of an Absolute. Hegel's Absolute is perhaps better understood heuristically. This does not get things quite right, but it indicates the role that the Absolute plays in Hegel's argument, as the totality of which everything is a moment.

A difficulty which besets any reference to Hegel in developing an argument about Vygotsky's work is the general inaccuracy, and sometimes the complete distortion, that prevail in common understandings of Hegel's philosophy. Pinkard (2000) notes how most short histories of thought or encyclopaedia entries make false statements about Hegel. Furthermore, most reactions to Hegel after Marx were intermingled with reactions to Marx. Misinterpretation of Hegel is communicated to readings of Vygotsky, where the influence of Hegel is read as evidence of hierarchical conceptions of abstract reason. The idea of the Absolute is often misunderstood as an entity rather than as a way of working through certain questions.

Instead of seeing Hegel's work as a frame in which questions of the nature of mind and its relation to world are pursued, the dualist tendencies of modern thought read it as mystical and speculative. A similar fate has befallen Vygotsky. Beiser warns against mistaking the absolute for a metaphysics of the soul, for God or for Providence. He notes that for Hegel there was no need for such a specific kind of entity: '[The] absolute is not a kind of thing, but simply the whole of which all things are only parts' (Beiser, 1995, p. 5). Misunderstanding of Hegel's Absolute is an important issue here especially because it relates to the argument that will be developed in Chapter 7 below concerning the anti-foundationalist epistemology in Vygotsky's work.[14] Not only did Hegel start from a Spinozist position of one substance, which includes both thought and extension; he also went back to Aristotle and Greek philosophy, and he rejected those claims to have clarified thinking that were made by early modern philosophers such as Bacon and Descartes. Significantly, where Descartes started from the separation of thought and being, Greek thought started from their unity.

Any attempt to understand the potential in Vygotsky's ideas must recognise the nature of the philosophy informing his work. This requires an uncompromising adoption of ways of thinking that overcome the dualist afflictions to which Prawat refers. At the same time a major obstacle blocks this approach: namely, that the world we actually live in is dualist in the sense that this is the mode in which it actually presents itself. Dualist misconceptions are not superseded because the presentations are continually renewed – for example, our dualist definition of an agent. The importance of dualism in the world today can be simply illustrated by the contemporary legal system in which 'individuals' who are all different from each other are recognised as persons with the same legal rights and responsibilities. The law does not fully attend to the way that reasons impact on particular individuals' actions but rather operates according to a common standard of what a 'reasonable person' would do.

This is why the development of Vygotsky's ideas may appear impractical, except insofar as they can be translated into a dualist frame. Dualism cannot be overcome by philosophy when the real-world existence of thought is dualist (Ilyenkov, 1977; Gergen, 1999). Hegel's crucial insight that philosophy arises after the event bears directly upon the relationship between thinking and the conditions that sustain it. Thought and word are so inseparably related that thought cannot exceed the bounds of what sustains it and what expresses it.

The dualist separation of mind and world, central to Kant's investigation of the possibility of reason and knowledge, is precisely what Hegel attempted to overcome. And although Kant's later work moved towards overcoming the rigid separation of concept and intuition and of spontaneity from receptivity, dualism remained (Pinkard, 2000, p. 339). As we have seen from Bowie's comments earlier, modern philosophers working on the same dualism make the same Hegelian move to deny the stark separation of receptivity and spontaneity, arguing that receptivity is already conceptual (McDowell),[15] or that it must be understood as taking an inferential form (Brandom).[16] In the same vein, a key contribution of Vygotsky was to emphasise the way that words and concepts represent or transmit: they do not merely reflect but actually structure thought. Concepts do not follow, but in fact precede, thought. Children enter a space in which concepts already have meaning beyond their grasp. Yet the very use of a concept, within the social space in which it is sustained meaningfully, allows children's activities to become meaningful within that space.

VYGOTSKY AND HEGEL

Deriving the categories of our understanding from what he took our thought to be, Kant sought to work out what would be the conditions of our reasoning; by contrast, Hegel worked through particular claims to knowledge *on their own terms*. He argued that it was necessary to go beyond what such claims to knowledge took themselves to be and to work through what is presupposed but unexamined, hence not justified, in any particular claims. This is significantly different from the approach that posits (however rigorously) what the conditions of our knowledge must be. Hegel's approach uses the activity of thinking to mobilise thought by pushing individual thoughts to their limits.

By contrast with Kant, who may be said to have attempted to establish universal criteria for knowledge, Hegel was aware that different criteria prevailed in different periods and that what counts as knowledge depends on these criteria rather than upon a universal measure. Hegel did not, however, let matters rest in what might have been a relativist position: he argued that reflection on the nature of knowledge occurred in every period and precipitated reflection on the nature of knowing. In other words, he linked knowledge to the movement of historical conditions. Consciousness is successively faced with contradictions (or antinomies) arising out of the relation between what it takes to be its object and its knowledge of this object. Hegel himself believed that thought, given its historical nature, achieved its fulfilment in the triumph of reason as he saw it in his time and place, but for Hegel this does not entail the Enlightenment conceit of reason cut off from its origins and conditions of development. The historical nature of knowledge effects the materiality of thought, because thinking always takes place within a definite historical space. According to Hegel, the thought that Kant assumed in deriving his categories was not thought *per se*, but thought at a particular historical point, dealing with particular questions and throwing up contradictions that appeared as antinomies. For Hegel, thinking outside this space, and hence outside of history (that is, thinking in terms of abstract reason), simply does not happen.

My purpose, following Hegel, is to show that Vygotsky was committed to reason not as abstract but as historical. I want to open questions about his work which the dualist approach forecloses: what counts as reason, what counts as knowing? The contextualist positions, considered in Chapter 2 above, claim to have a criterion for knowledge that is at odds with the criterion that Vygotsky drew from Hegel. In a peculiar parallel of the same point, contextualist or perspectivist positions want to give credence to the idea that knowledge is constituted by the available means of knowing. Moreover, to confuse the issue still further, those who favour an extreme version of contextualism reject history. In this way their critique of Vygotsky as embracing abstract reason is a reflection of their own view of knowledge.

In recent years there has been an attempt to move psychology away from mentalist positions, focusing on the solitary learner, in what amounts to a 'discursive turn': this emphasises the linguistic practices, discursive activities and semiotic mediations by which activities take place, and it attaches importance also to the sociocultural contexts in which activities occur. At present, it seems strange to consider thinking a material activity. In analytic philosophy, however, where there has been some concern about the reductive logical analysis of the way that language – and specifically sentences – picture the world, there has been a move away from mentalism and internalism, and towards externalism. The linguistic turn prompted by Wittgenstein precipitated a move away from mentalist conceptions of thinking. In the light of this, Harré and Gillet cite Wittgenstein to express what has become a prominent point of view: 'It is misleading then to talk of thinking as mental activity. We may say that thinking is essentially the activity of operating with signs' (Wittgenstein, cited in Harré and Gillet, 1994, p. 50). Explaining thinking in terms of an activity using signs can be only a small step, however, towards an alternative to the internalist and mentalist model of mind (see Chapter 3 above).

While Vygotsky is interested in the role of signs he resists any simple conception of signs as representations. Representations (scientific concepts) arise, on his view, neither because they reflect a world that exists independently of human thought, nor because they construct the world in their own image. Rather they arise through the continual reciprocity between the constitution of ideas through activity and their successive re-formation in thought. In 'The Historical Meaning of the Crisis in Psychology' (Vygotsky, 1997, pp. 233–243), Vygotsky expounds this dynamic view of knowledge. In this exposition, knowledge formation takes the form of a cycle moving from a vital phase of early development to one of stagnation as its maturity changes its position vis-à-vis its own development.

Bakhurst writes that 'for Vygotsky, the identity of psychology as a science depended on the degree to which it contributed to the transformation of the object it investigates. Its tasks were not simply to mirror reality but to harness it' (cited in

Daniels, 1996, p. 24). In other words, Vygotsky's conception of knowledge cannot be reduced to a representationalist one, grounded in what Hegel, in his discussion of the Understanding, relegated to the unconditioned universal. By contrast, Wertsch argues that Vygotsky had a commitment to universal human rationality as the *telos* of development and that this is 'reflected in his claims about how increasing levels of abstraction and generalisation attach to "genuine" and "scientific" concepts' (Wertsch, 1996, p. 25). The problem here concerns what scientific concepts are taken to be. For example, Wertsch refers to scientific concepts as taking a propositional form: as purported representations of a demonstrated truth. This more common-sense representationalist understanding of scientific concepts differs from the inferential form proposed by Robert Brandom. This distinction between representationalism and inferentialism is significant since the cogency and validity of critique of both abstract rationality and, at the extreme, rationality *per se* turn upon the particular understanding of the role that concepts play within science and other domains (see Chapter 7 below).

Wertsch overlooks the possibility that the abstraction and generalisation to which Vygotsky refers are not artificial moves made by the mind. In other words, Wertsch misses the point: Vygotsky does *not* work in a Cartesian framework that claims to capture an unconditioned universal. For Hegel (and, following him, Vygotsky) the understanding of the universal is an integral development of one substance of which thought and extension are parts. To examine the logic of an argument that rejects dualist premises, it is helpful to grasp Hegel's critique of what he called the 'Understanding'. The Understanding could stand as an example of the common conception of knowledge. In the *Encyclopedia*, Hegel describes the characteristics of the metaphysical thinking (with which he takes issue) found in philosophers who assume that the true nature of things is knowable through thought alone. He comments that this is also the way 'in which *mere understanding views* the objects of reason' (Houlgate, 1998, p. 7). Hegel also criticised the Understanding in the *Phenomenology* when he advanced a radically different way of conceiving what it is to be human, to possess mind and to exercise free will. In Vygotsky's writings also it is possible to discern this radically different way of conceiving mind and will, as was considered in the discussion of Spinoza in the previous chapter. Hegel's critique will be considered more closely later. For the moment it can be noted that Hegel's critique of the Understanding was important to Marx, and that the use that Marx made of it reinforced its importance for Vygotsky. In the *Economic and Philosophic Manuscripts* Marx demonstrated his roots in Hegel when he wrote: 'The great thing in Hegel's Phenomenology and its final result … is simply that Hegel grasps the self-development of man as process … that he thus grasps the nature of work and comprehends objective man … as the result of his own work … he grasps labor … as man's act of self-creation' (Marx, cited in Wood, 1988, pp. 67–75). The idea that human beings and their higher mental functions are an ongoing creation of their own activity immediately places thought on a different footing. The radical break that Hegel made with dualism, and the space he opened for an investigation of mind that resists a cognitivist or mentalist approach, is credited by numerous thinkers:

In the view of T. W. Adorno, Hegel challenged the naive, positivistic belief that experience renders 'something immediately present ... free, as it were, of any admixture of thought', and showed that there is in fact nothing in our experience that is not mediated in some way by reflection and understanding. In the view of Charles Taylor, Hegel's achievement is to have undermined the idea that human consciousness can be understood in the abstract and to have insisted that we situate subjectivity by relating it to our life as embodied and social beings. (Houlgate, 1998, p. 3)

In the *Phenomenology*, Hegel worked through the problems of what it is to know by examining different forms of historical consciousness. This is not, however, a simple examination but the realisation of an ontological logic, where each successive moment arises out of the partiality of the previous one. Hegel was concerned with different forms of consciousness not in terms of simple comparisons but as moments in a process of development, through which successive forms arise out of the inadequacies and one-sidedness of those that precede them.

Whereas the problem of knowledge – how we can claim to have knowledge and on what basis – was previously a matter of epistemology, Hegel turned knowledge into a matter of ontology. 'Ontology', in his thought, refers to the actual movement of being rather than to the analysis separately of the objects of understanding on the part of a subject. Hegel subsumed these separate analyses into the actual process of the development of thought. This development is neither a simple comparison nor a simple linear progression. Each form of thought is taken as the thought of a real age, and the movement from one form to the next is precipitated by the inadequacy of a particular form to grasp what it has set itself to grasp. To see this schematically as a simple, inevitable process of development does not do justice to the richness of the original conception. Or, it might be said in passing, a simple understanding that claims that all forms of thought that exist at this moment are somehow equal to all others does not do justice to the complexities of the contemporary world.

Hegel praises Kant for beginning the move to ontology by dealing with knowing as a logic. But at the same time he criticises Kant for assuming the categories rather than deriving them from thought itself as the necessary outcome of self-reflection. Unlike Kant, Hegel was concerned not with the foundations that might be discerned as the basis of any knowledge, but with the actual process through which these foundations were laid in the process of the development of thought itself. As Houlgate puts it:

> Hegel understands his logical study of categories to be also an ontology in the strongest possible sense. Hegel agrees with Kant that our categories contain the meaning and structure of objectivity; but against Kant, he thinks the categories contain the structure not just of objectivity *for us*, but objectivity *as such* ... not just the objective structure of *our* world but the objective structure of being itself ... Hegel's post-Kantian examination of what it is to *think* ... is thus ... a pre-Kantian, quasi-Spinozan examination of what it is to *be*. He proceeds through Kant to his new 'Spinozism'. (Houlgate, 1998, p. 12)

Hegel argued that Kant's 'thing-in-itself' could be understood only as an abstraction. As explained in Chapter 5, his Spinozism entailed a radically different understanding of what had previously stood as epistemology. The representative relation of an appearance standing in place of a reality was at odds with the idea of one substance (the Absolute). Instead, and in accord with a Spinozist conception of truth, the real is what has been fully actualised rather than what is merely existent as one-sidedness and not fully actual. A specific peculiarity of Hegel's approach is that it takes the appearance of a thing as an expression and not as a disguise. According to Houlgate again:

> Hegel's derivation of the categories in the Logic proves Kant's conception of the thing in itself to be an abstraction, by demonstrating that what something is in itself has actually to be conceived as inseparable from its relations to other things and the way it appears ... there is in fact no good reason to contrast the appearance of a thing with what it is in itself, as Kant does. Appearance, rather, must be understood as manifesting what the thing is in itself. And experience thus must be understood as experience of what there ultimately is. (Houlgate, 1998, p. 13)

Sometimes the difference between Hegel's thought and the thought of the Enlightenment is posed as one between empiricism and speculation, each of which can, with wanton exaggeration, be simply opposed to the other, in what is in effect a meaningless caricature. Thus empiricism is characterised as an almost mindless recounting of fact, and contemplation as thought totally separate from any object. Rockmore (1993) implicitly attacks this polarity by distinguishing different forms of empiricism, arguing that, although Hegel criticises sense-certainty for its one-sidedness, he can himself be seen as an empiricist insofar as he held to the general position that knowledge comes from our experience.

Many confusions result from the oversimplification of philosophical labels. The philosophical position of empiricism – that nothing can be known independently of experience – is taken in such diverse ways that the term loses meaning. The reading of Hegel as a mystical thinker would find it hard to conceive of Hegel as an empiricist. Yet in his anti-foundationalism, he shares with Quine (a renowned empiricist) the position that a merely analytical resolution of epistemology – how we can claim knowledge – is mistaken. Knowledge ultimately emerges world-historically. The separation of knowing from what is to be known has led to paths in philosophy that have thrown up antinomies, and these in turn reveal those paths to be dead ends. Quine's classic 'Two Dogmas of Empiricism' exposes the failure of the Kantian separation of analytic and synthetic statements – the claim that some statements are true by definition and others true as matters of fact. Quine questions whether anything is ever a priori. In relation to Quine's discussion of empiricism, it must be noted that the distinctive feature of Hegel's empiricism is its ontological character. For Hegel all theory, even 'common or garden' sense-certainty, already belongs to historical forms of thought and is, therefore, ontological in the sense of belonging to being in one or other of its various historical moments.

Empiricism, which Hegel calls sense-certainty, sees experience as the cause of knowledge and the senses as the means for acquiring such knowledge insofar as our representations coincide with the object that they purport to represent. For Vygotsky, following Hegel, the process of acquiring knowledge is reversed. What is commonly called a correspondence theory of knowledge is rejected,[17] and eventually what come to be our representations arise over a long process of development during which they are at no point separate from their process of coming-to-be. Under the influence of Hegel, Vygotsky is bound to reject the representationalist view of knowledge, which presupposes a terminus where knowledge is complete. When discussing word meaning, for example, Vygotsky notes that, when a word is first learnt, the process of the development of its meaning has only just begun. Words are used in a rough-and-ready way to perform particular jobs, and in the context of their use and reception their meaning is expanded and deepened.

Hegel's peculiar conception of how our representations arise and relate to the world is clear in his arguments about the requirements of science. As regards these requirements, Hegel certainly made clear what was *not* necessary: (1) the type of knowledge claimed for by the Understanding; (2) the assumption of a Given (what Sellars calls the Myth of the Given) against which the validity of our knowledge claims may be assessed; (3) any idea that cognition exercises certain categories that allow it to relate to an assumed Given; and (4) the idea of a fixed subject and fixed object separated by a void. He puts it as follows:

> Now in order to raise oneself to the standpoint of Science one must give up the presuppositions [*Voraussetzungen*] which are contained in the already mentioned subjective and finite modes of philosophical cognition: (1) the presupposition of the firm validity of limited and opposed determinations in general, of the Understanding in general; (2) the presuppositions of a given, represented, already complete substratum, which is supposed to be a standard for determining whether one of those thought-determinations is adequate to it or not, (3) the presupposition of cognition as merely relating of such ready and fixed predicates to some substratum or other, (4) the presupposition of the opposition between cognising subject and its object, which cannot be united with it – each side of which opposition is supposed once again, as in the case of the opposition just mentioned, to be independently [*für sich*] something fixed and true. (Hegel, *Encyclopedia*, par. 35, cited in Forster, 1998, p. 635)

This rejection of presuppositions informs his critique of Kant:

> The demand which has become customary through the Kantian philosophy, that before actual cognition the cognitive faculty be subject to critical investigation, appears plausible at first sight. However, this investigation is itself cognition; that it should be performed without cognition is senseless. Moreover, even the assumption of a cognitive faculty before actual cognition is a presupposition both of the unjustified category or determination of faculty or power and of subjective cognition. (Hegel, *Encyclopedia*, par. 26, cited in Forster, 1998, p. 635)

Hegel's philosophy can be distinguished from Kant's, and indeed from all other philosophies, by its starting point. For instance, in contrast to Kant, whose approach to the question of knowing is logical, Hegel takes an ontological position and starts his philosophising from what we take ourselves to be doing in knowing. He then works through the implicit 'takings' that, once expressed, lead beyond the original claim. The pertinent point is that rather than starting from a position that tries to determine what consciousness must consist in if it is to 'know', he starts from the forms of consciousness themselves and takes seriously what each of their claims to know comprises. By doing so and by examining what is authoritative in each claim to know, Hegel shows that: (1) more is claimed than at first sight would appear to be the case; (2) each claim, when fully considered, undermines itself and generates within its own terms a further form of consciousness; and (3) this further form of consciousness retains implicit elements that are exorcised once what is claimed is made explicit.

In the *Phenomenology*, Hegel traces the movement of reason through different forms: reason where the subject apprehends the world as it is; reason that involves tools or categories for getting to grips with how the world is; and reason that knows the world of objects in their existence for its own purposes.

He starts his examination of the forms that consciousness takes with sense-certainty and shows how once we reflect upon what this means – knowledge arising in our senses from a direct effect of experience – it becomes clear that there is more to it than first appears: to recognise an object is immediately to place it within a system. Thus sense-certainty is not quite what it claims to be for itself. Something further is required for acceptance of even the barest claim resulting directly from impingement on our senses. Sense-certainty claims for itself a knowledge of the world that is immediate – that is, a singularity that does not depend on any contribution from us in order to count as knowledge. Once this claim is fully expressed it undermines itself when it becomes apparent that this is inferential knowledge rather than noninferential. It is in fact not immediate but mediated. What are required are complexes of individual things – a system, not merely a singular object. This system Hegel calls 'perception', where the truth of what seemed to be immediate being is not given immediately to the senses but rather perceived by the mind. Here consciousness is distinguished into subjective and objective aspects. No longer do the two coincide. Instead the question arises of the difference between the individual's perception and the object itself, the distinction of appearance from reality. Terry Pinkard, explaining the development of mind – which he terms 'the sociality of reason' – in Hegel's *Phenomenology*, explains the issues as follows:

> The subject ... originally understood himself purely as apprehending subject, someone who stood in relation of acquaintance with the objects of knowledge. The guiding metaphor is that of the subject viewing the object. With the collapse of that idea, however, an alternative picture of the subject has emerged – namely that of a practical, living subject who deals with objects in terms of his cognitive capacities and for whom his concepts are more like tools with which he can deal with his environment. (Pinkard, 1996, p. 48)

Hegel's working through of claims to know takes us to a very different position from which to consider what it is to experience or to know. As Pinkard writes:

> To see the subject as part of life is to see the object of knowledge not as being like the kind of metaphysically construed objects of 'sense-certainty' or 'perception' that we can only apprehend; it is rather to see how these objects fit into the demands of the life of the subject himself – that is, into his various practical projects. (Pinkard, 1996, p. 49)

The important point here is that the world is not given to us, nor is it simply apprehended through categories; rather, it comes to us through our own purposes and intents coming to expression or realisation: 'Our conceptualising activities are not to be construed on the model of our apprehending objects; knowing something is construed instead as a form of acting. The agent has various desires that demand satisfaction, and his conceptualising activities are tools for the satisfaction of those desires' (Pinkard, 1996, p. 49).

What may appear to be an esoteric discussion in philosophy about epistemology, or what is actually, in the case of Hegel's account, a detailed and rigorous investigation of the appearances (phenomenology) of consciousness, has in fact direct implications for the work of Vygotsky. Vygotsky draws explicitly on the Hegelian dialectic in his work on the education of children with special needs. Writing in 1931, he takes issue with the pedagogue of the blind who attempts to replace vision with 'visual images' through other senses (e.g. touch) without understanding the nature of perception. He describes a famous tale used by A. A. Potebnia to show that a single generalisation is not knowledge: 'The blind man asks a series of questions which lead to an infinite regress "What is milk like?" – "It is white." – "What is white?" – "Like a goose." – "And what is a goose like?" – "It is like my elbow." The blind man felt the guide's elbow and said, "Now I know what milk is like!"' (Vygotsky, 1993, p. 203). Following Hegel, Vygotsky's argument is that perception and representation are not the sphere of compensation for the effects of blindness: 'compensation occurs not in the realm of elementary functions but in the sphere of concepts' (Vygotsky, 1993, p. 203). Given that much of contemporary educational practice is still conducted on the basis of assumptions about what Hegel called sense-certainty and perception, and without appreciating that more is involved even at what appears to be this elementary level of 'knowing', this is a crucial point.[18]

Arguing that knowledge is not based on sense impressions or on what we perceive, but instead arises in thought, Vygotsky insists that the lack of a sense changes nothing in human cognition and thought:

> both the blind man and the seeing man, in principle, know much more than they can imagine; they know more than they can absorb with the help of their five senses. If we really knew as much as we can absorb directly though our five senses, then not a single science (in the true sense of that word) would be possible. (Vygotsky, 1993, p. 203)

Emphasising the counterintuitive character of science and following a Hegelian line of thinking, he goes on to argue:

> For the links, dependencies, and relationships among things which are the content of our scientific knowledge are not the visually perceivable qualities of things; rather, they come to light through thought. This is also the way it works for the blind child. Thought is the basic area in which he compensates for the inadequacy of his visual perceptions. (Vygotsky, 1993, p. 203)

This comprehension of the character of thought is drawn from Vygotsky's understanding of Hegel and the social nature of mind. Vygotsky recounts how in formal logic:

> a concept is nothing other than a general representation ... [There is an] inverse proportionality between the extent and the content of the concept. The path to generalisation is thus a path which leads away from the riches of concrete reality toward the world of concepts, the kingdom of empty abstraction, far from living life and from living knowledge. (Vygotsky, 1993, pp. 204–205)

Vygotsky maintains that in dialectical logic it is quite the opposite:

> A concept seems richer in content than does a presentation. Thus the path to generalisation is not a path formally divided into separate indications. Rather, it is an uncovering of the links of the relationship of a given matter with another. If the subject becomes truly intelligible, not through immediate experience, but in all the many links and relationships which define its place in the world and its connection to the rest of reality, then one's understanding is a deeper, more real, truer and more complete reflection than the envisaged one. (Vygotsky 1993, p. 205)

This argument made in relation to his discussion of the education of the blind is surely sufficient to indicate that the criticism of Vygotsky as an abstract rationalist is unfounded.

Ilyenkov worked in the same philosophical tradition. He was a significant figure in the Mescheryakov experiment, which achieved results that challenged the empiricist version of knowledge (see Bakhurst and Padden, 1991). Mescheryakov's work, which showed how children deprived of sight and hearing could reach high levels of intellectual development, lent support to the Vygotskian idea that intellect 'is formed under the influence of society, through tools, speech and rules of behaviour' (Levitin, 1982, p. 216). An important conclusion reached by Mescheryakov and Ilyenkov was that knowing is not dependent on the senses as understood by empiricism, but arises in a *humanised* environment. Levitin tells how, in his booklet *Learn to Think from Youth*, Ilyenkov came to write:

> When Mescheryakov's four pupils kept a packed audience of hundreds of students and teachers enthralled for three hours, one of the many notes from the

audience read, 'Doesn't your experiment refute the old truth of materialism whereby there is nothing in the mind that wasn't first in sensations? They don't see or hear anything, but they understand everything better than we do.' I conveyed that question, letter by letter, through the finger (tactile) alphabet to Sasha Suvorov. I was sure he could answer it better than me. And indeed, Sasha replied promptly and clearly, speaking into the microphone: 'Who told you that we don't see or hear anything? We see and hear with the eyes of all our friends, all people, the whole human race'. (Levitin, 1982, pp. 216–217)

Ilyenkov uses the example of Meshcheryakov's four pupils to illustrate the significance of the 'humanised environment' of 'objectivised human capacities' that we inhabit. This environment extends to material objects, codes of behaviour and the ordering of life in time and space. The possibility of the experience of sensing for the blind or deaf child arises not by a mind directly interacting with a world but by a mind that is immediately social.

Bakhurst judges Ilyenkov's work to have major significance in revealing the way in which traditional questions of knowledge have been circumscribed:

> No doubt we should grant Ilyenkov that considerations about the nature of our 'humanized' environment must figure in any remotely adequate account of the human condition and the powers of our mind and language. This is something much philosophy, particularly of the analytic stripe, has failed to appreciate, relegating such considerations to the contingent context of thought and language, rather than the very medium of the mental. (Bakhurst, 1997, p. 39)

These limitations of analytic philosophy and the recent Hegelian turn within it suggest a connection between, on the one hand, Vygotsky and Ilyenkov and, on the other, contemporary philosophers such as McDowell and Brandom.

Hegel's historical location, associated – like that of Marx – with the failures of what has been seen as a political project of Enlightenment rationality, has compromised the reception of his work. Where his significance as a philosopher has been doubted, his influence on Vygotsky has been seen in a more negative light – that is, as evidence of an atavistic commitment to a concept of reason that stands above context, summoning to its own end all multiplicity and variety. In fact, as we have seen, Hegel was the greatest critic of abstract rationality. It is nonetheless something of a paradox that Hegelianism should find a renaissance in the tradition of analytical philosophy, a tradition so much at odds with his form of philosophising.[19] Given the popular caricature of Hegel, it is not surprising that he should be associated with the idea of an abstract rationality, nor that this should come to be seen as the hallmark of poor educational practice, nor that Vygotsky should be tarred with the same brush. McDowell's 'Hegelian' claim that receptivity is already conceptual involves a conception of 'reason' fundamentally different from what Wertsch quite correctly takes to task – that is, an extreme version of a decontextualised schooled knowledge, presented without regard to its genetic development, ignoring all sense of learning as the actualisation of concepts.[20] But, if the argument of this chapter is sound, this is a world apart from Vygotsky.

Chapter 7 continues the efforts of this book to establish sufficient links with Hegel's philosophical approach to sustain the argument that Vygotsky's concept of rationality did not conform to the version of Enlightenment thought found in contemporary accounts of his work.

NOTES

1 Kant's transcendental idealism maintains, for example, that spatial features are not qualities of things in themselves but objects of our representations: 'If the object (the triangle) were something in itself, apart from any relation to you, the subject, how could you say what necessarily exist in you as subjective conditions for the construction of a triangle must of necessity belong to the triangle itself?' (Kant, *Critique of Pure Reason*, A48/B65).

2 The active transformation of the world creates the possibility of mind/consciousness, which is not pregiven.

3 'Kant defines representations as "inner determinations of our mind in this or that relation of time" ([*Critique of Pure Reason*] A197/B 242) ... [He] argued that sensibility and its sensations were "the appearance of something and the mode in which they are affected by that something" (A44/B51). [subjective perception] ... Objective perception is further divided into intuition and concept, the former relating "immediately to the object and is single [while] the latter refers to it mediately by means of a feature which several things may have in common" (CPR A320/B377). Both are produced in an "act of spontaneity" with intuition being "given prior to all thought" (B132) but while the intuition provides a field within which the manifold of intuition may appear as a representation, it is the concept which synthesises these representations into experience and knowledge' (Caygill, 1995, p. 355).

4 The characterisation of Kant as being a representationalist thinker is open to serious questioning. For instance, Rorty takes Kant as an inferentialist as opposed to Descartes, on the grounds that Descartes took 'concepts to be representations (or putative representations) of reality rather than, as Kant did, rules that specify how something is to be done. Kant's fundamental insight, Brandom [1994] says, "is that judgements and actions are to be understood to begin with in terms of the special way in which we are *responsible* for them"' (Rorty, 1997, p. 9).

5 In one way Smith's insight is correct in that he has recognised that Vygotsky's work invokes a social Platonism that can also be found in McDowell's argument concerning the space of reasons and its existence in the world rather than in a purely ideal realm.

6 Knowledge is a priori if it is knowable without recourse to experience.

7 Houlgate notes how Kant's 'Copernican revolution' aimed to justify rather than just take for granted the assumption that a priori concepts tell us about things. 'Kant wrote in the preface to the second edition (1787) *Critique of Pure Reason* that "it has been assumed that all our knowledge must conform to objects. But all attempts to extend our knowledge of objects ... *a priori* by means of concepts, have on this assumption, ended in failure. We must therefore make trial whether we may not have more success in the task of metaphysics, if we suppose that objects must conform to our knowledge"' (Houlgate, 1998, p. 8).

8 Copernicus improved on Ptolemy's explanation of the motion of heavenly bodies by referring to the observer's own motion rather than attributing motion solely to the bodies themselves. Kant explained many of the features of objects by referring to the characteristics of the observer rather than to those of the objects themselves (Van Cleve, 1994).

9 According to Kant: 'If intuition must conform to the constitution of objects, I do not see how we can know anything of the latter *a priori*; but if the object (as object of the senses) must conform to our faculty of intuition, I have no difficult in conceiving such possibility' (Kant, *Critique of Pure Reason*, B.xvii).

10 Kant defines receptivity, intuition, spontaneity and the understanding in the following way: 'If the *receptivity* of our mind, its power of receiving representations in so far as it is in any

wise affected, is to be entitled sensibility, then the mind's power of producing representations from itself, the *spontaneity* of knowledge, should be called the understanding. Our nature is so constituted that our *intuition* can never be other than sensible; that is, it contains only the mode in which we are affected by objects. The faculty, on the other hand, which enables us to *think* the object of sensible intuition is the understanding' (Kant, *Critique of Pure Reason*, B75, A51).

11 Pinkard relates how Hegel originally called the *Phenomenology of Spirit*, the *Science of the Experience of Consciousness* but changed his mind during negotiations with the printer (Pinkard, 1996, p. 1).

12 Rorty comments on the Hegelian character of the work of his former research student Robert Brandom as follows: '[Wilfrid Sellars] described [his project] as an attempt to usher analytic philosophy out of its Humean and into its Kantian stage ... Brandom's work can usefully be seen as an attempt to usher philosophy from its Kantian to its Hegelian stage – an attempt foreshadowed in Sellars's wry description of "Empiricism and the Philosophy of Mind" as "incipient *Meditations Hegeliennes*" and his reference to Hegel as "that great foe of immediacy"' (Rorty, 1997, pp. 8–9).

13 Although Hegel's work bears the title *Phenomenology of Spirit*, laying it open to the belief that it is a mystical work, Pinkard has aptly subtitled his reading of the *Phenomenology*, 'The Sociality of Reason'. While Hegel was teaching his work to high school pupils he characterised it in his dictation notes as 'a study of "modes of consciousness, knowing (*Wissens*) and cognizing (*Erkennens*)"' (Pinkard, 2000, p. 333). See also Stewart (1996).

14 While a rejection of pregiven foundations cannot lead to any foundationalist concept of knowledge in itself, when linked to a notion of totality it is perfectly consistent with a foundationalist position construed as one in which the foundations do not come in advance but are part of the process of the unfolding of being.

15 Receptivity is already conceptual in the sense that it occupies a conceptual sphere.

16 Brandom explains how the interrogation of the assumptions of empiricism has led to an appreciation of a more rationalist way of thinking (i.e. where the conceptual is not separated from the empirical): 'Classical empiricist philosophy of mind takes immediate perceptual experiences as the paradigm of awareness or consciousness. Classical empiricist epistemology takes as its paradigm those same experiences, to which it traces the warrant for and the authority of all the rest. As the tradition has developed it has become clearer that both rest on a more or less semantic picture, according to which the concept of experience, awareness, and knowledge is understood in the first instance in *representational* terms: as a matter of what is (or purports to be) represented by some representing states or episodes. ... Empiricism attempts to understand the content of concepts in terms of the origin of empirical beliefs in experience that we just find ourselves with, and the origin of practical intentions in desires or preferences that in the most basic case we just find ourselves with.' According to Brandom, Sellars was motivated by a classically rationalist thought that 'what was needed was a functional theory of concepts which would make their role in reasoning, rather than their supposed origin in experience, their primary feature' (Brandom, 2000, pp. 24–25).

17 It should be noted that Hegel can be called a correspondence theorist but that, for Hegel, correspondence arises only on the completion of a process and this is at odds with the more familiar usage in philosophy (Harris, 1994).

18 Bruner (1996) refers to these misconceptions as the general folk psychologies underlying teacher practice.

19 R. J. Bernstein suggests that John McDowell's 'analytic' and former Oxford colleagues must have thought McDowell's reference to Hegel, informing his work *Mind and World*, a joke. For 'Hegel is a philosopher that few "analytic" philosophers have taken seriously (or even read) – a philosopher typically held up for ridicule, as someone who epitomizes the intellectual vices that "analytic" philosophers have sought to overcome' (Bernstein, 2002, p. 9).

20 Although I have called this McDowell's *Hegelian* claim, McDowell exploits Kant's terminology to make his case of the unboundedness of the conceptual. He clarifies that in answer to the

question: 'Does Kant credit receptivity with a separable contribution to its cooperation with spontaneity?' it is possible to answer in both the affirmative and the negative. However, it is possible to take from Kant's conception of experience that 'reality is not located outside a boundary that encloses the conceptual sphere' (McDowell, 1996, p. 41).

REFERENCES

Bakhurst, D. (1997) Meaning, Normativity and the Life of the Mind, *Language and Communication*, 17:1, 33–51.

Bakhurst, D. and Padden, C. (1991) The Meschcheryakov Experiment: Soviet Work on the Education of Blind-Deaf Children, *Learning and Instruction*, 1, 201–215.

Beiser, F.C. (ed.) (1995) *The Cambridge Companion to Hegel* (Cambridge: Cambridge University Press).

Bernstein, J.M. (2002) Re-enchanting Nature. In: N.H. Smith (ed.) *Reading McDowell on Mind and World* (London: Routledge), pp. 217–245.

Bird, G. (1996) McDowell's Kant: Mind and World, *Philosophy*, 71, 219–243.

Bowie, A. (ed.) (1998) Introduction. In *Schleiermacher: Hermeneutics and Criticism and Other Writings* (Cambridge: Cambridge University Press), pp. vii–xxxi.

Brandom, R. (1994) *Making it Explicit: Reasoning, Representing, and Discursive Commitment* (Cambridge, MA: Harvard University Press).

Brandom, R. (2000) *Articulating Reasons: An Introduction to Inferentialism* (Cambridge, MA: Harvard University Press).

Brockmeier, J. (1996) Construction and Interpretation: Exploring a Joint Perspective on Piaget and Vygotsky. In: A. Tryphon and J.N. Vonèche (eds) *Piaget – Vygotsky: The Social Genesis of Thought* (Hove: Psychology Press), pp. 125–143.

Bruner, J.S. (1996) *The Culture of Education* (Cambridge, MA: Harvard University Press).

Caygill, H. (1995) *A Kant Dictionary* (Oxford: Blackwell).

Daniels, H. (ed.) (1996) *Introduction to Vygotsky* (London: Routledge).

Forster, M.N. (1998) *Hegel's Idea of a Phenomenology of Spirit* (Chicago: University of Chicago Press).

Gergen, K.J. (1999) *An Invitation to Social Construction* (London: Sage).

Harré, R. and Gillet, G. (1994) *The Discursive Mind* (London: Sage).

Harris, H.S. (1994) Hegel's Correspondence Theory of Truth, *Bulletin of the Hegel Society of Great Britain*, 29, 1–13.

Houlgate, S. (ed.) (1998) *The Hegel Reader* (Oxford, UK: Blackwell).

Ilyenkov, E.V. (1977) The Concept of the Ideal. In: *Philosophy in the USSR: Problems of Dialectical Materialism* (Moscow: Progress Publishers), pp. 71–99.

Kant, I. (1973) *Critique of Pure Reason*, N. Kemp Smith trans. (London: Macmillan).

Levitin, K. (1982) *One Is Not Born a Personality: Profiles of Soviet Education Psychologists*, Y. Fillipov trans. (Moscow: Progress Publishers).

McDowell, J. (1996) *Mind and World* (Cambridge, MA: Harvard University Press).

Piaget, J. (1995) *Sociological Studies*, L. Smith ed. (London: Routledge)

Pinkard (1996) *Hegel's Phenomenology: The Sociality of Reason* (Cambridge: Cambridge University Press).

Pinkard (2000) *Hegel: A Biography* (Cambridge: Cambridge University Press).

Pippin, R. (1997) *Idealism as Modernism: Hegelian Variations* (Cambridge: Cambridge University Press).

Prawat, R.S. (1999) Cognitive Theory at the Crossroads: Head Fitting, Head Splitting, or Somewhere in Between?, *Human Development*, 42:2, 59–77.

Quine, W.V. ([1951] 2001) Two Dogmas of Empiricism. In: A.P. Martinich and D. Sosa (eds) *Analytic Philosophy: An Anthology* (Oxford: Blackwell), pp. 450–462.

Rockmore, T. (1993) *Before and After Hegel: A Historical Introduction to Hegel's Thought* (Berkeley: University of California Press).

Rorty, R. (1997) Introduction. In: W. Sellars *Empiricism and the Philosophy of Mind* (Cambridge, MA: Harvard University Press), pp. 1–12.

Sedgwick, S. (1997) McDowell's Hegelianism, *European Journal of Philosophy*, 5, 21–38.

Sedgwick, S. (2012) *Hegel's Critique of Kant: From Dichotomy to Identity* (New York: Oxford University Press).

Smith, L. (1996) The Social Construction of Rational Understanding. In: A. Tryphon and J.N. Vonèche (eds) *Piaget – Vygotsky: The Social Genesis of Thought* (Hove: Psychology Press), pp. 107–123.

Stewart, J. (ed.) (1996) *The Hegel Myths and Legends* (Evanston, IL: Northwestern University Press).

Van Cleve, J. (1994) Kant. In: J. Dancy and E. Sosa (eds) *A Companion to Epistemology* (Oxford: Blackwell).

Vygotsky, L.S. (1993) *The Collected Works of L. S. Vygotsky, Volume 2, The Fundamentals of Defectology (Abnormal Psychology and Learning Disabilities)*, J. Knox trans., R.W. Reiber and A.S. Carton eds (London: Plenum Publishers).

Vygotsky, L.S. (1997) *The Collected Works of L. S. Vygotsky, Volume 3, Problems of the Theory and History of Psychology*, R. Van der Veer trans., R.W. Reiber and J. Wollock eds (New York: Plenum Press).

Wertsch, J. (1996) The Role of Abstract Rationality in Vygotsky's Image of Mind. In: A. Tryphon and J.N. Vonèche (eds) *Piaget – Vygotsky: The Social Genesis of Thought* (Hove: Psychology Press), pp. 25–42.

Wood, A. W. (ed.) (1988) *Marx: Selections* (New York: Macmillan).

7
Vygotsky, Hegel and Education

Previous chapters have examined the philosophical background of Vygotsky's work in order to show that his notion of reason was far more sophisticated than the expression 'Enlightenment rationality' suggests. This chapter considers four areas in the differences between Vygotsky's concept of reason and 'Enlightenment rationality' in its familiar characterisation. These areas cover: (1) foundationalism and anti-foundationalism, (2) the conception of science, (3) the conception of development and (4) idealism and materialism. The last is developed more by Ilyenkov, although, given its Hegelian and Spinozist provenance, it can be reasonably interpreted as part of the general direction of Vygotsky's work.

These areas are treated here as though they were separate, but this is only for ease of exposition. In point of fact, they are not simply interrelated but are facets of a totality. Since demonstrating this point would require a longer excursion into Hegel than is possible here, suffice it to say that questions concerning rationality and questions concerning starting points – whether conceived as foundations or data – are really part and parcel of one another.

FOUNDATIONALISM AND ANTI-FOUNDATIONALISM

Although abstract rationality tends not to be considered in terms of foundationalism and anti-foundationalism, it *is* helpful to bring these issues together: they interconnect with those other aspects of the critique of rationality that favour multiple 'knowledges' as an alternative to what is taken to be the logocentrism of rationality.

In characterisations of postmodernist thought, foundationalism and anti-foundationalism are posited as a simple opposition: on the one side, foundationalism as a denial of human creativity; on the other, anti-foundationalism as recognition of infinite variety and creativity. However, two problems arise with this opposition: first, anti-foundationalism conceived as a simple opposite does not eradicate all the

Vygotsky Philosophy and Education, First Edition. Jan Derry.
© 2013 Jan Derry. Editorial organisation © Philosophy of Education Society of Great Britain.
Published 2013 by John Wiley & Sons, Ltd.

elements of foundationalism; and second, rejecting foundationalism and advocating anti-foundationalism as its alternative does not imply free human creativity to the extent that postmodernists imagine. As already suggested, underlying the criticism of abstract rationality is an untheorised conception of freedom. While foundationalism is understood as a denial of human creativity and a representative of logocentric rationality, anti-foundationalism is promoted as allowing space for infinite human variety and creativity: such is the position of postmodernists such as Gergen. But what is missing from this conception of anti-foundationalism is the possibility of material constraints on our thinking imposed by our cognitive activity in the world.

Foundationalism and anti-foundationalism are concerned with the way in which knowledge is obtained. The one starts from the secure ground of what is known to be certain and builds upon it; the other denies the existence of such a secure starting point. But this direct opposition has not been universally accepted, and Hegel rejected it out of hand. Although Vygotsky is explicit about the importance of Hegel for his work, Wertsch takes it for granted that Vygotsky is a foundationalist in the sense of operating with presuppositions to the effect that the nature of knowledge is given in advance of any activity and that development is determined teleologically. Wertsch argues repeatedly (Wertsch, 1991, 1996, 2000) that Vygotsky has a deep philosophical commitment to Enlightenment traditions of abstract rationality and that, with colleagues involved in 'the first grand socialist experiment in the form of the Soviet Union', he shared 'a belief in some form of universal rationality and a belief in the possibility of progress towards such rationality' (Wertsch, 2000, p. 22). Similarly, in their introduction to the *Cambridge Companion to Vygotsky*, the editors reiterate this claim, suggesting that 'an important starting point [of a productive reading of Vygotsky] … is that he was an "ambivalent Enlightenment rationalist" … deeply committed to the kind of abstract reasoning … that would be a credit to the strongest advocate of the Enlightenment' (Daniels, Cole and Wertsch, 2007). Wertsch takes as evidence for this view what he believes to be the foundational assumptions underlying Chapters 5 and 6 of *Thinking and Speech*. These are the assumptions of 'referential relationships between signs and objects' and 'increasing generalization and abstraction', which together lead inevitably to the conclusion that the 'decontextualisation of mediational means' is the aim of development: 'In Vygotsky's view assumptions about meaning [in language] provide the foundation for defining human development and telos' (Wertsch, 2000, p. 22). To avoid these presuppositions, which he sees as typical of the Enlightenment conception of rationality, Wertsch emphasises local meaning-making:

> I shall argue that there are some major inconsistencies in his writings, in that he sometimes espoused abstract rationality as *telos* of development but on other occasions assumed that other forms of mental functioning occupy that role … such inconsistencies reflect a struggle between basic philosophical commitments, on the one hand, and the results of analysing complexities of human speech, on the other. (Wertsch, 1996, p. 26)

In a later work he writes that 'Vygotsky was deeply committed to Enlightenment traditions of abstract rationality'. Wertsch equates abstraction with the 'decontextualisation of mediational means': it is the semiotic potential available in abstraction (and the systematicity of interrelationship of signs), which 'yields increasingly powerful ways to categorize, reflect and control this world' (Wertsch, 2000, p. 22). This characterisation of rationality and its rejection, however, leaves the alternative position open to charges of relativism and the devaluation of knowledge.

What must be noted here is that the nature of rationality has an important bearing on the relation of theory and practice. While rationality is deemed a universal abstraction, theory is viewed as applicable to practice in such a way as to 'categorize, reflect and control the world'. It was this view of theory that was denounced by Schon (1983) when he commented on the dissonance between the swampy low-land of practice and the high ground of theory. It was Schon's comment, illustrative of the inadequacies of the competency approach to teacher education, that prompted the 'conversation' Joseph Dunne undertook with philosophers, a conversation with the aim of finding out what rationality could mean if it were *not* to be applied as a technique to achieve specified ends – the all-too-familiar contemporary aim of control through regulation and accountability.

The critique of 'the Enlightenment project', as a version of abstract reason applied to the world in an authoritarian way, has proved influential in educational research, leading many commentators to question the status of knowledge. When he criticises formal logic,[1] Vygotsky himself recognises a view of rationality as controlling and regulating at the expense of richness and diversity:

> It is completely clear that if the process of generalizing is considered as a direct result of abstraction of traits, then we will inevitably come to the conclusion that thinking in concepts is removed from reality … Others have said that concepts arise in the process of castrating reality. Concrete, diverse phenomena must lose their traits one after the other in order that a concept might be formed. Actually what arises is a dry and empty abstraction in which the diverse, full-blooded reality is impoverished by logical thought. This is the source of the celebrated words of Goethe: 'Gray is every theory and eternally green is the golden tree of life'.
> (Vygotsky, 1998, p. 53)

As his commentary on the generalisations of formal logic shows, however, Vygotsky's conception of rationality is different from any construal of 'the development of meaning [as] a matter of increasing generalisation and abstraction' (Wertsch, 2000, p. 20). In contrast to this impoverished version of reason, Vygotsky argues that:

> A real concept is an image of an objective thing in all its complexity. Only when we recognise the thing in all its connections and relations, only when this diversity is synthesised in a word, in an integral image through a multitude of determinations, do we develop a concept. According to the teaching of dialectical logic, a concept includes not only the general, but also the individual and particular.
> In contrast to contemplation, to direct knowledge of an object, a concept is filled with definitions of the object; it is the result of rational processing of our

existence and it is mediated knowledge of the object. To think of some object with the help of a concept means to include the given object in a complex system of mediating connection and relations disclosed in determinations of the concept. (Vygotsky, 1998, p. 53)

Wertsch's concern with Vygotsky's treatment of rationality centres on what he takes to be that conception of truth in which words are designative of things. Some of Vygotsky's statements do indeed look like examples of a suspiciously simple correspondence theory of truth. Statements such as those that suggest that once children have appropriated scientific concepts, they have grasped reality, would be a case in point. However, by taking such statements at face value and taking them out of their philosophical context, these readings tend to miss Vygotsky's use of a Hegelian and Spinoza-inspired conception of reason, a conception that rejects simple ideas of correspondence out of hand. Put simply, for Vygotsky a concept does not correspond to an object but enables thinking by including the object 'in a complex system of mediating connections and relations disclosed in determinations of the concept' (1998, p. 53). Unlike the caricature of abstract reason, Vygotsky's conception of reason is embedded in the historical processes involved in the genesis of concepts: 'Thus the concept does not arise from this as a mechanical result of abstraction – it is the result of a long and deep knowledge of the object. ... Psychological research is disclosing that in a concept we always have an enrichment and deepening of the content that the concept contains' (p. 54).

The link between reason and the world implied here is also at odds with the abstract caricature of reason found in popular commentary on Hegel. Previous chapters have stressed how a dualist conception survives unnoticed in the presuppositions of critiques of abstract rationality. This implicit dualism conjures up a version of rationality in which reason is so divorced from the world that it can be easily dismissed as a grandiose gesture. Yet, in fact, Hegel dismissed this version as 'the vanity of reason'. Statements such as 'what is rational is actual; and what is actual is rational' have exposed Hegel to accusations of a hierarchical, logocentric form of reason,[2] where what is known also happens to coincide with Hegel's version of events – for example, the superiority of the Prussian state. The understanding of Hegel outside Hegel scholarship and the accounts of his philosophy that have arisen from the Communist party dogma of dialectical materialism complicate matters further. In particular Hegel's anti-foundationalism has not been appreciated. Pinkard deals with the misapprehensions of Hegel in the introduction to his biography, and his remarks there are worth quoting at length:

Hegel is one of those thinkers just about all educated people think they know something about. His philosophy was the forerunner to Karl Marx's theory of history, but unlike Marx, who was a materialist, Hegel was an idealist in the sense that he thought reality was ultimately spiritual, and that it developed according to the process of thesis/antithesis/synthesis. Hegel also glorified the Prussian state, claiming that it was God's work, was perfect and was the culmination of all human history. All citizens of Prussia owed unconditional allegiance to that state, and it could do with them as it pleased. Hegel played a large role in the growth of German nationalism, authoritarianism, and militarism with his quasi-mystical celebrations of what he pretentiously called the Absolute.

Just about everything in the first paragraph is false except for the first sentence.

What is even more striking is that it is clearly and demonstrably wrong, has been known to be wrong in scholarly circles for a long time now, *and* it still appears in almost all short histories of thought or brief encyclopaedia entries about Hegel. (Pinkard, 2000, p. ix)

In Pinkard's caricature of the common conception of Hegel's philosophy, all the elements of the familiar criticisms of Vygotsky can be found. What stands out in particular are: (1) the idea of a *telos* of abstract rationality towards which all cognition develops (Wertsch); and (2) the idea that Vygotsky was an idealist dealing with concepts and symbols rather than matter and tools (Zinchenko, 1985). Pinkard points out that Hegel's philosophy has not been understood beyond a small field of scholars. But while the idea that Hegel's approach was crudely foundational is in error, it is also the case that it was not simply anti-foundational. For Hegel the absence of a pregiven foundation does not mean the absence of all foundations. Rockmore explains Hegel's position as follows:

The justification is then, not already there, present from the beginning, so to say, like something that is preserved and unchanged through the reasoning process ... the justification is created or produced during the development of the theory ... To begin, it is not enough to begin, for there is and can be no privileged beginning point. We ... encounter the relation between system and history. The true only becomes true in and through its development, its real unfolding in the course of which it actualises itself. (Rockmore, 1993, p. 63)

We start as anti-foundationalists, but, having built our foundations as we go along, we finish as foundationalists. As Otto Neurath famously put it, 'We are like sailors who have to rebuild their ship in the open sea, without ever being able to dismantle it in dry dock and reconstruct it from the best components' (Neurath, cited in Cartwright *et al.*, 1996, p. 89). Both Hegel and Neurath were fully aware that their view of knowledge had a socio-cultural or historical dimension. Creating and transforming the ground of knowledge as we go along (i.e. history) comes to have a central role. The rejection of foundations of thought entailed in this position is effectually also a rejection of abstract reason. In the same way that Hegel has been mistakenly believed to have a commitment to an abstract, foundational notion of reason, so Vygotsky is misunderstood by criticism that does not take account of his anti-foundationalism.

Vygotsky's discussion of Spinoza's 'theory of method' shows clear evidence of anti-foundationalism:

A theory of method is, of course, the production of the means of production, to take a comparison from the field of industry. But in industry the production of the means of production is no special, primordial production, but forms part of the general process of production and itself depends upon the same methods and tools of production as all other production. (Vygotsky, 1997, p. 253)

Vygotsky endorsed Spinoza's argument that we should not commit ourselves to a search going back to infinity. In order to discover the best method for finding truth, we do not need to find a method of finding a method:

> By such proceedings, we should never arrive at the knowledge of the truth, or, indeed, at any knowledge at all. The matter stands on the same footing as the making of material tools, which might be argued about in a similar way. For, in order to work iron, a hammer is needed, and the hammer cannot be forthcoming unless it has been made; but in order to make it, there was need of another hammer and other tools, and so on to infinity. We might thus vainly endeavour to prove that men have no power of working iron. But as men first made use of the instrument supplied by nature to accomplish very easy pieces of workmanship, laboriously and imperfectly, and then, when finished, wrought other things more difficult with less labour, and greater perfection; and so gradually mounted from the simplest operations to the making of tools, and from the making of tools to the making of more complex tools, and fresh feats of workmanship, till they arrived at making, with small expenditure of labour, the vast complicated mechanisms which they now possess. So, in like manner, the intellect, by its native strength, makes for itself intellectual instruments, whereby it acquires strength for performing other intellectual operations, and from these operations gets again fresh instruments, or the power of pushing its investigations further, and thus gradually proceeds until it reaches the summit of wisdom. (Spinoza, cited in Vygotsky, 1997, p. 254)

Two indications of the importance of Hegel for understanding Vygotsky are: first, the absence of an unbridgeable epistemological chasm between thought and world, and following from this, second, the conception of development as a non-linear process embedded in historical resources. In particular Vygotsky took on board Hegel's position that, while we must be anti-foundationalist at the start, we cannot help but develop foundations for our knowledge as we proceed. Hegel rejected all claims to a priori knowledge and to knowledge apart from experience. As Rockmore puts it:

> According to Hegel, philosophy, that he, like Kant, regards as the highest form of knowledge, and that he later in a famous passage in the *Philosophy of Right* will compare to an owl, can only take wing afterwards, or after the fact. The point is that for Hegel, knowledge, including philosophy, is not and cannot be *a priori*; on the contrary, it emerges in and is the product of collective effort of human beings over the course of recorded history to come to grips with their world and themselves. (Rockmore, 1993, p. 85)

When the Hegelian dimension of Vygotsky's thought is acknowledged, it becomes clear that Vygotsky's understanding of the concept is far richer than that often attributed to him. Far from having a decontextualised view of abstract rationality, Vygotsky's reason is ontological. Like a snowball rolling down a mountainside, his concept grows through the material it picks up in its descent: 'Thus the concept does not arise from this as a mechanical result of abstraction – it is the result of a long and deep knowledge of the object ... Psychological research is disclosing that in a concept we always have an enrichment and deepening of the content that the concept contains' (Vygotsky, 1998, p. 54). A concept's relation to the world is not one of correspondence. If ultimately Hegel can be understood as a correspondence theorist (see Harris, 1994), his form of this view is not the one against which Wertsch reacts in his concern with the designative approach to word-meaning. A concept's development cannot be separated from the world of which it is a part and in which it plays a role of constituting conditions for knowing. Unlike some constructivist understandings of word-meaning, however, these conditions are not arbitrary but are intricately connected to the formations in which the concept functions.

Vygotsky's understanding of the concept offers the possibility of grasping the gap between mind and world – and its mediation – as creative. The concept is a result of a complex process of development in which thought and the world are never categorically separated. Vygotsky demonstrates his deep understanding of Hegel's approach to philosophy on this matter when he states: 'In Hegel's view, the word [by which Vygotsky means concept] is existing vitalised thoughts. The connection between thought and word is not a primal connection that is given once and forever. It arises in development and it itself develops' (Vygotsky, 1987, p. 285).

THE CONCEPTION OF SCIENCE

Scientific concepts are not the apex of abstract rationality in the way that commentators such as Wertsch and Lemke suppose. Criticism of abstract reason often coincides with a criticism of science, which in postmodern thought is frequently seen as an authoritarian claim to knowledge. The conception of science underlying this position is not, however, unchallenged. For instance, interesting positions taken up in the philosophy of science by authors such as Nancy Cartwright, Roy Bhaskar and Ian Hacking consider scientific theory as something other than generalisation and abstraction (representation). In different ways each of these authors takes issue with the simple idea that theory represents the world and describes real events. Claims of this type do not, however, necessarily lead to a view of theory as a social construction (viewing it as just one more 'perspective') or to its devaluation, since they open the way to seeing the relation between scientific concepts and the world in iterative terms: at some points theory and the world are isomorphic,[3] at others they are dissonant.

The idea that scientific concepts are the expression of an abstract reason applied to the world is not what Vygotsky had in mind. Attempts to interpret what he actually thought in these terms fail to appreciate his understanding of science. In discussing the character of science and the misunderstandings of it, Vygotsky refers to Marx: 'The essence of any scientific concept was defined in a profound manner by Marx: "If the form in which a thing is manifested and its essence were in direct correspondence, science would be unnecessary"' (Vygotsky, 1987, p. 193). Vygotsky has a particular concern for the value of theory, abstract thought and the possibilities inherent within it: 'It may seem that analysis, like experiment, distorts reality by creating artificial conditions for observation' but, as he goes on to maintain, 'The strength of analysis is in abstraction, just as the strength of experiment is in its artificiality' (Vygotsky, 1997, p. 320).

Vygotsky's appreciation of science as a practice that cannot be set apart from our engagement with the world and that has a normative character (our transactions with nature carry significance) is illustrated by his view that 'each word is already a theory' and that the 'real and the scientific fact' do not coincide:[4]

> while the highest scientific abstraction contains an element of reality ... Even the most immediate, empirical, raw, singular natural scientific fact already contains a first abstraction. The real and the scientific fact are distinct in that the scientific fact is the real fact included in a system of knowledge ...The material of science is not raw, but logically elaborated, natural material which has been selected according to a certain feature. The fact itself of naming a fact by a word is to frame this fact in a concept. ... it is an act toward understanding this fact by including it into a category of phenomena which has been studied before. Each word is already a theory. (Vygotsky, 1997, p. 249)

The emphasis on artificiality and abstraction resonates with an argument made by Ian Hacking that phenomena, and more specifically 'effects', on the whole, do not occur without our intervention in nature but are created by a careful effort of theory and experimental design. It is through the activity, procedures and techniques of experimentation that we are able to express matter such that its characteristics are amenable to the form of conceptualisation that creates regulative and predicative capacity: 'To experiment is to create, produce, refine and stabilise phenomena' (Hacking, 1983, p. 230). This line of argument has little in common with the representational view of reality, in which laws describe effects in the world.[5] In this view, intervention *prises reality* into expressing itself in particular forms that do not exist without it. Hacking explains his position as follows: 'the phenomenon of physics – the Faraday effect, the Hall effect, the Josephson effect – are the keys that unlock the universe. People made the keys and perhaps the locks in which they turn' (Hacking, 1983, p. 229). It is important to note that while making the case for the manufacture of phenomena, Hacking maintains that this approach is firmer ground for a hard-headed scientific realism than the conventional view of theories as representations.

Bhaskar and Cartwright are similarly ill-at-ease with a simplistic hypothetico-deductive conception of science. Cartwright (1983) distinguishes different orders of scientific theory on the basis that there is a trade-off (or inverse proportionality) between the explanatory power of fundamental theoretical laws and their predictive capacity. Bhaskar (1978) for his part, echoing Bacon's claim that experiment is twisting the lion's tail, argues that the relation between laws and events is not one of constant conjunction; rather it is what we do in science that *produces* the regularities.

Crucially, Vygotsky's appreciation of science not only differs from that which relates theory directly to observable empirical objects in the world, but it is tied to a different appreciation of intellect. The fact that humans possess a second nature, which allows a different sort of contact with the world from that of animals or machines, makes it possible for them to overcome the limitations of their physical characteristics. The specific nature of scientific knowledge, as Vygotsky, following Marx, understood, prevents the lack of any sense from necessarily impairing the development of the intellect. This development does not depend upon the 'receptivity' of a bare 'given': 'the links, dependencies and relationships among things which are the content of our scientific knowledge are not the visually perceivable qualities of things: rather they come to light through thought' (Vygotsky, 1993, p. 203).

Vygotsky was well aware of the argument, taken up later by philosophers of science, that the relationship of knowledge to the world is one neither of induction nor of mere description. As would be expected of someone well read in Hegelian philosophy, Vygotsky rejects a correspondence theory of truth in which our knowledge arises from the world and immediately maps on to it isomorphically. He is at pains to emphasise that this is not the way in which a scientific concept relates to knowledge: 'The scientific concept necessarily presupposes a different relationship to the object, one which is possible only for a concept' (Vygotsky, 1987, p. 193). The difference between scientific concepts as they are commonly understood, as descriptions of the world, and as they are understood by Vygotsky, drawing upon Marx, is that in the latter case they are constituted historically rather than abstractly. When Marx speaks of abstractions in the *Grundrisse*, he understands them as 'forms of being'. The possibility of universalising abstractions arises then 'world-historically':

> As a rule, the most general abstractions arise only in the midst of the richest pos-
> sible concrete development, where one thing appears as common to many, to all.
> Then it ceases to be thinkable in a particular form alone. On the other side, this
> abstraction of labour as such is not merely the mental product of a concrete total-
> ity of labour. Indifference towards specific labour corresponds to a form of soci-
> ety in which individuals can with ease transfer from one labour to another, and
> where the specific kind is a matter of chance for them, hence indifference. Not
> only the category of labour, but labour in reality has here become the means of
> creating wealth in general, and has ceased to be organically linked with particular
> individuals in a specific form ... therefore this society by no means begins only
> at the point when one can speak of it as such. (Marx, 1973, pp. 104–106)

Marx criticises the abstract application of categories without regard either to their origin in, or their expression of, their real-world context. He points instead to the way that categories emerge historically:

> This example of labour shows strikingly how even the most abstract categories,
> despite their validity – precisely because of their abstractness – for all epochs, are

nevertheless, in the specific character of this abstraction, themselves likewise a product of historic relations, and possess their full validity within these relations. (Marx, 1973, p. 106)

Marx writes of how modern society is the most developed and complex organisation of production and of how its development makes features of other forms of production understandable. This understanding is not achieved, however, by the mere application of a category: 'Human anatomy contains a key to the anatomy of the ape … The bourgeois economy thus supplies a key to the ancient, etc. But not at all in a manner of those economists who smudge over all historical differences and see bourgeois relations in all forms of society' (1973, p. 106). This is a more subtle point than it appears when read simply as an argument for there being a *telos* of development. In the sentence just quoted, Marx attempts to distinguish this ontological conception of development from one that merely imposes abstract categories in order to construct explanation. Vygotsky makes a similar criticism of assumptions about method when he refers to the way in which psychologists (like Marx's bourgeois economists) take concepts derived from one perspective and apply them to others as though they represented constants of reality rather than variables that developed with reality historically. Such an approach reduces concepts (as though they were identical in transfer) to 'round and empty zeros' (Van der Veer and Valsiner, 1993, p. 145).

Although particular concepts arise historically, their relation to the world is not isomorphic in the sense of corresponding directly to particular instances of an empirical given. Thus, in rejecting an empiricist way of deriving categories, Marx continues:

It would therefore be unfeasible and wrong to let the economic categories follow one another in the same sequence in which they were historically decisive. Their sequence is determined, rather, by the relation to one another in modern bourgeois society, which is precisely the opposite of what seems to be the natural order or which corresponds to historical development. (Marx, 1973, p. 107)

In dealing with our possibility of knowing in this way, Marx shares with Hegel a rejection of the dualism of a distinct mind and world. Vygotsky's sociogenetic conception of mind entails this same conception of the development of knowledge and this same conception of the nature of science. Vygotsky cites passages from Marx's *Grundrisse* quoted above in 'The Historical Meaning of the Crisis in Psychology', and he uses it against Pavlov's understanding of how science proceeds when – repeating Marx's statement that 'the anatomy of man is the key to the anatomy of the ape' – he argues for what he terms 'this methodological principle of the "reverse" method' (Vygotsky, 1997, p. 235).

THE IDEA OF DEVELOPMENT

Marx's and Hegel's ideas of history and development influenced every aspect of Vygotsky's thinking on concepts. Vygotsky rejects the notion of a linear development from the everyday to scientific concept in favour of an approach in which scientific concepts, in their formation, act back on everyday concepts. The way Vygotsky works with these ideas counts as further evidence against the accusation that he is a 'recapitulationist' or 'stageist' in terms of his conception of development. Scribner (1985) has provided a strong case for refuting this reading, and Vygotsky's use of Marx's argument clearly indicates that he does not hold to the conventional notion of development often attributed to him (see Smith, Tomlinson and Dockrell, 1997). It is necessary to have some knowledge of the Hegelian notion of development in order to understand the potential in Vygotsky's ideas and to appreciate that he did not subscribe to the caricature of evolutionism mistakenly attributed to both Hegel and Marx. But it is difficult, if not impossible, to take account of this Hegelian sense of development when Vygotsky is assimilated into the paradigm of contemporary psychology.

A particular instance of the misreading of Vygotsky is evident in a recent text that identifies similarities between his ideas and those of Piaget. What is striking about the text in question is the fact that the authors are so influenced by their assumption that Vygotsky shares their unproblematised narrative of development that they misquote him. Claiming that there is a common view that intellectual development occurs as a sequence of stages,[6] they align two passages, supposedly drawn from the relevant text, in order to support their argument that Vygotsky and Piaget shared the same view on development. Thus Smith *et al.* write:

> A commitment to this view is made explicitly by both Piaget and Vygotsky, for example:
>
> 'we do in fact find, in the analysis of forms of social equilibrium, these same structures ... (just as the) cognitive mechanism in children involve three distinct systems' (Piaget, 1995 [*Sociological Studies*], p. 56).
>
> 'Development consists in three intrinsic stages' (Vygotsky, 1994 [Van der Veer and Valsiner, *Vygotsky Reader*], p. 216). (Smith *et al.*, 1997, p. 2)

The two passages are presented as definitive, but they are not accurately presented quotations and are misleading. The text from which the second statement has been extracted actually translates the relevant passage as follows:

> If one were to attempt to make any *schematic* inferences from our research, they would basically reveal that the road which leads to concept development consists of three intrinsic stages, each of which in turn, can also be subdivided into separate parts or phases. (Vygotsky, in Van der Veer and Valsiner, 1994, p. 216, italics added)

What we see here is that Vygotsky speaks of stages only with the cautious qualification: 'If one were to attempt to make any schematic inferences ...'. So what is the frame of reference that has sanctioned this adjustment of quotations? It is not only that the syntax is altered. It is also that it omits to point out that it is 'concept development' that Vygotsky is talking about and not development in general. This is clear not only in Van der Veer's translation but also in Norris Minick's rendition of *Thinking and Speech*, in Volume 1 of *The Collected Works of L. S. Vygotsky*. Here once again one finds the expression 'an attempt to represent ... schematically' cautiously qualifying what is said, and here once again the reference is to concept development rather than to development in general: 'If we attempt to represent the genetic implications of our research *schematically*, it indicates that the course of concept development is composed of three basic stages, each of which breaks up into several distinct phases' (Vygotsky, 1987, p. 89).

The omission of words from Vygotsky's text obscures the distinctive character and subtlety of his views on development. It is in virtue of such omissions and errors that Vygotsky comes to be subsumed into common-sense understanding within cognitive psychology.

By contrast, Bakhurst's study of Soviet philosophy in relation to consciousness is more amenable to a Hegelian idea of development in Vygotsky's work. As opposed to the idea that psychological faculties themselves exist prior to experience, Vygotsky's position is to be explained as follows:

> He denies that the child enters the world naturally equipped with embryonic forms of higher mental functions from an understanding of more basic psychological mechanism (of the kind, perhaps, with which animals and human children are endowed by nature). The higher mental functions, he claims, are irreducible to their primitive antecedents, either phylogenetic or ontogenetic ... The complex is the key to the comprehension of the simple. He argues that a proper understanding of elementary capacities rests on a grasp of higher mental functions and not vice versa ... 'the anatomy of man is the key to the anatomy of the ape'. (Bakhurst, 1991, p. 66)

Adopting the phrasing of Marx concerning the anatomy of men and apes, Bakhurst's argument points to a rejection of a foundationalist approach to mind – that is, a conception of the development of intellect as evolutionary process, from lower to higher stages.

THE IDEAL AND THE REAL

It is useful at this point to take stock. So far I have argued that neither the view that there are foundations on which knowledge may be built, nor a conception of scientific theory as corresponding to the world as it is, nor a hierarchical idea of development, do justice to Vygotsky's work. A further point needs to be added: that polarising the ideal and the real as mutually exclusive opposites also leads to misunderstanding. Such a polarisation is integral to the Cartesian dualism of mind and world. In spite of their intention to transcend it, contemporary critiques of Vygotsky have been based on this dualism, while in the Soviet Union attacks on Vygotsky during his lifetime were framed in terms of the opposition of the ideal and real. In the Soviet Union the philosophical presuppositions of Cartesian dualism took the form of a Stalinised 'Marxism', in which the material was conceived as brute matter and the ideal was opposed to it as mystical and bourgeois. This clearly led to a profound misreading of Vygotsky. It is here that we can grasp the significance of Ilyenkov who, by challenging the presuppositions of Stalinised Marxism, and in particular by rejecting the polar opposition of the real and the ideal, returned to a similar understanding of Marxism to Vygotsky's.

Ilyenkov is a particularly significant figure in this connection because, as David Bakhurst has demonstrated, his work is a link between Vygotsky and John McDowell: this shows McDowell's relevance for the understanding and interpretation of Vygotsky. What is it about Ilyenkov's work that connects with McDowell? Both turn to Hegel as a means for rejecting any categorical distinction between the ideal and the real. Working within a quite different tradition from McDowell, Ilyenkov addresses what he calls 'the problem of the ideal' in a way that provides an important insight into the social nature and sociogenesis of mind. But it should be noted that his conception of universal reason is again distinctively different from that caricatured in critiques of reason. For it involves not a particular form of reason that is able simply to depict the world but rather the ability of the 'thinking body' to move in such a way as to make the form of any other body (Ilyenkov, 1977a, pp. 44–47). Its key point is an appreciation that our ability to think, our second nature, is part of nature and not distinct from it, and this is precisely the position that McDowell adopts. We are mistaken when we equate nature with whatever is amenable only to scientific investigation, for human activity – that is, free activity – is also part of nature.

Ilyenkov follows Vygotsky in arguing that higher mental functions are the realisation of human potential through activity. At this point the extremely difficult problem arises of how it is that the brain can be realised as mind only through activity. For Ilyenkov this emerges from his considerations of Kant's idea of 'transcendentally inborn' forms of operation of the individual mentality as a priori 'internal mechanisms'. Against this position, but in line with Vygotsky and also Hegel,[7] he insisted that 'the self-consciousness of *social* man [is] *assimilated from without* by the individual', stressing that 'It is these forms of the organisation of social (collectively realised) human life activity that exist *before, outside* and *completely independently* of the individual mentality' (Ilyenkov, 1977b, pp. 80–81). To put it in simple terms, we have here a concept of reason in which individuals participate rather than one that is constructed by individuals. For Ilyenkov the rejection of the simple opposition of idealism and materialism is explicit and unqualified:

> It will readily be appreciated how much broader and more profound such a positing of the question [the ideal and the material] is in comparison with any conception that designates as 'ideal' everything that is 'in consciousness of the individual' and 'material' or 'real', everything that is outside of the consciousness of the individual, everything that the given individual is not conscious of, although this 'everything' does exist in reality, and thus draws between the 'ideal' and the 'real' a fundamental dividing line which turns them into 'different worlds' that have 'nothing in common' with each other. It is clear that given such a metaphysical division and delimitation, the 'ideal' and the 'material' cannot and must not be regarded as opposites. (Ilyenkov, 1977b, p. 81)

A simple example of the materiality of thinking activity is that of tying a knot in a handkerchief as an *aide-mémoire* – that is, constituting a material thing as an ideal object. The most important ideal object is, of course, money – a thing of no intrinsic significance but the very stuff of wealth, an ideal object that clearly has the most massive material implications. One implication is its conditioning of the way we think about the world. Reference to this aspect of money features prominently in Ilyenkov's argument concerning the materiality of the ideal. What we might normally think of as separate and distinct from the world that we inhabit (a preconceptual given) is, although ideal, constitutive of our activity. As humans, we inhabit a world constituted not only by causes but also by reasons.[8]

McDowell deals with the same issues as those raised by Ilyenkov's consideration of the ideal and the real through his examination of the limits of contemporary epistemology. The crux of his argument is first, that epistemology is not best conceived in terms of a separation of mind and world, and second, that humans are constrained by reasons as well as causes. In a typically Hegelian way, McDowell exposes what he calls the philosophical anxieties present in contemporary epistemology. He argues that the way in which the problem of epistemology is outlined in contemporary writings produces a philosophical anxiety about the very possibility of thought. He utilises the distinction in modern philosophy between impressions (empirical description) and knowledge in order to expose an implicit problem or tension in what we take to be the conditions or foundations of our knowing. On the one hand, he argues, we are faced with the thought that what we conceive as the empirical world could not (by our very conception) stand in judgement over our thought, and yet, on the other hand, the retreat to a form of coherence theory to avoid this difficulty leaves us equally anxious about the purchase that any self-defining system might have on anything that is external to its own internal coherence. The key point of McDowell's argument here is the breaking down of the barrier between mind and world, which is effected through his formulation of the 'unboundedness of the conceptual'. What follows from his engagement with contemporary philosophy is that 'the space of reasons' can be conceived of as part of nature. This offers a possibility of seeing the world as 'enchanted' again, but not in the way that it was seen as enchanted in premodern times.

McDowell has not actually spelled out what he means by 're-enchantment' (see Testa, 2007), but it is clear from his writings that this must entail recognition that reason is a force in the world. For in rejecting the tradition of Cartesian dualism, McDowell sees reason on both sides of the divide, so to speak: indeed it is because there is a space of reason in nature that human beings are capable of grasping it by exercising their rational capacities. This presence of reason on both sides of the divide allows McDowell to resist the charge of idealism – that is, that the world is simply what thought takes it to be. The crucial move that McDowell makes is to argue that to be in touch with the world at all (as a human being) assumes a normative context.

McDowell's work has greater sophistication and subtlety than these few sentences can convey. The purpose here is not to summarise it but simply to show that the philosophical tradition within which he is developing his ideas about epistemology is the same as that within which Vygotsky and Ilyenkov worked – namely, the Hegelian tradition. What can be said of the work of McDowell can also be said of that of Robert Brandom: again this is a highly elaborate innovation in contemporary philosophy that looks back to the Hegelian tradition within which Vygotsky and Ilyenkov worked. The fact that leading contemporary philosophers are turning to Hegel does not endorse a particular reading of Vygotsky; it does, however, provide support for taking Hegelianism more seriously and thus, at one remove, for us to take seriously Vygotsky's statements about the importance of Hegel for his work. The issues at stake come into focus over the question of reason, where a sharp distinction exists between its conceptualisation by Hegel and his followers, on the one hand, and the target of the critics of logocentrism and 'the Enlightenment grand narrative', on the other.

IMPLICATIONS FOR EDUCATION

In bringing Hegel back onto the agenda of contemporary philosophy, McDowell and Brandom are also bringing back, although not as part of their immediate project, the philosophical tradition that shaped the work of Vygotsky and Ilyenkov. The aim of this book has been not only to argue that Vygotsky's work was influenced by Hegel but that his work cannot be properly understood outside this influence: when it is assimilated into the alternative Cartesian tradition of Western thought, it is positively misunderstood.

The connections between contemporary philosophy and the philosophical tradition framing Vygotsky's work are of interest in their own right. The work of McDowell and Brandom adds strength to the claims that Vygotsky's work should be considered within this Hegelian frame of thought and that reading it against a different background will lead to serious misinterpretation. Even if the argument that forms a major part of this book is accepted, however, questions remain concerning the practical implications of Vygotsky for contemporary education or, to be absolutely precise, whether seeing Vygotsky's work through a Spinozist and Hegelian lens has practical consequences.

In bringing Hegel back onto the agenda of contemporary philosophy, McDowell and Brandom are also bringing back the philosophical tradition that shaped the work of Vygotsky and Ilyenkov, even though concern with the work of these Russian thinkers is not an immediate part of their project. The work of these neo-Hegelians has particular interest because it illustrates how philosophy is reworked again and again in different periods, thinking itself anew in very different contexts from the one in which it originally arose. Brandom says of philosophy that it is 'a discipline whose distinctive concern is with a certain kind of *self-consciousness*: awareness of ourselves as specifically *discursive* (that is, concept-mongering) creatures' (Brandom, 2009, p. 126); or, to quote Aristotle, it is a matter of 'thought thinking itself'. For Hegel, the movement of thought is not distinguished from the world of which it is part. It is within the framework of this approach, and read through Vygotsky and the neo-Hegelians, that the contemporary influence of Hegel on practical issues about education can be explored. Contemporary debates concerning the nature of curricula illustrate the point. It is here that one can find those presuppositions underpinning common conceptions of mind and world that characterise much of the contemporary educational theory and practice criticised in this book.

The nature of the curriculum is a perennial concern for educational research and practice, and in the UK and America during the last half-century the issue of subject knowledge has received a great deal of attention. With much at stake, positions are often polarised. If recent Hegelian-influenced developments in philosophy concerning the nature of awareness and understanding were taken into account, the general understanding of subject knowledge and its relation to pedagogy would surely benefit. Robert Brandom is especially interesting here because, in stressing the inferentialism in Hegel's thought, he has, like Vygotsky, brought to the fore those aspects of the human condition that concern *coming to know*.

It is generally agreed that quality of teaching and learning is affected by teachers' content or subject knowledge, but how, to what extent and in what way remains largely unexplored (Ball, Lubienski and Mewborn, 2001). In research so far, possibly because insufficient attention has been given to teachers' *orientations* to the knowledge domains with which they are concerned, the *structure* and *form* of content knowledge has not been studied in its own right. The relationship between knowledge and pedagogy has long been recognised. For example, Whitty (2010) argues that 'some of the key challenges in giving disadvantaged pupils access to powerful knowledge – and giving it meaningful and critical purchase on their everyday lives – are pedagogic ones'. However, the focus of attention has generally been on pedagogy or on knowledge but not on their integral relation. Hence the debate on the curriculum is all too often polarised through focusing on one to the neglect of the other.

Brandom's work offers a way out of this opposition. On the basis of his *inferentialism* (Brandom, 2000) it is possible to see that the all-too-common conception of *coming to know*, evident in the practice of teaching, is founded on a mistaken prioritisation of representation over inference – that is, on the assumption that initial awareness takes the form of a representation and that only once this is grasped can inferences be made. This prioritisation of representation arises from a misunderstanding about the nature of representation – to the effect that it is immediate and that its meaning arises solely from its relation to the object, event, or whatever, that it represents. If Vygotsky's Hegelian characterisation of a concept as developing 'only when we recognise the thing in all its connections and relations' is taken seriously, then, as educational research has shown, it would not be reasonable to expect to teach by conveying atoms of meaning in the absence of encouraging awareness of the inferential connections constituting the concepts involved. On the contrary, teaching would need to be sensitive to, and based upon, the 'complex system of mediating connection and relations disclosed in determinations of the concept' (Vygotsky, 1998, p. 53)

When an *inferentialist* approach to knowledge is adopted (Bakker and Derry, 2011), students' primary focus involves the inferential connections that constitute concepts such that representations are already connected, through reasons, to other aspects of the knowledge domain to which they belong. What does this entail? Inferentialism demonstrates that grasping a concept involves commitment to the inferences implicit in its use in a social practice of giving and asking for reasons. This has clear implications for how teachers organise learning. If teachers adopt an inferentialist orientation to knowledge, they will necessarily emphasise the inferential relations between the concepts that constitute representations rather than conveying 'facts' in an atomistic way. It is generally agreed that good practice involves teachers situating concepts in meaningful contexts and engaging in rich questioning and dialogue in order to develop learners' competence in a subject area. But inferentialism offers the possibility of going a step further and indicating ways that could prevent less experienced teachers from following practices, such as discussion-based activities and 'active learning', without being fully aware of the form such practices need to take if they are to be effective.

There are countless examples of teachers adopting an 'active' or 'constructivist' approach to learning without appreciating what this involves in either the design of what they do or the manner of their own responses. It is well understood that, when teachers engage with a wide range of learners, they cannot assume that the words that they use bear the same meanings for learners. Margaret Donaldson's classic work *Children's Minds* opens with this very point, when she quotes from Laurie Lee's account of his childhood in *Cider with Rosie*. Lee recounts the experience of his first day at school. On arrival the teacher says: '"You're Laurie Lee, aren't you? Well just you sit there for the present." I sat there all day but I never got it. I ain't going back there again' (quoted in Donaldson, 1978, p. 17). However, although there is general acceptance that shared meaning between teachers and students cannot be relied upon, inadequate attention is given to the means by which the teacher assists the learner in coming to share common knowledge (Edward and Mercer, 1987). There is a serious neglect of the extent to which the form and structure of the knowledge domain (i.e. the inferential connections between concepts) is relevant to participation in common knowledge. While it is understood that learners have different meanings for the same words, what that difference actually consists in is rarely unpacked. The idea that when learners use a word, they have already made a commitment to a set of concepts that support the meaning of that word is not precisely attended to, and as a result the teacher's questioning often supports learning poorly, in spite of the fact that it is known that the quality of questioning plays a major role.

By explaining how propositional content and, in particular, how objective meanings are constituted in the social practice of what Brandom terms the 'giving and asking for reasons', inferentialism opens new ground for thinking about the nature of learning. In particular, an inferentialist approach can assist in resolving the apparent opposition between constructivist ideas about learning, which emphasise the learner's construction of meaning, and the more traditional approaches that stress the knowledge domain as a discipline. While constructivist ideas, where attention is given to meaning construction on the part of the learner, can lead to a neglect of the domain of knowledge within which it takes place, traditional approaches can fail to take sufficient account of how learners make sense of concepts.

By reversing the conventional order of explanation, which privileges representation over inference, what was initially at odds – the 'inference making' of learners versus the 'facts' of the knowledge domain – becomes one and the same. Knowledge domains have a particular inferential structure, and learners' induction into domains involves their becoming responsive to a new inferential structure by modifying their use of concepts. For Brandom, Hegel achieved the inversion of the traditional order of semantic explanation begun by Kant. He did this 'by beginning with a concept of experience as inferential activity and discussing the making of judgments and the development of concepts entirely in terms of the roles they play in that inferential activity' (Brandom, 1994, p. 92). Brandom's approach is fundamentally different from any conception of thought in terms of individual mental states and words that are understood exclusively as the names for things, events or states of affairs. Teachers may approach meaning in terms of the relations between representations and what is represented, and they may support this by additional explanation to clarify the initial thought of what is represented. However, even where the meaning of a word is intimately associated with its referent, the question of how this association arises is a matter of pedagogical importance. In line with Brandom's approach, the forming of the association between word and object involves reversing the conceptual framework in which a great deal of conventional pedagogical practice takes place. It involves emphasising instead the way that the learner must be brought into those inferential relations that constitute a concept, before the concept is acquired.

Like Hegel and Vygotsky before him, Brandom is concerned with what is distinctive about human beings. He contrasts human knowing with the responsiveness of a parrot or a thermostat. For instance, he asks:

> What is the knower able to *do* that ... the thermostat cannot? After all they may respond differentially to *just* the same range of stimuli. ... The knower has the practical know-how to situate that response in a network of inferential relations – to tell what follows from something being ... cold, what would be evidence for it, what would be incompatible with it, and so on. (Brandom, 2000, p. 162)

The knower is capable of making a judgement, whereas the thermostat is not, and this distinguishes the response of the knower from that of the thermostat. The thermostat's response is simply a moment in a series of causal stimuli, whereas human responsiveness involves reasons and not just causes: that is to say that humans, however poorly informed about the real nature of a situation, have an appreciation of its significance – they locate their 'response in a network of inferential relations' (Brandom, 2000, p. 162). No machine can, or indeed needs, to do this. The machine, so long as it is working properly, is compelled to respond, whereas humans need not respond if they have reasons for not doing so – that is, they have choice.

Thermostats and parrots do not, like humans, have concepts of temperature or redness. Humans know that saying 'That is cold' is not compatible with 'That is hot', or 'That's red' is not compatible with 'That's green'. Humans, as Vygotsky understood, are born into what Sellars, in a Hegelian vein,[9] called the 'space of reasons', and their induction into linguistic practices initiates children into the inferential relations that constitute concepts, that is, what they follow from and what follows from them. As children develop, they are in a position to take responsibility for attributing their own concepts; they have become responsive to the particular reasons that constitute their use of any concept. In Wittgenstein's terms they have learned to take part in 'language games'.

Once it is understood that grasping a concept involves a commitment to the inferences implicit in its use in a social practice of giving and asking for reasons, definite pedagogical implications follow. According to a Vygotskian approach, effective teaching involves providing an opportunity for learners to work with a concept in the space of reasons within which it falls and within which its meaning is constituted. *Participation* can develop without an immediate and full grasp of the reasons constituting the use of a concept; initially all that is required is the ability to inhabit the space in which reasons and concepts operate. For Brandom, as for Hegel and indeed Vygotsky, grasping a single concept requires simultaneously grasping many concepts (Vygotsky, 1998, p. 53). For Vygotsky, concepts depend for their meaning on the system of judgements (inferences) within which they are disclosed. Instead of understanding the meaning of a concept primarily in terms of its representation of an object, it is the system of inferences in which the object is disclosed that has priority.

When inference is privileged over representation, awareness needs to be understood in terms of the inferential space that is inhabited by thinking creatures rather than in representational terms. In these conditions the primacy of teachers and their knowledge of the relevant inferential domain assume major significance. As opposed to being facilitators who encourage learners' own meaning-making, teachers assume a standing of authority as regards the relevant knowledge domain. However, this authority is in terms of their *orientation* to the relevant domain, and it involves a conception of subject knowledge that does not presuppose the priority of representations. If subject knowledge is represented as 'facts' without regard to the inferential structure constituting the facts in the first place, learning will not be achieved. As Vygotsky remarked, in relation to Tolstoy's recognition of the futility of his own attempt to teach concepts directly, 'direct instruction in concepts is impossible. …The teacher who attempts to use this approach achieves nothing but a mindless learning of words' (Vygotsky, 1987, p. 170).

This leads back to contemporary debates about knowledge:[10] it concerns the emphasis to be given to disciplines and facts as against the constructivism of learners' engagement in their own *meaning making*. Most of these debates are unnecessarily polarised owing to a failure to appreciate the extent of the ground the two sides share. The belief that knowledge pure and simple matters, and that learners should have access to *powerful knowledge*, finds expression too often as a return to the canon and the teaching of 'facts'. The conviction that learners need to be active in their own development as knowers is seldom supported by a clear understanding of the conditions necessary for that development. Each pole of the debate would benefit from the insights drawn from Hegel, such as are expressed through the work of Vygotsky and articulated in terms of inferentialism by Brandom. In the case of subject knowledge, an inferentialist account forces attention onto the systematic character of disciplinary domains while, in the case of learner-centred meaning-making, it serves to highlight precisely what meaning-making involves.

The questions that can be raised about these presuppositions call for new enquiry. Exploring the problems raised by different readings of Vygotsky – in particular those that neglect what might be termed the inferential background to his work – sheds light on more fundamental problems arising from the presuppositions underpinning current educational practice.

Once the distinctive relation of humans to the world is recognised, a bald empiricism that sees concepts as standing in representational relation to their objects will no longer provide the basis for sound educational theory and practice. Philosophy is not a simple and direct solution to the problems of education. Vygotsky's work provides no blueprint for teachers and educational administrators, but it does provide a frame of ideas within which questions concerning education can fruitfully be pursued. Yet this depends crucially, as this book has tried to show, on reading Vygotsky in the light of the philosophical tradition he explicitly endorsed, the tradition in which Spinoza and Hegel were such notable members.

NOTES

1 'From the point of view of formal logic, the development of concepts is subject to the basic law of inverse proportionality between the scope and the content of the concept. The broader the scope of the concept, the narrower its content. This means that the greater the number of objects that the given concept can be applied to, the greater the circle of concrete things that it encompasses, the poorer its content, the emptier it proves to be' (Vygotsky, 1998, p. 53).

2 Translated from 'Was vernünftig ist, das ist wirklich; und was wirklich ist, das ist vernünftig', in G. W. F. Hegel, *Grundlinien der Philosophie des Rechts*. According to Longuenesse, 'Hegel's notion of *Wirklichkeit*, actuality, is known above all through the sentence that appears in the Preface to the *Principles of the Philosophy of Right*: What is rational is actual; and what is actual is rational. (S. 7, 24; R. 20) A scandalous statement, and even more scandalous in the translation that long prevailed: What is rational is real and what is real is rational. For in identifying Hegel's notion of *Wirklichkeit* with the more familiar notion of reality, this translation makes plausible an interpretation according to which, by elevating "the real" to the dignity of "the rational," Hegel indulges in the speculative sanctification of what is, of the existing world. But in fact, Hegel's notion of *Wirklichkeit* has a quite specific content which resists any overly simplistic interpretation of the sentence just cited' (Longuenesse, 2007, p. 110). Stern notes that the phrase had been 'seized on by Hegel's critics as a summation of his conservatism and quietism' and argues instead that Hegel's 'intention is not to offer a normative assessment of what is actual … rather it is to suggest that genuine philosophy must be committed to reason in its methods of inquiry, if it is to properly undertake an investigation into the "spiritual universe" as well as the "natural" one' (Stern, 2006, pp. 235–236).

3 Hofstadter remarks that: 'It is a cause of joy when a mathematician discovers an isomorphism between two structures which he knows. It is often a "bolt from the blue", and a source of wonderment. The perception of an isomorphism between two known structures is a significant advance in knowledge – and I claim that it is such perceptions of isomorphism which create *meanings* in the mind of people' (Hofstadter, 1980, p. 50).

4 Feynman in *The Character of Physical Law* offers a sense of this lack of coincidence when he argues: 'There is … a rhythm and a pattern between the phenomena of nature which is not apparent to the eye but only to the eye of analysis; and it is these rhythms and patterns which we call Physical Laws' (Feynman, cited in Cartwright, 1983, p. 55).

5 There is a dissonance, even an asymmetry, between thought and world. Hacking (1983) repeats Paul Feyerabend's point that events do not serve well as the basic building blocks of matter.
6 The authors are aware of the complexities in providing a characterisation of development but what stands out in their text, from their more subtle consideration, is a stageist view of development common to Vygotsky and Piaget.
7 To put the point in Hegelian terms: 'the self *results from* interacting with the world . . . "only this self-*restoring* identity or this reflection in otherness within itself – not an original and *immediate* unity as such – is true" . . . the self is a *result* and not an "absolute beginning" . . . Hegel states that subjectivity is the conceptual sum and unity of its own entire development. What constitutes this unity is . . . the process of "its own becoming." Hegel describes this process as the "path of enculturation" (*Bildung*)' (Bykova, 2009, p. 267).
8 'The interest in Ilyenkov's work is that he aspires to reconcile the space of reasons and the space of causes, to portray us as minded beings who are inhabitants in a natural world, but whose distinctiveness resides in the fact that our mode of existence cannot be exhaustively explained in causal terms' (Bakhurst, 1997, p. 39).
9 Sellars described his *Empiricism and Philosophy of Mind* as 'incipient *Meditations Hegeliennes*'. Bernstein notes that a 'careful reading of his work . . . reveals how close his orientation is to the opening sections of Hegel's *Phenomenology*. Sellars's critique of the Myth of the Given reads as if it were a translation of the opening section of the *Phenomenology* into what Sellars called the 'new way of words' (Bernstein, 2010, p. 97).
10 For relevant works on the topic of knowledge in the context of education, see Young (2007), Muller and Young (2007) and Guile (2010).

REFERENCES

Bakhurst, D. (1991) *Consciousness and Revolution in Soviet Philosophy: From the Bolsheviks to Evald Ilyenkov* (Cambridge: Cambridge University Press).
Bakhurst, D. (1997) Meaning, Normativity and the Life of the Mind, *Language and Communication*, 17:1, 33–51.
Bakker, A. and Derry, J. (2011) Lessons from Inferentialism for Statistics Education, *Mathematical Thinking and Learning*, 13:1–2, 5–26.
Ball, D.L., Lubienski, S. and Mewborn, D. (2001) Research on Teaching Mathematics: The Unsolved Problem of Teachers' Mathematical Knowledge. In: V. Richardson (ed.) *Handbook of Research on Teaching*, 4th edn. (New York: Macmillan), pp. 433–456.
Bernstein, R.J. (2010) *The Pragmatic Turn* (Cambridge: Polity Press).
Bhaskar, R. (1978) *A Realist Theory of Science* (Hassocks: Harvester Press).
Brandom, R. (1994) *Making it Explicit: Reasoning, Representing, and Discursive Commitment* (Cambridge, MA: Harvard University Press).
Brandom, R. (2000) *Articulating Reasons: An Introduction to Inferentialism* (Cambridge, MA: Harvard University Press).
Brandom, R. (2009) *Reason in Philosophy: Animating Ideas* (Cambridge, MA: Harvard University Press).
Bykova, M. (2009) Spirit and Concrete Subjectivity in Hegel's *Phenomenology of Spirit*. In: K.R. Westphal (ed.) *The Blackwell Guide to Hegel's Phenomenology of Spirit* (Oxford: Wiley Blackwell), pp. 265–295.
Cartwright, N. (1983) *How the Laws of Physics Lie* (Oxford: Oxford University Press).
Cartwright, N., Cat, J. Fleck, L. and Uebel, T.E. (1996) *Otto Neurath: Philosophy Between Science and Politics* (Cambridge: Cambridge University Press).
Daniels, H., Cole, M. and Wertsch, J.V. (2007) *Cambridge Companion to Vygotsky* (Cambridge: Cambridge University Press).
Donaldson, M. (1978) *Children's Minds* (London: Fontana).

Edward, D. and Mercer, N. (1987) *Common Knowledge: The Development of Understanding in the Classroom* (London: Methuen).

Guile, D. (2010) *The Learning Challenge of the Knowledge Economy* (Rotterdam: Sense).

Hacking, I. (1983) *Representing and Intervening: Introductory Topics in the Philosophy of Natural Science* (Cambridge: Cambridge University Press).

Harris, H.S. (1994) Hegel's Correspondence Theory of Truth, *Bulletin of the Hegel Society of Great Britain*, 29, 1–13.

Hofstadter, D.R. (1980) *Gödel, Escher, Bach: An Eternal Golden Braid* (London: Penguin Books).

Ilyenkov, E.V. (1977a) *Dialectical Logic: Essays on Its History and Theory* (Moscow: Progress Publishers).

Ilyenkov, E.V. (1977b) The Concept of the Ideal. In: *Philosophy in the USSR: Problems of Dialectical Materialism* (Moscow: Progress Publishers), pp. 71–99.

Longuenesse, B. (2007) *Hegel's Critique of Metaphysics* (Cambridge: Cambridge University Press).

Marx, K. (1973) *Grundrisse* (London: Penguin Books).

Muller, J. and Young, M. (2007) Truth and Truthfulness in the Sociology of Educational Knowledge, *Theory and Research in Education*, 4:2, 173–201.

Pinkard, T. (2000) *Hegel: A Biography* (Cambridge: Cambridge University Press).

Rockmore, T. (1993) *Before and After Hegel: A Historical Introduction to Hegel's Thought* (Berkeley: University of California Press).

Schon, D. (1983) *The Reflective Practitioner* (New York: Basic Books).

Scribner, S. (1985) Vygotsky's Uses of History. In: J.V. Wertsch (ed.) *Culture, Communication and Cognition: Vygotskian Perspectives* (Cambridge: Cambridge University Press), pp. 119–145.

Smith, L., Tomlinson, P. and Dockrell, J. (1997) *Piaget, Vygotsky and Beyond: Future Issues for Developmental Psychology and Education* (London: Routledge).

Stern, R. (2006) Hegel's *Doppelsatz:* A Neutral Reading, *Journal of the History of Philosophy*, XLIV, 235–266.

Testa, I. (2007) Criticism From Within Nature: The Dialectic Between First and Second Nature From McDowell to Adorno, *Philosophy and Social Criticism*, 33:4, 473–497.

Van der Veer, R. and Valsiner, J. (1993) *Understanding Vygotsky: A Quest for Synthesis* (Oxford: Blackwell).

Van der Veer, R. and Valsiner, J. (1994) *The Vygotsky Reader* (Oxford: Blackwell).

Vygotsky, L.S. (1987) *The Collected Works of L. S. Vygotsky, Volume 1, Problems of General Psychology*, N. Minick trans., R.W. Reiber and A.S. Carton eds (New York: Plenum Press).

Vygotsky, L.S. (1993) *The Collected Works of L. S. Vygotsky, Volume 2, The Fundamentals of Defectology (Abnormal Psychology and Learning Disabilities)*, J. Knox trans., R.W. Reiber and A.S. Carton eds (London: Plenum Publishers).

Vygotsky, L.S. (1997) *The Collected Works of L. S. Vygotsky, Volume 3, Problems of the Theory and History of Psychology*, R. Van der Veer trans., R.W. Reiber and J. Wollock eds (New York: Plenum Press).

Vygotsky, L.S. (1998) *The Collected Works of L. S. Vygotsky, Volume 5, Child Psychology*, R.W. Reiber ed. (New York: Plenum Press).

Wertsch, J.V. (1991) *Voices of the Mind: A Sociocultural Approach to Mediated Action* (London: Wheatsheaf).

Wertsch, J. (1996) The Role of Abstract Rationality in Vygotsky's Image of Mind. In: A. Tryphon and J.N. Vonèche (eds) *Piaget – Vygotsky: The Social Genesis of Thought* (Hove: Psychology Press), pp. 25–42.

Wertsch, J.V. (2000) Vygotsky's Two Minds on the Nature of Meaning. In: C.D. Lee and P. Smargorinsky (eds) *Vygotskian Perspectives on Literacy Research* (Cambridge: Cambridge University Press), pp. 19–30.

Whitty, G. (2010) Revisiting School Knowledge: Some Sociological Perspectives on New School Curricula, *European Journal of Education*, 45:1, 28–45.

Young, M. (2007) *Bringing Knowledge Back In: From Social Constructivism to Social Realism in the Sociology of Education* (London: Routledge).

Zinchenko, V.P. (1995) Cultural-Historical Psychology and the Psychological Theory of Activity: Retrospect and Prospect. In: J.V. Wertsch, P. del Rio and A. Alvarez (eds) *Sociocultural Studies of Mind* (Cambridge: Cambridge University Press), pp. 37–55.

Index

Vygotsky Philosophy and Education, First Edition. Jan Derry.
© 2013 Jan Derry. Editorial organisation © Philosophy of Education Society of Great Britain.
Published 2013 by John Wiley & Sons, Ltd.

semiotic mediation 10, 99, 113
Sennett, Richard 57–58
sense-certainty 116–117, 118–119
   see also empiricism
Shayer, Michael 72
Shif, Zhozefina I. 76
situated cognition *see* cognition, situated
Sloman, Aaron 43–44, 63n25
Smith, Leslie 45, 106–107, 135
sociogenesis 8, 40
   of meaning 37–38
   of mind, theorisation of 32, 33–34, 80
   see also epistemology, problems of
Soviet Marxism 8, 13, 35, 68, 98, 99–100, 129
   under Stalin 137–138
Soviet Union 13–14
   attacks on Vygotsky 137
   philosophy 9, 137
   psychology 13, 99, 137
   see also Third International, Communist
Spencer, Herbert 98
Spinoza, Baruch
   and Descartes 85, 88–89, 96, 100
   and determinism 99–100
   and dualism 88, 110–111
   on freedom/free will 24, 64n47, 85–88,
      92–93, 99–100
   and Hegel 110–111, 115–116
   influence 4, 23, 24, 31, 85, 110–111
   and modernity 102n4
   on truth 93–94
   works: *Ethics* 23, 82n14, 87
spontaneity 106, 109, 123n10
   and receptivity 106, 109, 112
Stalinism 8, 9, 13
   see also under Soviet Marxism
Starke, August der 58
Stoics 88
street children 18

Taylor, Charles 38, 39, 62n16, 115
teachers 141–142
   authority of 3, 49, 50
   capabilities 14
   and knowledge 21, 27n20, 49, 141
   role of 74
   training 128
teaching 21
   classroom *see* classroom practice
   and factual knowledge 141
   inferentialist 142

methods 18, 21, 27n20, 50, 141–142
   scientific 7, 21, 76–77
   see also education; learning; teachers
terminology, problems of 12–13, 19
Third International, Communist 9
Tolstoy, Leo 70
   Vygotsky on 70–71, 81n3
Toulmin, Stephen 44–45
   Cosmopolis 63n26
transcendental idealism 108, 109
transfer problem, the 17–22
Tulviste, Peeter 25

universalism 8, 10, 25, 26n4, 57, 114, 134
   see also abstract rationality

Valsiner, Jaan 9, 33, 68, 71
   Understanding Vygotsky 62n9
Van der Veer, René 9, 33, 68, 71, 136
   Understanding Vygotsky 62n9
Vygotsky, Lev Semyonovich
   conception of history 13, 53, 77, 112–113
   debt to Hegel vii, 1, 31, 35, 36, 68,
      105–124, 127, 129, 131, 132, 134
   debt to Spinoza 1, 4, 24, 31, 36, 68,
      82n14, 85–100, 129, 131
   extracts from 21, 38, 51, 74, 78–79, 80,
      86, 87, 90–91, 92, 97, 119, 120,
      128–129, 130–131, 133, 144
   literature on *see* Vygotskian studies
   misquotation of 136
   neglect of vi
   philosophical context 6, 32–33, 34–36, 68–70
   Stalinist attacks on 137
   works: 'The Historical Meaning of the
      Crisis in Psychology' 113, 135; *The
      Psychology of Art* 85; *Thinking and
      Speech* 70, 73, 127
Vygotskian studies vi, 10–14, 17, 20–21, 31, 39
   see also individual scholars

Walkerdine, Valerie 27n18, 52
Wells, Gordon 43, 49, 51–54, 58, 64n42
Wenger, Etienne 15, 21
Wertsch, James 3
   abstract rationality 45, 114, 130
   agency 24–25, 27n23, 28n24
   artificial intelligence 17
   Cartesian mechanics 36
   decontextualised rationality 6, 26n1, 38,
      121, 127–128